CREATED AND PRODUCED BY TOTAL TELEVISION PRODUCTIONS

Oct 31 '68

Total TeleVision productions
Inc., 386 Madison Avenue, New York 17, N.Y., OXford 7-4123

Dear Mark —

You've been very patient — however what is sent to you I'm afraid isn't exactly "stop the presses" info — hope it will be useful in some way.

Best — Tread

CREATED AND PRODUCED BY TOTAL TELEVISION PRODUCTIONS

THE STORY OF UNDERDOG, TENNESSEE TUXEDO AND THE REST

BY MARK ARNOLD

Created and Produced by Total TeleVision productions:
The Story of Underdog, Tennessee Tuxedo *and the Rest*
©2009 Mark Arnold and Fun Ideas Productions. All Rights Reserved.

All prominent characters from *The King and Odie, The Hunter, Tooter Turtle, Tennessee Tuxedo, Underdog, The World of Commander McBragg, Go Go Gophers, Klondike Kat and The Sing-a-Long Family, Cauliflower Cabby, Gene Hattree, Rocky and Bullwinkle* and *Hoppity Hooper* mentioned in this book and the distinctive likenesses thereof are copyrighted trademarks and properties of Classic Media, LLC, a Boomerang Media, LLC company.

All prominent characters from *The Beagles, The Otter Side, The Colossal Show, Parrot Playhouse, Manley's Marauders, The Clock, Noah's Lark* and any other unrealized TTV projects mentioned in this book and the distinctive likenesses thereof are copyrighted trademarks and properties of Total TeleVision productions.

All prominent characters from Twinkles, Trix, Cocoa Puffs and FrostyO's mentioned in this book and the distinctive likenesses thereof are copyrighted trademarks and properties of General Mills Cereals, LLC.

All additional material is their respective copyright holder. The material used in this book is used for historical purposes and literary criticism and review and is used by permission. It is not designed to plagiarize or in any other way infringe on the copyrights of any copyrighted materials contained herein.

Permission is granted to other publications or media to excerpt the contents contained herein for review purposes provided that the correct credit and copyright information is included for any materials reproduced.

Published in the USA by:
BearManor Media
P O Box 71426
Albany, Georgia 31708
www.bearmanormedia.com

ISBN 1-59393-345-2
Printed in the United States of America.
Cover Art by Mike Kazaleh. Book design by Brian Pearce.
Interior graphics courtesy of Buck Biggers, Bradley Bolke, John Bruszewski, Tread Covington, Joe Harris, Michael Hayde, Mark Arnold, and various locations on the web.

TABLE OF CONTENTS

"DON'T TOUCH THAT DIAL!" 9
"THAT'S THE MOST UNHEARD OF THING I'VE EVER HEARD OF" 33
"I AM THE HUNTER!" 73
"HELP, MR. WIZARD!" 97
  ALL ABOUT GAMMA 119
"TODAY OUR STORY IS ABOUT...TWINKLES" 125
"TENNESSEE TUXEDO WILL NOT FAIL!" 137
"THERE'S NO NEED TO FEAR, UNDERDOG IS HERE!" 161
"GO GO GOPHERS WATCH 'EM GO GO GO!" 179
"DID I EVER TELL YOU ABOUT...?" 189
"KLONDIKE KAT ALWAYS GETS HIS MOUSE!" 197
"LOOKING FOR THE BEAGLES" 201
"BUT FIRST, TIME FOR A LITTLE SONG." 211
"LOOKS LIKE THIS IS THE END!" 215
  WITHER UNDERDOG? 245
  APPENDIX: TOTAL TELEVISION EPISODE GUIDE 251
  APPENDIX: PUBLISHING 361
  APPENDIX: A WHO'S WHO OF TOTAL TELEVISION PRODUCTIONS . . 363
  BIBLIOGRAPHY 367
  INDEX 369

Also by Mark Arnold:

The Best of the Harveyville Fun Times!

DEDICATION

This book is dedicated to my mother, Jean Arnold (April 16, 1943–October 7, 2008), who passed away during the writing of this book.

Special thanks to Frank Andrina, Roman Arambula, Jerry Beck, W. Watts "Buck" Biggers, Bradley Bolke, Jerry Boyd, Christie Brehm, John Bruszewski, Jesus Christ, Treadwell Covington, Susan D'Antilio, Dave Downey, Todd P. Emerson, Mark Evanier, Rick Goldschmidt, Joe Harris, Michael Hayde, Tom Heintjes, Lee Hester, Dave Holt, Mike Kazaleh, Jeff Little, Leonard Maltin, Bill Morrison, Ben Ohmart, Patrick Owsley, Shelley Pleger, Keith Scott, Bruce Schwartz, Scott Shaw!, Linda Simensky, Larry Storch, Chet Stover, Allen Swift, Joe Torcivia, Mark A. Yurkiw, and anyone else I may have forgotten...

Interviews conducted specifically by the author for this book were completed on the following dates:
Buck Biggers, August 24, 2006
Chet Stover, August 24, 2006
Frank Andrina, December 15, 2007
Bradley Bolke, December 16, 2007
Allen Swift, January 5, 2008
Roman Arambula, January 5, 2008
Joe Harris, January 13, 2008
Tread Covington, January 19, 2008

CHAPTER 1

"DON'T TOUCH THAT DIAL!"

In Keith Scott's book, *The Moose That Roared*, Scott asserts his opinion about the TTV output: "These shows — *King Leonardo and his Short Subjects, Underdog, Go Go Gophers, Tennessee Tuxedo and his Tales* — were pleasant diversions, but definitely not up to Jay Ward's cartoon caliber. Some, like the short filler *Commander McBragg*, simply didn't work well, quickly proving repetitious and screamingly unfunny."

This book will set out to prove otherwise.

The Total TeleVision productions (TTV) (yes, it's large "V," small "p") story is one that is not well known. For various reasons, it has been confused over the years with Jay Ward Productions, yet their best-known creations of Tennessee Tuxedo and Underdog are as fondly remembered as any other major animated star. The company's founders got their start after branching off from their positions at General Mills' advertising agency called Dancer-Fitzgerald-Sample (DFS) and with an animation studio that produced animated commercials called TV Spots, and later with Gamma. The complete story of how TTV came to be was first detailed in a magazine cover story in *Animato!* #38 Summer-Fall 1997 by David Krell, and by Buck Biggers and Chet Stover's *How Underdog Was Born*, but what really happened to that successful company was a mystery...until now. And now (to quote the late Paul Harvey), here's the rest of the story...

According to Wikipedia, "Handling the General Mills account as an account executive with the Dancer-Fitzgerald-Sample advertising agency in New York in 1960, Buck Biggers teamed with Chet Stover, Tread Covington and artist Joe Harris to create TV animation (*King Leonardo, Tennessee Tuxedo*) as formats to sell General Mills breakfast cereals. With the success of *Underdog*, Biggers and his partners left Dancer-Fitzgerald-Sample to form their own company, Total TeleVision, with animation produced at Gamma Studios in Mexico." This statement is not entirely correct, as they left to form TTV a lot sooner than *Underdog*. With this book, it is hoped that the true story will finally and completely be revealed.

W. Watts "Buck" Biggers was born on June 2, 1927, in Avondale Estates, Georgia. His bio on Wikipedia states, "He went to Avondale High where he was member of a debating team which won the state championship. Skipping his senior year of high school, he edited the school newspaper at North Georgia Military College and went on to Emory University Law School. At age 20, he headed for New York City where he struggled unsuccessfully as a pianist and vocalist, singing his own original songs. At the advertising agency Dancer-Fitzgerald-Sample, he began as a mailroom trainee and rose to the position of VP Account Supervisor on General Mills and Corn Products/Best Foods accounts, handling millions in billing.

"In 1968, Ballantine Books published Biggers' *The Man Inside* as an original paperback. In 1999, it was reissued by Bamberger Books as a hardcover. It was optioned as a feature film by One Brick Films." (A film is in development as of 2009. Although Biggers is a published author, he claims no relation to Earl Derr Biggers, the author of the *Charlie Chan* novels.)

"His novel *Hold Back the Tide* concerns a lovelorn police chief who wants a hypnotist to eliminate his obsessions so he can continue solving crimes. It was published February 2001, as a 1st Books Library eBook.

"Biggers is vice-president and co-founder of the Boston-based Victory Over Violence 'dedicated to creating a positive force in the media to offset the cynicism and negativity, which create a climate of violence,' and has used Underdog to promote the organization."

Chester A. "Chet" Stover was born on April 19, 1925, in Scranton, Pennsylvania. His grandmother was a painter, and Stover originally aspired to follow in her footsteps. He eventually took art classes at the University of Minnesota.

After being in the service for three years, he resumed his scholastic career on the G.I. Bill and went to Dickinson College in Pennsylvania and graduated from the Union Seminary, a division of Columbia University, with an emphasis in writing by majoring in English.

After dabbling in some door-to-door selling, Stover landed his first job at DFS and worked there from 1951-1961, starting out as a cub writer, and eventually rising through the ranks to become Senior VP Creative Director, before leaving for TTV.

He currently lives in Richfield, Connecticut, and has a wife and two children.

One of Chet's early successes was the Trix Rabbit, a character created by Joe Harris. "The Trix Rabbit was a commercial and I was the creative director on that. Joe designed the Trix Rabbit, too," remembers Stover.

Harris recalls how he created the rabbit mascot that has longevity second only to Tony the Tiger of Frosted Flakes: "I created the rabbit and I created the line 'Trix are for kids' and also 'silly rabbit' and it all seemed to just flow out on the page. I don't know, Buck could probably tell you better about this, he was also involved with General Mills, and could probably tell you what product market share it was for Trix, but it was way down, something like 1.6, and when the Trix commercial came out, it was an instant hit, and the market share soared and I got a raise of 1500 bucks. It may not sound like much, but a new Volkswagen at that time was only 1200. So, I went out and bought a new Volkswagen.

"As I said, there was a dichotomy in my life. One of them is that I draw, but I also write, and I began to write much more afterwards, after Dancer. At the time I was writing commercials as well as illustrating the storyboards and producing them, and I never know which will come first, whether I will have a writing story or whether I will be having a visual idea. That's the way it's always been with me, so I can't tell you what came first, the words or the pictures. Very frequently they come together. I will draw a character and say, 'Talk to me,' and the rabbit will say, 'Trix are for kids!' Stuff like 'silly rabbit,' that stuff just came out Sunday night, and I walked in the next day and I showed it to Chet and he looked at it and he said, 'Uh...' (And, by the way, I have this letter from Chet which I still keep as a precious treasure.) He said, 'What is the selling line?' And I said, 'It's 'Trix are for kids!' Who else is going to buy a three-colored cereal?' And so, he thought about it and said, 'Ok, I'm going to the Mills and I'll see what we can do.' So he went, they bought it, we did the commercials, and that was the beginning of the story. That has not changed — now this is 2008 — it's the same line, the same characters, the same everything. As far as I know, it's one of the longest, if not *the* longest, running commercials — with no changes except upgrading the style — in advertising history. Pillsbury Doughboy is a close runner, but Trix, I don't know, I've got to talk to Saatchi and Saatchi.

"Most of the stuff I did for Dancer was yeoman's stuff. In other words, there were already established brands like Bounty towels. I did a lot of work that was in the mainstream for General Mills. I did the Cheerios Kid, I did Kix, I did Twinkles the Elephant. I don't think any of them are so memorable. I did the Cocoa Puffs Kids. That was created by a guy named Frank Aarondale. He had created them, and I simply worked on them. We were all doing each other's work back then, so I did a number of commercials for that and for the Cheerios Kid. But the Trix I guess you would call my shining moment. I hired Mort [Marshall] to play the Trix rabbit. That was an extraordinarily successful commercial. The Cocoa Puffs Kids went [from] 'puff, puff, Cocoa Puffs' to 'Cuckoo for Cocoa Puffs.' It had changed over the years, but the Trix rabbit stayed the same.

"I went to Gifford & Kim for the Trix commercials. Paul Kim, who was an animator who was working for Disney, and Lou Gifford, a businessman, had a very, very lovely studio, and I went to them with all my work. I never took any commercials except to studios of my choice, and they were always top people. I used people who had worked on *Fantasia*, Lars Colonius and Duane Crowther. Lars was an old-time animator. Duane worked on "Yellow Submarine." Now, those are the kind of people I'd look for, and Chris Ishi, who was also a Disney guy."

W. Watts "Buck" Biggers formed TTV with his partner Chet Stover. Biggers recalls, "Chet was there from the start. [One] of my driving forces was in 1959. I visited Cape Cod and told my late wife that we were going there to live. Then I didn't know how, but when I got back to New York very shortly thereafter, Gordon [Johnson] called me into his office and asked me to go find a creative team so that he could help keep [Jay] Ward and [Bill] Scott on the straight and narrow, and I took that as kind of fate."

According to *How Underdog Was Born*, the entire TTV project was originally just another new assignment from Gordon Johnson, but what it turned out to be was a competition between them and the already established Jay Ward Productions from Hollywood, to turn out the best made-for-TV cartoons that they could manage. They claim that the TTV story starts on May 13, 1959, in the offices of DFS.

Regarding Ward, Biggers stated, "Only met him in person once, talked to him two or three times on the phone. He was a very gracious and a very nice guy and a terribly creative guy." When asked if there was a real rivalry or creative difference or was it "We're all in the same boat. We're making some great shows!," Biggers said, "I don't think I felt either of those things. I don't think for a long time he knew who we were or wanted to know who we were. He was just interested in his own stuff. He kind of kept himself apart in a way. Very creative guy."

Tread Covington comments on Jay Ward Productions. "That was because of General Mills. I don't believe that we had any creative people that did the storyboards for both. We don't have the same look. I think that the Jay Ward cartoons were much more stylized, really, than ours. Ours was far more in the category of old-fashioned traditional cartoons with animal characters. When the shows were paired together, we were like cousins. We were a separate family. Of course. If we were very presumptuous, we would say that we were their rivals. But they had huge success before us.

"It was different. I was always amazed at how it seemed that they missed the boat in getting their right audience. I think that so much of their stuff went totally over the heads of the little children who were watching, and they did develop a following among the more hip and older kids. They were aiming at our crowd — the young kids crowd — as far as their times of day on the air. I just kept thinking, 'If I was involved with their program, I would try to get those college kids who really went for their kind of crazy humor.' I think it was very collegiate humor, and ours wasn't. You could like it as a child, but most of their little nuances were going right over young heads.

"It is quite ironic because the producers were the same. Of course, they made a mark. We made a mark, too, but they made a fantastic mark such as *George of the Jungle* coming from them; all that kind of nuttiness."

May 13, 1959, was the day that Biggers informed Stover of the idea Johnson proposed. According to Johnson, General Mills was paying for an assembly line of animators in Mexico at Gamma Productions, and with all of these people on the payroll, couldn't afford to shut the assembly line down.

The show was Jay Ward's *Rocky and his Friends* and the entire enterprise was based upon having a tight delivery schedule, but now Ward and his staff were starting to get behind due to the fact that some of the show's scripts were considered inappropriate for children by General Mills and ABC, the network airing the shows.

It was all very time consuming for Johnson to make these edits and when the discussions between Johnson and Jay Ward and Bill Scott were underway about these changes, the production line in Mexico shut down, until a resolution could be agreed upon.

The solution was to utilize another studio to work to accommodate the requirements necessary to make shows acceptable for all ages. The studio was to be named "Total TeleVision" and Biggers clinched the deal with a one-page press release which described the concept in succinct detail, offering "Total Concept," "Total Entertainment" and "Total Flexibility." This concept was presented to Johnson who was immediately sold on the idea, although, according to Biggers and Stover's book, Biggers acted like he was referring to a company he found, rather than one he founded. Ultimately, Johnson was convinced and the presentation of the *King Leonardo* concept clinched the deal. The only problem was that Johnson asked for artwork, and Biggers had none to show. In a panic, Biggers contacted Stover who suggested they hire a storyboard man and cartoonist. Biggers didn't want to bring in another person until the deal with Johnson was solidified and countered that Stover, being a painter, could produce the required artwork needed. Stover rejected the idea, so Biggers countered that if Stover wouldn't do it, he would draw the artwork himself. This threat convinced Stover to take out his pen. The relieved Biggers turned his attentions to the shows' theme songs, which turned out to be a masterstroke as the various theme songs of the TTV shows are some of the most memorable themes ever composed for television.

Another issue was that Gamma only worked on the one show, so when the assembly line shut down, there were no other productions to work on. This also necessitated a need for more shows and Jay Ward Productions was unwilling or incapable of producing another series while *Rocky and his Friends* was in production.

The only other show Ward attempted during *Rocky's* original run (later called *The Bullwinkle Show*) from 1959-1964 was *Fractured Flickers*, which consisted entirely of live-action silent-movie footage and celebrity interviews hosted by Hans Conried, better known as the voice of Snidely Whiplash on the *Dudley Do-Right* segment.

There was also a third reason behind Johnson's concern over Gamma: he had personal financial interest in the company and did not wish to see it go under.

Creating TTV solved all of these problems. While Ward and company were hashing it out, production could continue on the TTV productions, which were initially episodes of *King and Odie, Tooter Turtle* and *The Hunter*, and, as a result, Gamma would thrive and so would Johnson's (and General Mills', DFS's and ABC's) fortunes.

Johnson sought out the services of Biggers as he was a trusted colleague and friend, and he knew that Biggers had the contacts necessary to come up with a complementary show that he could control. This was not the case with Ward's production house.

The plan was always to get a new team to produce some new cartoon shows, not to take over Ward Productions or take away *Rocky and his Friends*, but a non-confrontational rivalry began and, as a result, drove the competing studios to produce some of the most fondly remembered cartoon series of the 1960s.

While TTV created the shows that will be revealed and discussed in the upcoming pages, Jay Ward Productions came up with not only the aforementioned *Rocky and his Friends* and *The Bullwinkle Show* series with its accompanying segments of *Fractured Fairy Tales, Dudley Do-Right of the Mounties, Aesop and Son, Bullwinkle's Corner, Peabody's Improbable History, Mr. Know-it-All*, and *The Bullwinkle and Rocky Fan Club*, but Ward followed up this success with *Hoppity Hooper* (a.k.a. *Uncle Waldo*) and *George of the Jungle* with its accompanying segments, *Superchicken* and *Tom Slick*.

Ward did make other shows but retreated into the world of advertising, specifically promoting the brands of Quaker Oats, and helping cereals with names like Cap'n Crunch, Quisp, Quake and King Vitaman achieve success and sometimes legendary status.

None of Ward's internal staff had anything to do with anything at TTV. Harris explains, "To this day, a great number of people think Jay Ward did it. That was the result of all that mix and match. Besides, Jay Ward had a name. If Jay Ward were a Russian, he would have been censured for the cult of personality. He put his name on everything. It was Jay Ward Studios, Jay Ward this, Jay Ward that. They had the big Bullwinkle moose out in front of the studio. *Rocky and Bullwinkle* was a great show, and a great idea. The only problem I had with it is that it was all topical humor, and once you got over the fact that the Kirwood Derby had a reference to it. I knew kids would laugh but they wouldn't get it, and we didn't do any of that. We didn't do topical humor."

For a more in-depth analysis of Ward, his studio and his productions, one should consult Keith Scott's excellent *The Moose That Roared: The Story of Jay Ward, Bill Scott, a Flying Squirrel, and a Talking Moose*. The book is admittedly a bit disparaging in its comments about TTV, but Biggers had this to say about the book: "I'm going to be honest with you, I liked the book and I read it, but I never got past the middle, not because of the book, it was business things that took me away."

After Johnson proposed the idea to Biggers, Biggers then turned to his longtime business partner, Chet Stover, who reacted favorably to the news: "Have you lost your mind? What the hell do we know about creating a cartoon series?"

Biggers explained that the situation wasn't as folly as Stover believed, and soon was allied with him after he convinced Stover that because they had created the Cheerios Kid, they could easily expand a cartoon character idea into a half-hour series. Biggers also told Stover that there was a few times when Biggers was brought in to make revisions to the *Rocky* show, so he basically learned on the job.

Stover was still worried that they had no business or experience writing 30-minute scripts when all of their previous scripts were only 30 seconds long. Biggers assured him it could be done, because the series would be comprised of a combination of shorter segments, none totaling longer than 4½ minutes in length. The rest of the show would be padded out with commercials and the opens and closes to the shows and the regular segments.

Stover was still concerned about leaving a steady paycheck for the adventurous world of freelancing and owning your own business, and felt that Biggers' work on *Rocky* was not enough to justify creating an entire company and cartoon series. It was Biggers' confidence and tenacity that finally allowed him to take a risk. That, and a phone call before an important meeting with Biggers when changes to one of his accounts were not heeded. So the ad campaign was released without Stover's approval.

Biggers had personal reasons for taking the risk. Although he did like his position at DFS, it also created marital difficulties due to his lengthy commute. Stover, too, was tired of living in the "big city" and so the TTV opportunity offered them both the opportunity to stabilize their lives and to fulfill their dreams away from Manhattan. He also was not crazy about continuing to support ad campaigns for products like cigarettes.

Stover was still concerned about his mortgage, but the opportunity was too good to pass up, coupled with the fact that the TTV business would be done on the side while keeping their jobs at DFS. If TTV was a success, they could leave DFS confidently. If it failed, all Biggers and Stover wasted was their time, but at least they would still have their jobs, and would have to sort out their personal lives and goals at another time and another way.

Biggers and Stover did not wish to put their DFS jobs in jeopardy so they agreed to discuss things regarding TTV offsite through a series of martini lunches. Though foreign today, in the 1950s and 60s, it was a common business practice.

Biggers explains, "I just spoke to a writer's conference on Tuesday and they were a wonderful audience. When I got off the podium and we were driving home [my partner] Nancy said to me, 'Maybe you ought to go a little softer on that martini business.' What we did was that we worked — we'd get there about nine o'clock — work 'til about 12:30, touching up the writing we had done during the week individually and then plotting the two new or four new episodes: couple *Hunters*, couple *Tennessee Tuxedos*, we'd plot those, and then our work was really done and so then we'd go to lunch. Then we'd come up with all sorts of ideas, some of them very good. We kept notes on our lunch and we had to because a lot of times we'd change opinions. But, they were always a three-martini lunch. Always the same thing: double shrimp cocktail and three martinis! Oh God, yes! [It is] very outdated! And that was it. We only met once a week, it wasn't like something we did every day. It was a fun time. We laughed like hell! When I say we should have paid people to let us do the work, I mean we really had fun!"

Stover concurs, "My son read our book and said, 'My God, you did everything with martinis!' That was an era in the industry when Madison Avenue lived on martinis. Yes, it's incredible. I know for a fact that there were times when in the agency it was no use to talk to some guys after lunch because they were out."

The concern was one of conflict of interest, but in reality, it was an unfounded fear mainly because General Mills and DFS were partners in many advertising campaigns and they had already established the relationship with Jay Ward Productions. But Biggers and Stover decided to play it safe anyway; probably more for privacy than anything else, as what they were doing was quite different than anything else anyone else in the ad agency was doing.

Though Stover finally agreed to the plan, he reminded Biggers that he didn't know the first thing about cartoons. Although he was an accomplished artist and had created some characters previously, he admitted to not watching them or TV at all. Biggers again assured Stover not to worry as he did watch cartoons and he was watching the two big hit series of the time, the aforementioned *Rocky* as well as Hanna-Barbera's *Huckleberry Hound Show*. Biggers recommended that Stover do the same, to learn by watching. The ever-skeptical Stover complied. "I had left the agency, and Joe [Harris] did, too."

Another decision was to research prior successes and failures of previous children's TV shows and cartoon shows. Not such an easy task in 1959 as the history literally was being made at the time, and no books existed on the subject. Also, the Internet did not exist to quickly grab up-to-the-moment information, so they had to delve quietly in the DFS media files to see what information they could find about ratings.

What they discovered was that from 1952-1959, more children's shows were created for the weekdays than on Saturday mornings where their first show was set to debut. As a result, precious little information was available on how well any show would do in those time slots. TTV's show was scheduled to premiere in the fall of 1960 on Saturday mornings, so they were truly pioneering virgin territory. In fact, the only new animated show that had debuted on Saturday morning previously was Hanna-Barbera's *Ruff and Reddy* in 1957, but even then there was a live-action host. The yet-to-be-created TTV show would have no host, much less a live-action one.

They also learned that although shows could be repeated, they couldn't be repeated too often, or else ratings fell. They also found the same problems if animation was too limited, or if the show's demographic was aimed too young. At the time, most homes had only one TV set, and it was usually the older child that made the programming decisions for children's time slots.

As a result of all of this research, Biggers and Stover knew that they had to create a show that appealed to kids, but would be appreciated by adults and older kids as well, but not to the degree that *Rocky and his Friends* had. They did not seek to alienate the smaller children.

An additional result from all of this research was to create animal characters that hadn't been used previously for other starring cartoon characters, so animals such as mice, ducks and bears were off limits. (Strangely, this rule didn't seem to apply to dogs, as there have been many dog characters in the past, including Huckleberry Hound, Pluto and Reddy [from *Ruff and Reddy*], but that didn't seem to deter Biggers and Stover from creating *The Hunter* and later *Underdog*.)

The decision was made early on to form their own company with Biggers and Stover as principle owners and head writers, Stover supplying the "highbrow, head laughs" and Biggers supplying the "lowbrow, belly laughs." They also decided to employ a front man to relay business decisions, so that work could continue on during the day for TTV while Biggers and Stover worked for DFS. It took them four weeks to come up with a basic storyline, character summaries and a pilot script.

As a result of these informal offsite meetings, TTV didn't have an office at first, although they did have a gas station. It was a deserted one midway between the two owners' homes where they could meet on weekends and evenings and not have to go downtown to discuss their plans.

In looking through a *Life* magazine book about the Macy's Thanksgiving Parade, there's a blueprint showing the Underdog balloon and stating that TTV's address was 366 Madison Avenue, New York. (This balloon, incidentally, was designed by Joe Harris and was the first to "fly" in a horizontal position as opposed to vertical.)

Stover reflects, "What we used to do when we were still working at the agency, you could rent office space for just a day or you could have it as a mail drop, so that's what we did a number of times."

Adds Biggers, "That was just a mail drop and a place where you can go up and use the conference room if you want to. It was not a real address. We finally did have an office address, but I'm not even sure where it was. That was Tread, the great guy that we brought in to front the company, because we couldn't. He became our New York rep and our man for recording soundtracks, so he was the only one who was there, so if you think about it, our address was wherever we were."

Claims Covington, "There was an office near the agency. We started with a mail drop just to get going but then we rented an office on Madison Avenue right across the street from Dancer-Fitzgerald-Sample. Then, we had a secretary. Actually, we had several secretaries. They were all terrific gals. I was there every day."

Born July 9, 1926, Treadwell Covington was the third of the four principle owners of TTV brought into the fold. Despite his unusual name, he possessed the skills absolutely essential to the success of all the TTV shows. Over the years, there had been rumors that he was a fictitious person like Jay Ward's "Ponsonby Britt" only from the standpoint that he has a rather unique name. Biggers and Covington both laughed at the claim.

Recalls Biggers: "Yes, he does [have a unique name]. He sounds and kind of looks like his name. He's tall and with grey hair, even then, and is very dignified looking and he's from Chapel Hill, North Carolina, and speaks with almost a British-type accent. I knew he'd be very impressive to Gordon and he was. He was a very good one to present to Gordon. We couldn't do it ourselves, so we chose Tread and he went in and showed the first scripts and first models." (These were the models that Stover had done in a moment of desperation, when no one else was available, over a period of eight days.)

Covington adds, "I was known as just Tread Covington in the cartoons, because it seemed simpler. I thought 'Tread Covington' was the simplest name. I may have used 'Treadwell.'

"I was born in Miami, Florida — Coral Gables — and grew up in that area. After the service, I completed my degree at the University of North Carolina. Then, I had a brief job in advertising in New York and then returned to North Carolina, where I was married and worked in advertising in Charlotte. I went back to Miami for a couple of years, again in advertising. From there, my family and I went to New York City because my wife had a newspaper and magazine career and we both agreed that NY was probably the best place for us because we would both be able to find jobs that we were interested in without moving again. I continued my advertising activities in New York and met again with one of my good friends from college, Buck Biggers. We used to have a weekly lunch as advertising people used to do, and we would just catch up and talk about advertising and about ideas we had for creative activities. One day Buck presented the idea for *King Leonardo and his Short Subjects*. He thought General Mills might be interested in the cartoon. We went to work on the idea and, happily for us, Buck was associated with the advertising agency for General Mills. Two other partners joined us — Chet Stover and Joe Harris. Joe was predominately our artist and art director. Chet and Buck were the writers. I was in charge of business management as well as voices and the voice tracks, music and effects, and that was pretty much the setup that we established. *King Leonardo and His Short Subjects* aired on NBC and was a success. We worked as an independent company called Total TeleVision productions; a company that delivered cartoon shows sponsored by General Mills. Every time we were about to spread our wings and go in an independent direction, General Mills would need a new property. That was great for us, and we wouldn't consider not giving our full attention to it. Eventually, when General Mills' marketing directions changed, we decided to close shop."

Biggers continues, "Tread handled the voice tracks. We would decide who we wanted and either have pre-selected them or have Tread do some auditions and also tape some selections. But we practically never went in there. We talked to the voice people but they didn't know us from a hole in the wall.

"He recorded all of the soundtracks. He's a very good man in the booth and he did all the New York recording of soundtracks. You understand that a lot of the tracks were done wherever a person was. Wally Cox could go into a studio out in Hollywood or wherever and record his part. The actors seldom worked together. They'd go in and do their parts. Don Adams would go in somewhere and then ship that tape in and then it would be put together with others. The New York sessions Tread supervised. Usually, though, we were doing two a week."

Stover concurred, "That was something Treadwell [Covington] handled. We decided on who the voices would be, and got their agents to do that. We didn't get involved with that. I went down for a couple of sessions."

Covington remembers how he started working for TTV. "I worked for another advertising agency. Buck Biggers and I were good friends. I worked for Gaynor & Ducas, a small agency in New York, and from that agency I went to a direct mail agency. That's where I was working at the time Buck called me. Dickie-Raymond was based in Boston. I worked in the New York office. And then from that job, I went full time into Total TeleVision."

According to Biggers, Covington was dissatisfied with his current position at his agency and was interested in something new. Admittedly, Covington was their second choice after a man named Eli Feldman, but Feldman was out of the running as he preferred to stay in his lucrative position at Pelican Films, despite being close friends with both Biggers and Stover. Ultimately, for reasons already stated, Covington turned out to be the best choice for the job.

Covington continues, "It was totally new to me other than having directed voice commercials. We operated pretty much a la Gilbert and Sullivan. We were all over the map when we started our company with an office in New York primarily as a meeting place for the four of us whenever we were in the city, and, of course, in my case, my full-time office. I loved casting the voices and the voice recording sessions and the music and effects work in the studio in New York. I always liked this. As a child, it was fun to put on a play and things like that. I loved the opportunity of working with scripts and voice talent and characters, so I delighted to do this part of the work."

Covington recalls whether casting and recording voices was a career goal. "I really wanted to aim for creative writing. I thought it would make sense to try advertising copywriting. I did specifically study journalism at the University of North Carolina, but my plan was to try something in the creative writing field. I had a newspaper job briefly before my first job in advertising copyrighting. Then with Total TeleVision productions, I thoroughly enjoyed being the director of the voices for the characters, working along with the voice actors and engineers.

"After Charlotte, North Carolina, I worked for another ad agency in Miami, Florida. In those days, I was known as a copy-contact person. In smaller agencies, if you were a copywriter, you were also the account man or account woman, and so it was called copy-contact. I was doing the copywriting, and also the account work. In New York, I thought it would be a smart thing to try for the account side, which struck me at that time as where the better money was, and, of course, as often happens, no sooner did I get established as an account man, then agencies started paying enormous money for the copywriters." Covington turned out to be the key element in selling the show to Gordon Johnson, but the final piece of the puzzle had to be added when Johnson requested a complete storyboard of *King Leonardo* for the presentation in front of General Mills in Minneapolis. A few names were mentioned by Biggers and Stover of who would take on the awesome responsibility of drawing and executing the storyboards, including Chris Ishi, but ultimately the job went to another man currently working at DFS, Joe Harris.

Harris explains how he got to work for DFS, which ultimately led to his tenure at TTV. "I looked around and figured that I'd like to work in advertising, so I started with a list of the advertising agencies and I figured that everyone else would do the same thing, so instead of starting with the ones beginning with 'A,' I decided to start with the ones beginning with 'Z' and worked backwards. And when I got to Dancer-Fitzgerald-Sample, you can tell how many I tried.

"Dancer-Fitzgerald-Sample really changed my life. They had been called, by some people, an insurance company with artists. They were really old school. They were really tough. I met the head art director, Bob Peterson, who said, 'I like your portfolio.' Once again I got off to a rocky start, and then one day a fellow by the name of Andy Love — you might have heard some of his records — came up with a song about Gold Medal flour. He played a banjo and had a real country tune, 'It will be your finest hour, when you switch to Gold Medal flour.' It was a beautiful little tune, and Bob Peterson said to me, 'I don't know what we're going to do with you. We've had some trouble with some of the stuff you've done, but see what you can do with this.' I did a cartoon thing for it, and that was what the music said to me. I did animation and it was a big hit. The Gold Medal flour thing is the first thing I ever did.

"In those days you had producers who actually went out and shot whatever you did. You had writers who wrote everything and came up with the ideas, and you had a row of people who were the art directors, who only did storyboards. Three distinct, never to mingle, groups. There was just an absolute separation among the three. So, when I got this project, I had music, but I didn't have any words, except the lyrics, so I didn't have to deal with a writer. I had this thing of a storyboard that I had done and they said, 'OK, go ahead and produce it.' And that was the beginning. I asked around and said, 'Where do you get this stuff produced?' They had a whole list of people. Disney had suffered a revolution back in the early '50s and a lot of the people left because of the low pay and the lack of union rules and so on, and they all opened up little shops in New York. Some of the finest illustrators and some of the finest animators of our time were in little shops there. I'm talking people like Ernie Pintoff, Lars Colonius, Duane Crowther, Chris Ishi. Jack Nander was one of them. You name somebody on the top of the heap, and they were there. I was introduced to a group of people over the years that were the top people at Disney, and I just reveled in it. I became the supervisor of animation after that for General Mills. I did Gold Medal Flour, and I did all of the cereals. Of course, people were ahead of me on that, so I met a lot of the guys in the agency, who had also done lots of other things. Some of them had done Cheerios, because Cheerios was a big number at General Mills. The upshot of it was, I became the writer, the art director and the producer, the first time anybody had ever worn a triple hat, and I realized that I could write, so that's what I did.

"One day, Chet Stover came down to me and said, 'We've got a problem at General Mills. They have a product called Trix, which is the same thing as Kix, only they made it in three colors, dyed three colors. So this thing called Trix, we don't have any ideas for it. Can you come up with something?' That was Friday night, and I said, 'What do you want?' So he said, 'See what you can bring in on Monday morning.' So, I had a very heavy weekend that weekend, I had my wife and daughter. I was booked, so to speak, and Saturday went by, I did as much as I could. Then Sunday I kind of goofed off a little bit and then Sunday night I sat down and thought, 'Come on, you've got to do this.' I ran off a storyboard and a script, and that was the first Trix commercial. That was in 1958.

"It was a funny time. It was still the 'Wild West' in advertising. I can't tell you what fun I had meeting all the people I met. The sum of it all came when Buck and Chet came to me and said, 'The General Mills people want to do a kids show for television. Would you be interested in working on it?' Buck had already gotten word from Gordon Johnson, who was the 'Punjab' of General Mills and the agency, and Gordon had said to Buck, 'Let's put it together,' and Buck went to Chet and Chet came to me. I said, 'Of course. Let's do it,' and so we did. Later on, I found a very strange thing. We had success with *King Leonardo*, but in order to do it, we decided that we would form Total TeleVision — now, I don't know if Buck told you this — but we wouldn't leave the agency. So there are three guys, who are now saying that they're going to create a top show for NBC daytime all by themselves, while also carrying on a full-time career at an agency."

Covington describes Johnson, as "one of the account supervisors who was very high up at Dancer-Fitzgerald and he had a lot of different contacts because that was one of his things. He was very important to both sides. The creative side and the producer side."

Harris continues, "It was insane! Yeah, most of the agency didn't know what was going on. Obviously, Gordon Johnson knew and we had his blessing. We decided, eventually, that we should peel off from the agency, not all together, but one at a time, because we had clients, and we had the agency, and in those days, you didn't just go and say, 'I'm going to AT&B, and then I'm going to go to HM&H.' We were Dancer-Fitzgerald people. We had loyalty to our agency and also a loyalty to our clients. To make it short, I was the last one to leave. I spent a year doing both full-time jobs, doing full-time storyboarding and production in my apartment, and I think if you read the article that I wrote in *Animato*, I wrote about that. Three hours of sleep a night; get on the train and go into work. Come back and come home at 6:30 or 7 or so. Go immediately into a back room I had set up and work until 4 in the morning. Get up at 7 and go into work and do the same thing. I did it for a year, and I did not realize what the limits of the human mind and body were until I had tried that, and after a year, I left and went to the comparative ease of living in a house — 'cause I had bought a house by that time — and only working for 12 hours a day. It was like a retreat, and, of course, working in that business, there were long periods in between seasons where you didn't really have to work much, so I bought a little beach house, took my family out there every summer, and lived a good life. That was the beginning of Underdog."

Harris continues, "You'll have to ask Buck and Chet who they were looking for before they asked me to join them. It was Chris Ishi and he would have been a better choice. He was a full-fledged animator. He knew his business backwards and forwards. He had worked for Disney. He started with Disney in 1940, and when the war broke out, they interned him, and he was in a camp, and he became the cartoonist for the camp newspapers. When he got out, he joined the army in 1943, fourth brig relief in the China-Burma-India sector, found a lovely Chinese girl and married, and came back, and then started his own studio. Chris would have been a perfect example, and he could have done a great job. It was funny, but after the holocaust of getting dumped by General Mills, I got a call from Chris Ishi and he said, 'Joe, how would you like to come work for UPA?' And I said, 'Are you kidding?' He said, 'No, I'd like you to come on board. You know I like your work and I like what you've done.' And I said, 'Well, just tell me what to do, I'd love to work with you,' and he said, 'Ok, meet me tomorrow in New York.' He called me the next day and said, 'Joe, don't come in to New York.' I said, 'Why not?' He said, 'We've just been bought out,' and so UPA went to different hands. He was no longer at the helm. It's funny how life works, isn't it? It was the exact day, and I would have loved to work with him. He just died in 2001. He was born in 1919-1920, so he had a long, long run."

"Joe is a fine, fine storyboard man," Biggers described Harris. "Excellent! On our first series, Chet did the models (Chet is more of a painter than a cartoonist) and then Joe took those models and made them more 'cartoony.' Then Chet would work with him on each of the model sheets. In truth, we would say, 'We want a penguin. Don Adams is a penguin, because we thought he looked like a penguin, or we want Wally Cox as a dog,' and so forth. So, he would do initial models and send them in and Chet and I would look at them. He originally thought that Underdog got larger muscles when he made his change from Shoeshine Boy, but we explained that the 98-pound weakling remained a 98-pound weakling."

Harris comments on who designed the various TTV characters. "Everyone. All 97 or whatever there are. Let me qualify. I know at one time, there was a guy by the name of Sy Plattes, in General Mills, and he wanted to have a character named after him, so I turned it over to somebody — might have been Pete Dakis — and he designed a character called Platypus. That was our little kiss on the ass for Sy, and then there might have been one or two other characters in *Tennessee*, I'm not sure. But all of the major characters, I did."

Stover adds, "We were equals, [but] Buck did the music. The way that [we] worked was, I talked to Joe Harris and I brought him in to the company and he and I worked together. I would tell Joe exactly what we wanted, for instance, sketching Underdog. And then Joe would do a whole bunch of sketches and since we worked so far apart, he would mail them and then Buck and I would go over them and make any corrections. Sometimes I remember putting some of his drawings up on a window in a hotel we used to work in and we'd trace on them, making changes and then we'd send them back to Joe."

Harris talks about his role in the process of creating a TTV show: "I got the script, but that didn't mean anything to me, until I got the tracks, because you have to animate tracks, and that's where Tread came in. He would supervise people, and what I would get now was the script, but it was more of a reinforcement of the tracks, so that I knew what was going on, and then I would break it down into panels and movement. So, like any storyboarder, you read what is there, you feel what is there, and then you figure out how the action should be broken up. Do I have that person or character stand there and just deliver it, or do I cut to a reaction shot or part of another character? Do I have a change of scenes in the middle from a close-up to a long shot? All of those things have to go through your head when you hear the track. Then I would mark off the script into segments of what I was doing. I just built a little notes down and say, 'ECU = Extreme Close-Up; MCU = Medium Close-Up; LS = Long Shot.' Then I would have a little record on my scripts of what was going on. Then, after I had done my storyboard, the preproduction guy would come in, that would be Lu Garnier or Pete Dakis and Bob Schleh was the other guy. There were one or two others who came and went. Those three primarily, we would sit down together and he would have the bar sheets. We got the bar sheets. We'd go over every single piece of information on all the bar sheets and then Bob Schleh, who was the one I worked with the most and most continuous, he did not like to draw even though he was supposed to be an animator, and so if it came to a hand gesture, or a mouth, or a turn of the head, he would say, 'What do you want to do here?' and I said, 'Well, I want the hand to come up and point like he was shooting somebody,' and he said, 'For what?'

"Bob would say, 'Well, then draw it!' Now I spent all this time drawing what I hadn't drawn on the storyboard, but assumed that it was obvious and Bob would make me draw everything on the margins. So that's how we went through it. It was a little more lenient than it would be working with Lu. Lu had been president...I think he had an administrative role, but I don't know, and he's in the union. Anyway, Lu and I got along very easily. He loved to draw and he was very fast at it. Pete was a fine artist. Bob, I never saw him draw. That's how we went through it. Now, once the bar sheets were finished, the storyboards were keyed to it, then we'd ship those off to Mexico, and that was the process."

Covington remembers that eventually Harris needed help with his heavy workload. "Gary Mooney was one of our storyboard artists. When we would storyboard the scripts, he was under Joe Harris' official tutelage. He would draw the characters for the storyboards. Initially, Joe did all of that. Then, we farmed it out among others like Gary. He worked in our New York office." Mooney was to be interviewed for this book, but sadly passed away at the age of 78 in August 2008.

To handle the merchandising of the upcoming TTV series, Biggers turned to Peter Piech, who had success merchandising Jay Ward's *Rocky and his Friends* through P.A.T. "Leonardo was actually P.A.T. or Producers Associates of Television. That was Peter Piech's company and also Gordon's company and they were almost always co-producers with us. They handled Mexico [Gamma Productions]," explains Biggers about the situation.

Piech was born in Brooklyn, on June 30, 1918. He began in journalism, with P.A.T. from 1958. Later, he joined forces with Covington and Biggers to form TTV. After leaving P.A.T., Piech formed his own company, Filmtel International Corporation, which distributed the cartoons of both Ward and TTV until 1979. "Although he lacked the clout of Columbia Pictures TV subsidiary Screen Gems, who funded the early Hanna-Barbera material, it should be pointed out that Piech ended up producing over 400 original half-hour animated TV shows," Keith Scott proclaims in *The Moose That Roared*.

Covington remembers Piech, "I had a lot of dealings with Peter. He worked at our co-producers. He was sort of my counterpart in the production part of our work."

Harris adds, "Peter Peich and Charlie [Hotchkiss] were a little empire unto themselves, and I don't know what the payback was to Peter or why. Buck could probably tell you. Buck was on the accounting end, so he was involved in the politics and the strategy. I never wanted to get into that, and Chet, to a degree, was pretty savvy about politics himself, but Buck would probably have known more. At any rate, the company at that time was the top merchandising company in the country. Why I can't think of the name, I don't know. At one time I knew it. I think it was because in my mind, they were a total failure. They came out with sheets and pillowcases with Underdog and various characters, and they came out with some cheap-looking games — you know, the cardboard games that you have to put together — that you throw away the day after Christmas. And they came out with a few items like that, and they came out with glasses. I still have one of the glasses with Underdog on it, but I always was disappointed and I kept saying, 'Why don't they come out with this and that,' and I kept seeing all the things that they didn't do. After a while, that just disappeared. I don't know what happened to the merchandising after 1969."

P.A.T. was formed in October 1958, with Len Key and Peter Piech as a distribution and merchandising arm for Jay Ward Productions, which is why Bullwinkle merchandise bears the legend "P.A.T.-Ward." When TTV was formed, a second name was created to differentiate the properties from Ward's, which is why TTV merchandise bore the legend "TTV-Leonardo." Piech's duties for both companies were administrative, such as advancing production money, along with the merchandising. Their address during that time was at 500 Fifth Avenue, New York. Both Ward and TTV were hired as independent contractors by P.A.T.

Although Piech was the head of P.A.T., it really was Gordon Johnson who called the shots. Johnson was the top decision maker at DFS, as Senior Vice President and Account Executive for General Mills. As a result, DFS really controlled P.A.T. and was in effect the Executive Producer for all of the shows Ward and TTV produced. Len Key and Roger Carlin settled the deal with Gamma and became partners with the Mexican studio. Johnson (as well as Piech) was also a part owner of the operation.

Key (in an interview from *The Moose That Roared*) explained, "When we did the *Rocky* deal, we had mentioned the feasibility and low price of admission in either Japan or Mexico to Charlie Hotchkiss, our contact at Mills' ad agency. Of course he got very enthused. Then when Japan bombed out on us, Roger Carlin said that Piech knew someone in Mexico — this rich general contractor named Gustavo Valdez. Valdez really wanted to get into the animation business, so we both flew down to meet him. Valdez was a multimillionaire, and I can remember having lunch at his magnificent home. We discussed our pickup with General Mills, and he agreed to join the project. He would build a brand-new cartoon studio, from scratch!"

Peter Piech passed away on May 25, 1999.

Buck Biggers and Chet Stover in the 1970s from a page of their letterhead at the time.
LETTERHEAD CONTRIBUTED BY BUCK BIGGERS.

Buck Biggers is also an accomplished author. Three of his books include *The Man Inside*, *Hold Back the Tide* and *How Underdog Was Born*, the latter co-authored with Chet Stover.

Above: Buck Biggers has become more prominent in recent years, appearing at the Los Angeles Comic Book and Science-Fiction Convention in 2006. PHOTO BY MARK ARNOLD.
Below: Another recent photo of Buck Biggers.

CREATED AND PRODUCED BY TOTAL TELEVISION PRODUCTIONS

Joe Harris was the first of the four TTV co-founders to "break the ice" about TTV in an article in *Animato!* magazine in 1997. He later was featured on various Underdog tapes and DVDs discussing his co-creation. FROM THE AUTHOR'S COLLECTION.

Joe Harris today.

CREATED AND PRODUCED BY TOTAL TELEVISION PRODUCTIONS

CHAPTER 2

"THAT'S THE MOST UNHEARD OF THING I'VE EVER HEARD OF"

TTV's first show was called *King Leonardo and his Short Subjects*, which debuted on NBC at 10:30 a.m. on October 15, 1960. It was the second color cartoon series on the network's Saturday morning schedule, according to Ron Kurer's very informative "Toontracker" website.

Recalls Biggers, "All our shows were in color, as was *Bullwinkle*. Everything that was done for General Mills out of Mexico was originally done in color. That was Gordon. He was very much a far-thinking man. He was very clever and that was his idea and General Mills bought the idea and they did it."

Stover comments, "On *King Leonardo*, I did the original drawings, but they're very crude!"

Before settling on the *Short Subjects* moniker, *King Leonardo* went through a couple of working titles, including *The King and his Kingdom* and *King Leonardo and his Kingdom*. *Short Subjects* was finally chosen for two reasons: the show was comprised of a number of short cartoons or short subject, as cartoons used to be billed in movie theaters; and, apart from Leonardo and Itchy, all of the characters on the show were based on animals that were rather small or "short," like a fox, a hound, a rat, a skunk, a turtle and a lizard.

The *King and Odie* segment featured good King Leonardo the lion and his faithful companion Odie Cologne the skunk. Leonardo's chief nemesis was Biggy Rat, whose sidekick Itchy Brother was indeed Leonardo's brother. It took a month to come up with the complete concept, which was completed by June 27, 1960. As Biggers and Stover were from the advertising world, they used concepts based on what they knew. They set the *King and Odie* stories in the jungle in a land called "Bongo Congo." The jungle was chosen as it was an affectionate nickname applied to the advertising business. Biggers and Stover were surprised to find out how many cartoon animals didn't live in their natural habitat.

In continuing the advertising references, Biggers and Stover wanted characters to represent a CEO and his "right-hand man," and so that's how Leonardo and Odie originated, with the name Leonardo coming from Leonardo da Vinci. It wouldn't be too much of a stretch to think that Biggers and Stover were thinking autobiographically, but they would not be the first to admit that. A skunk was chosen because who would argue with him?

Soon, with Harris' completed storyboards in tow, Johnson and Biggers made their final presentations to General Mills with Biggers supplying the voices and pointing to the storyboard drawings. The General Mills executives loved it all and green-lighted the series. General Mills' only concern was whether TTV could come up with enough plots. Biggers and Stover countered with the creation of 26 two-part plot summaries, enough for 52 episodes. GM's fears were abated.

Next came the voices. The character of King Leonardo was the first of many TTV characters to be based on real-life celebrities, in this case 1930s character actor Eugene Pallette while Odie was to be an imitation of dignified actor Ronald Colman. Biggers reflects on how each show got pitched: "I did the original presentations for the account executives that were handling the shows for Gordon. I didn't do them like I was with the company. It was mine. So, I did the presentations and we had to use voices that I could imitate reasonably, so that was the reason for Ronald Colman and Eugene Pallette. Guys like that that I could actually imitate. So the first person that we got that I couldn't imitate was Wally Cox. But it didn't matter because everybody knew Wally Cox's voice so well that it didn't make any difference." By the time the show was sold, longtime voice actor Jackson Beck was chosen to play the Eugene Pallette-based king. He also doubled as Biggy Rat, a character based on Edward G. Robinson.

Covington agrees. "We did have real people in mind, and we were also aware that we should not limit ourselves with obscure references and things that would really not register with children. Essentially, in the sense of jokes and humor, we wanted to keep it as timeless as possible, but also to have fun. All of us thought that a good way to have the cartoons come to life would be to have live character models for the different principals in the cartoons. For example, if Biggers and Stover had a particular kind of voice in mind or personality in mind, they would tell me this. For instance, Eugene Pallette, the actor, was a stocky, gruff-voiced actor and he was memorable in a lot of comedies. We thought that his type of voice, his personality would be very good for King Leonardo, sort of a blustering guy and very much in control. Then Jackson Beck made this the voice of King Leonardo. Ronald Colman — a very suave British actor of the '30s and '40s — was the inspiration for the voice of Odie Colognie. We saw the light of day in 1960. We were about a year from the time that we first started to get together.

"In our voice casting of the various miscellaneous characters, if we had no preconceived voice ideas, I would just go for voice actors I knew whom I had worked with who were talented and successful and could come up with a particular personality to fit the character's look. It wasn't so much whether the kids would know whom Eugene Pallette was so much as finding just the right kind of voice for the character.

"I had a good relationship with a studio in New York from being involved in commercial work that I had done for my agency as an account executive. I handled a small dairy company's advertising. The top writer in charge of that account and I worked very closely on that, doing the commercials so we got to know certain voices that worked for the commercials for the dairy company. Norman Rose comes to mind, Allen Swift, of course, and just different ones that I knew through that work. That helped in the casting. We used Norman Rose as sort of incidental character or narrator. I worked with him a lot in my ad agency days. We were always developing a troupe that we could rely upon."

"Allen Swift was our first voice selection. We always used him. He was always great. He did Itchy Brother and Odie Colognie on our first show," says Biggers. Itchy Brother's voice was an even more obscure imitation, that of "Slapsie" Maxie Rosenbloom, who was a former prize-fighter-turned-actor. This "punch drunk" sort of voice was perfect for the king's beatnik brother.

Allen Swift was born Ira Stadlin, on January 6, 1924, in New York City. He has done numerous voices outside of TTV, including such characters as Clint Clobber for Terry-Toons and many for Rankin-Bass, but is probably best known for doing Tooter Turtle, Riff Raff and Simon Bar Sinister for TTV. He had a long tenure on *The Howdy Doody Show* and hosted a *Popeye* Show in New York for many years. He remains good friends with Animation Director Gene Deitch, with whom he worked on every one of Deitch's projects.

Swift takes up his story here. "I was working as a stand-up comedian and booked at a nightclub. They had a marquee announcing who was on [the bill], but [the name] was different than my own. I went to them and said, 'My name is Ira Stadlin,' and I was kind of annoyed, I [had] a contract. 'Well, that's the name your agent sent me.' And I called the agent, his name was Marty Baum. Marty said, 'Oh yeah, we changed your name.' 'You changed my name?' 'Ira Stadlin sounds like a girl's name.' So for the week that I played at the club, I was Artie Moore. After I got back, I was already booked for a television show. For that television show I was Artie Moore, but I said to my dad [that I didn't] want it to be that stupid name. My father said his favorite humorist was Jonathan Swift. I said that mine was Fred Allen. Allen Swift. That's how it came about.

"I always wanted to be an actor. My dream was to make a living, and to make a living as an actor was second and that was it. I was never thinking about television and obviously I grew up in the radio period and all my heroes were radio actors. I was an entertaining person and a good comedian and that was an easy way to get into the business. I was not dependent on anyone else to work with. I did my own material. I stood up and performed it.

"My ability in mimicry was always there. It was always great. I could duplicate almost any role. Now, I never gave it much thought because at the very beginning of my career or semi-career as I thought of performing of doing my comedy, I did impersonations. I met a professional performer, who said, 'Ira, don't do impersonations. You will become known as an impersonator, while the actor comedians make a lot more money.' The impersonator is usually the first one on the bill, so using that information I did not do mimicry professionally. Actually, in the '50s, I started getting successful. I was getting better in nightclubs and theaters and I had finally got an agent who was Lew Grade of England. He booked me at the Palace, which, of course, was a great thing for comedians to play at. After the Palace, he booked me at the Palladium and more offers came through, including *The Howdy Doody Show*.

"A friend of mine named Jack Barron, Associate Producer at the Palace, set up the auditions and asked me to create voices for *The Howdy Doody Show*. They already had these voices and I asked, 'Whatever happened to the people who did this show?' They said, 'Forget about it. That's not important.' They were looking for a new voice to do them. They had given up on matching the voices. Everybody in that cast had apparently walked out on their contracts, and they decided to recast. That was what I was told, but I don't know if it was true or not.

"So Bob Smith, who owned most of the show, and did the voice of Howdy Doody, let them walk. The deal was that those characters would go to this island and they would all come back with different voices. He had no problem with Howdy; he had a problem with all the other characters. I said, 'Wouldn't you rather have voices that sound the same?' 'Look, we've gone through this already. We've had everybody.' So I said, 'Give me a record of it so I can listen to it and come back.' The main people who did the voices were gone. So there I was hired for a television show, but I couldn't get over the fact. I thought, 'Wow, I can be home with my son, and not have to be out on the road.' So that ended my stand-up comedy career and started me on the voiceovers. I replaced Dayton Allen and everyone — everyone who had walked off!"

Next to be hired was Jackson Beck. Born July 23, 1912, the man who would make his mark at the forefront of American broadcasting began his career against the wishes of his actor father, Max Beck. "He didn't want me to become an actor because he knew what kind of a tough business it was, but I persisted anyway."

Early in his career, part of Beck's bread and butter was performing for Columbia Pictures' condensed radio versions of their new films, which served as a kind of audio "coming attractions" for movies soon to be released to theaters. Hired on the strength of his impersonation skills of the leading actors of the time, Beck recalls that he had little competition in impersonating dramatic leading men like Fredric March or John Payne. "Who the hell goes around impersonating them? But I could do them, so I did them."

His quest for a regular berth took a side trip in 1944, when on a tip from an agent friend he learned that Famous Studios was hiring. He auditioned for the Fleischer brothers as a voice on the *Popeye* animated shorts and landed the role of Bluto.

Beck was not the first Bluto; that distinction belonged to William Pennell, who had passed away. Others tried their hand at the role until Beck secured it from 1944 through 1957, and again as Brutus in newly-made TV *Popeye* cartoons in the early 1960s.

He was also announcer on many "Little Caesar" pizza commercials and the 1980s *G.I. Joe* series, and was the voice of "Buzzy the Crow" for Famous Studios in the 1940s and '50s.

For TTV, his voice also appeared on various "Big G" cereal commercials and announcements and his talents were utilized again as bridging narrator for *The Dudley Do-Right Show*, a P.A.T. patch job utilizing repeat segments from both Jay Ward and TTV shows.

Beck passed away on July 8, 2004.

One of the "trademarks" of the various TTV shows is the establishment of catchphrases, originating primarily because of the four owners' extensive backgrounds in advertising.

As Biggers recalls, "We did it on purpose from the very start. For example, King Leonardo used to say, 'That's the most unheard of thing I've ever heard of.' We did those things from the beginning because kids love repetition. That's one reason why we could get by with doing only 17 shows and repeating them three times in a year, because kids love repetition. They almost love the repetition more than the original time because they almost like to know what's going to happen and even talk with it and almost say the lines. So, when you have repeat lines like that it also helps when they play make believe and they pretend that they are your character. If they don't have anything to say like, 'There's no need to fear, Underdog is here!' it's very hard for them to imitate the character. We wanted that because that's the stuff that will help build your show's ratings, so we purposefully went after that."

Biggers goes on to explain how their shows, though targeted toward children, were appealing to older ages as well. "There are two things there that go together. One is that when we did our shows, there were mostly one-TV homes. You didn't think of five TV sets in the house, you thought of one. And you thought we've got to do something here that not only appeals to little kids, but also to bigger kids, or they'll take the TV away from the little kids. And, you've got to do something if you can that has some appeal for adults. And also we had to sell to adults. You might not think that's important, but if they don't laugh, they don't think it's funny, you understand? You can say to them, 'Kids will love this!,' and if they don't laugh themselves, they don't think it's funny. So, in dealing with those things, we found out that it's wonderful if you use voices that mothers or fathers had seen in the movies. In other words, not the person but their voice, it gives them a feeling of familiarity and they kind of enjoy it, so we found that was true and so it was also easier with older kids so we developed that and used it whether they'd seen it on TV or seen it in movies or whatever."

It was also decided to make the *King and Odie* stories each run two parts rather than one in order to keep the viewers tuned in, but less than the multi-part stories that Jay Ward produced in order to allow more flexibility for programmers, who wouldn't be forced to run *King Leonardo* shows in any particular order after their initial run.

King Leonardo aired on NBC through September 28, 1963, when it was syndicated in reruns under the series title of *The King and Odie*. So popular was TTV's first series success that the named Leonardo stuck as their production company for subsequent series, so TTV and Leonardo were interchangeable production company names. New episodes continued to air on *Tennessee Tuxedo and his Tales* and ultimately 104 episodes of *King and Odie* were produced.

Gordon Johnson commented on the success of the first TTV show for *Animato*! "*The King Leonardo Show*, after only three national ratings, is the top rated children's program on daytime network television. As you know, the initial rating produced a 40% share of audience and we were very excited about this performance. The second and third ratings exceeded 50% in share which makes it by far the best performing new show of any type on television this year."

According to the Wikipedia, "Handling the General Mills account as an account executive with the Dancer-Fitzgerald-Sample advertising agency in New York in 1960, Biggers teamed with Chet Stover, Tread Covington and artist Joe Harris to create TV animation (*King Leonardo, Tennessee Tuxedo*) as formats to sell General Mills breakfast cereals. With the success of Underdog, Biggers and his partners left Dancer-Fitzgerald-Sample to form their own company, Total Television, with animation produced at Gamma Studios in Mexico." This is not correct as Biggers and company left DFS long before the creation of Underdog.

Frank Andrina (born in 1933) is one of the few surviving animators who worked on the three segments of *King Leonardo and his Short Subjects* at TV Spots, which was located on Cole, just below Santa Monica Boulevard in Los Angeles. This was only for a short time in the case of *King Leonardo*, as work on the show was soon transferred completely to Gamma Productions in Mexico. TV Spots also animated a number of *Fractured Fairy Tales* for Jay Ward before that, too, was transferred completely to Gamma.

TV Spots was a small commercial animation studio that Shull Bonsall had bought in 1954. Bob Ganon, General Manager of TV Spots, interested Bonsall in producing animated cartoons in addition to their regular TV commercial assignments. One of their earliest series was the 1957 color version of *Crusader Rabbit* that had no Jay Ward involvement, unlike the earlier 1949 black-and-white series, which was an early Jay Ward series.

TV Spots also did the animation for a number of other animated cartoons of the era, which resemble the TTV shows, but have no other affiliation. Andrina explains, "[There] was the *Calvin and the Colonel* and it was an hour-long show, and it was pretty good. It was opposite *Perry Mason* so it lasted about a couple weeks. It was on in primetime, originally.

"*King Leonardo* was done at another building and it was the 'B' animators. *King Leonardo* and that other show, *Tooter the Turtle*, I worked on those overtime at night. [TV Spots] did a pilot as I was leaving, for *Beetle Bailey*, but I don't think it went over well, and I quit there just toward the end.

"*Linus [the Lionhearted]* was the same studio, but it was in another building and it was with the 'C' animators, along with *Calvin and the Colonel* and *Tooter the Turtle* and so forth. They did overtime on them. I worked on [*Linus the Lionhearted*] overtime. None of the regular animators worked on *Calvin and the Colonel*.

"Gerry Ray was the director and I worked with him a lot, and Bob Ganon, who was one of the producers. We worked for about a year and a half and did 26 shows and they were an hour each.

"The animators [at TV Spots] went out every afternoon to watch the live-action show of *Amos 'n Andy* in order to get the feel for these characters. They had a lot of animators that were listed in the titles at the end of the episode. I looked at the end of the shows that I've got, and practically everybody's dead.

"There are some bad things that happened at TV Spots. There was an animator there named Pat Mackey. He was a very good animator at one time, and then he had an accident that affected his brain. They hired him and everything he did had to be changed, so that was funny. So they spent a lot of money on him and also a guy named Al Paisley, and everything he did had to be changed. I didn't know why we were paying this guy. That's the bad thing. They didn't do a thing he said, and they canceled the show.

"It was the first show aired in color because they planned to use it ahead. They said that *Calvin and the Colonel* was to be aired in color, but all I saw was black and white. It was a team effort of limited animation. At the time I was doing it, I thought it was full, but we saw some of it on the screen, and it was extremely limited.

"After *Calvin and the Colonel*, I went over to Snowball; they were working on *Beany and Cecil*, and then there was a layoff. Then, I must have gone to Hanna-Barbera."

Harris comments on TV Spots, "That was a company on the West Coast. We did start doing that until we found out that they were much too expensive and Gamma Studios was already in existence in Mexico, and they decided, as they will in their wisdom, that if it's cheap, it must be good. I don't know whether they took a lease on that building or what they did, but they decided that they were going to go to Mexico City. Why they didn't go to Korea or Czechoslovakia, I don't know, because those are two wonderful studios. Ernie Pintoff went to Czechoslovakia, and did incredible work there, and married a Czechoslovakian girl. For all I know, he's still there. I haven't heard. There was this TV Spots and they decided that that was going to be too expensive."

"Captain" Allen Swift" hosted a popular children's show in New York in the 1950s featuring *Popeye* cartoons.

Allen Swift's accurate imitation of Popeye's voice allowed him to voice the famous sailor on record on at least one occasion.

The cast of the *King & Odie* segment of *King Leonardo and his Short Subjects* included Itchy Brother, Biggy Rat, Odie Colognie and the King himself.

Above: The King made a sole children's book appearance in 1962 with *King Leonardo and the Royal Contest*. *Right:* King Leonardo appeared in seven Gold Key comic books from 1960-1962. FROM THE AUTHOR'S COLLECTION.

CREATED AND PRODUCED BY TOTAL TELEVISION PRODUCTIONS

King Leonardo was the first heavily-marketed TTV character with many toys, records and cereal boxes featuring his likeness. SOME ITEMS FROM THE AUTHOR'S COLLECTION.

The King and Odie -- Episode 2 -- "The Man From the Moon"

Narrator: And now back to Bongo Congo. The Brave king Leonardo, tricked into going up in the Whirl-a-scope by Biggy Rat and Itchy Brother, was feared lost when the whirl-a-scope hurtled back to earth and hit in a terrific explosion. But there was no doubt about where Biggy Rat and Itchy Brother were -- they had moved into the palace and put Itchy on the throne! Things looked bad for King Leonardo's loyal servant, Odie Colognie! ...
(UNDER NARRATION, FLAG WITH LEONARDO'S PICTURE IS PULLED DOWN FROM TOP OF PALACE, ITCHY'S PICTURE FLAG GOES UP IN ITS PLACE -- THEN SHOT TO THRONE ROOM WITH ITCHY SPRAWLED AND SCRATCHING ON THRONE -- BIGGY SMOKING CIGAR AND PACING NEARBY)
(ODIE BURSTS INTO THRONE ROOM) (SOUND: Doors Thrown Open)

ODIE: Ah hah! Just where I thought I'd find you scoundrels!

Biggy: Not so fast, big shot. Who let you in, anyway?

Odie: Imposters! My king will have your heads for this!

Itchy: Gee, Odie -- don't be square. Your king is like nowhere!

Odie: My duty is clear -- I must drag you from the throne.
(ODIE CHARGES THE THRONE ONLY TO BE PLUCKED UP BY BIGGY, WHIRLED AND TOSSED LIGHTLY INTO THE CHANDELIER ABOVE THEM)
(SOUND: SCUFFLING, THEN TINKLE OF CHAND)

Biggy: Now listen, guys -- you're both wrong. Look, Colognie, your king's right here. With Kingsy gone, his loyal brother is just doing his duty, see?

Odie: Traitors! My king lives and I shall find him! But first...
(ODIE SWINGS ON CHANDELIER AND LEAPS ON ITCHY SENDING HIM CRASHING THROUGH THE THRONE. (SOUND: CRASH) BIGGY CALMLY PINS ODIE BY HOLDING HIM DOWN WITH HIS FOOT)

Biggy: Now, look, Colognie -- don't get tough, see! (TAKES TOE AND GIVES COLOGNIE A PUSH -- HE ROLLS TO OTHER END OF THRONE ROOM BEING WRAPPED UP IN ROYAL RED CARPET AS HE ROLLS)
(SOUND: THUMP down STAIRS & ROLL)

The complete rough draft script for *The King & Odie,* episode #2, entitled "The Man From the Moon." SCRIPT COURTESY OF TREAD COVINGTON.

Itchy:	So long, Odie, hit the roadie!
Narrator:	And at this very moment as Odie Colognie struggled to free himself from the royal carpet, a strange sight was seen in a far-away part of Bongo Congo ...
	(THE WHIRL-A-SCOPE HAS LANDED IN ONE PEICE AND A CROWD HAS GATHERED. AS IT HISSES AND SPUTTERS, ONE FROM THE CROWD BOLDLY GOES UP AND PULLS THE DOOR OPEN)
King:	(STAGGERS OUT STILL WEARING SPACE HELMUT WITH MANE OVER HIS EYES, BUT LOOKING CONSIDERABLY BATTERED) Confound it! Can't see a thing! Where am I anyway?
Crowd voices or voices:	Bongo Congo -- the earth -- our country -- who is he? -- He's from Mars! -- No, the Moon -- the Man from the Moon!
King:	Of course I'm from the Moon! But you don't fool me -- you're no Earthlings!
Crowd:	Yes! Yes! This is Bongo Congo!
King:	Rediculous! If you were Earthlings you couldn't speak my language.
Crowd:	But you're speaking our language!
King:	I'll settle this, confound it! Take me to your leader.
Crowd:	Yes, yes! To King Leonardo!
King:	Leonardo, huh? Sounds more like a moon name to me ... well, let's go. (STARTS WALKING AND GOES BLINDLY INTO SIDE OF WHIRL-A-SCOPE) (SOUND: THUMP)
Crowd:	No, Moon Man, this way.
King:	(BEING LED AWAY) Confound it, don't you Earthlings ever have any daylight?
Narrator:	And so King Leonardo had returned, but had been so shaken up he'd lost his memory. In his space helmut, his people didn't know him and off they went with what they thought was a Man

from the Moon to meet their leader, King Leonardo! But ~~instead of Leonardo, there was~~ another King on the throne ... (THRONE ROOM - ITCHY IN SAME POSITION AS EARLIER -- SPRAWLING AND SCRATCHING ON THRONE, BIGGY WITH A CIGAR AND PACING)

Itchy: (AS KING ENTERS THRONE ROOM AND HEADS FOR WRONG DIRECTION UNTIL A GUARD TURNS HIM AND LEADS HIM TO ITCHY) Man! Dig that crazy ~~thing~~ face from outer space!

Biggy: Watch it, King -- this may be a plot! Guard, who is this guy?

King: I'm the man from the moon, of course -- and who are you?

Biggy: I'm the king's friend, see? And here's the king... (YANKS ITCHY FROM DOZING INTO REGULAR POSITION ON THRONE)

Itchy: (STARTLED FROM SLEEP) ~~Br~~-what? Oh, yeah! I am like the royal leader and all that jazz.

King: So you're Leonardo, huh? (ASIDE) These Earthlings look sick!

Itchy: Like no, Moon Man -- you're not hep with the latest!

Biggy: Meaning Kingsy blew up in the whirl-a-scope, and this is his loyal brother and next man on the throne, see?

King: (AS WE SEE ODIE STRUGGLING TO FREE HIMSELF FROM ROLLED UP CARPET IN THRONE ROOM CORNER) Well, I'm a busy man. Just point me toward Mars and I'll be on my way!

Odie: (BURSTING FREE FROM THE CARPET): Wait! Wait, your Majesty! This is all a dreadful mistake! (RUSHES TO KING AND TUGS AT HELMUT)

Biggy: Now look, Colognie, don't be a trouble-maker, see? (PLUCKS AT ODIE TO PULL HIM AWAY FROM KING) (YANK PULLS HELMUT FROM KING) (SOUND: CORK OUT OF BOTTLE)

Itchy: Dig that crazy resemblance! Haven't we -- like met before?

Odie: Yes, traitor! This is your brother, the King!

King: Rediculous! I'm the man from the Moon. Who are you?

Odie:	Never fear, your Majesty. You'll soon remember everything!
Biggy:	(SUDDENLY TURNING ON KING AND ODIE) All right you guys -- don't anyone move! (BIGGY SLAMS HELMUT BACK DOWN ON KING AS ITCHY PUSHES ODIE BACK INTO ROLLED-UP CARPET)
King:	Confound it, dark again! Turn on those lights!
Itchy:	Like right away, Moon Man. Hey, guards, like lead these two cats to the cooler!
Biggy:	Meaning the dungeon, see? (PUFFS CIGAR WITH VICTORY GLEAM)
Odie:	(FROM CARPET) You've gone too far, Biggy Rat! You'll pay for this! Your heads will (AT THIS POINT, BIGGY AGAIN KICKS CARPET WITH HIS TOE AND IT ROLLS OUT ROOM) r-o-l-l-l-l-l! (AND GUARDS TAKE KING AWAY AS ITCHY PLAYS A BONGO BEAT)
Narrator:	Is this really the end of King Leonardo and Odie Colognie? We'll know the answers when we see the exciting end of this story in the next episode, "All's well that Spins Well!"
Narrator:	it was touch-and-go in Bongo Congo. Deep in the dungeon Biggy Rat and Itchy Brother. Time was running out ... (SHOT OF ALARM CLOCK RUNNING OUT OF DUNGEON ONLY TO BE KICKED BACK IN BY GUARD. BOUNCES AND STOPS AT ODIE WHERE HE IS TALKING TO THE KING)(ODIE HAS JUST MANAGED TO PULL HELMUT OFF OF KING) again, surely you recognize your loyal servant.

(SCENE SHOWS ITCHY LAZILY PLAYING BONGO DRUMS WHILE BIGGY EMPTIES THE ROYAL SAFE OF ITS GOLD) (DOORS BURST OPEN AND KING ENTERS WITH ODIE AND GUARDS).

Biggy: All right, you guys, do some fast talking. Nobody gets out of that dungeon, see?

Itchy: Yeah, like how? Moon Man?

King: Moon Man? Rediculous! I'm the King.

Odie: There, your Majesty! The two traitors -- on your throne and stealing your gold!

King: Guards! Get those theives. (KING LEAPS ON BYCICLE AND SPEEDS TO THRONE)

Itchy: Gee, Big! It's my royal relative, all *right! Let's cut out of here!*

(SOUND: Screech of bycicle brakes.)
Guards throw Itch & Big at King's feet — Odie unfolds carpet from door — When carpet reaches throne, Odie hops off & side, King gives one kick to B & I with his royal toe — The two go rolling up in carpet (SOUND: swish of carpet out the room) (SOUND: Odie & King shake)

The complete rough draft and complete final script for *The King & Odie*, episode #10A, entitled "Royal Amnesia" and the complete final script for "The Man from the Moon," now numbered episode #10B. SCRIPTS COURTESY OF TREAD COVINGTON.

Royal Amnesia Ep #10-A

Narrator: It was a great day, ~~today,~~ in Bongo Congo. Not to be passed up by other countries, Bongo Congo entered the Space Race. For weeks citizens of Bongo Congo had worked on the great whirlea-scope and now it would soon be time for the countdown. ~~So far, xxxxxx only King Leonardo himself knew who the pilot would be for this first all-important test ...~~ and already there was trouble at the palace gates ...

(CLOSEUP OF A PLACARD WITH ITCHY'S HAND POINTING OUT THE WORDS)

Itchy: (READING)"The - king - flys - or - no - test!" Gee! Big, that's a really cool sign!

Biggy: OK, now listen, guy -- cross the draw bridge and march up and down in front of the gates until they open up, see?

Itchy: Yeah, Big, I dig.

(AS ITCHY GOES TOWARD BRIDGE, SHOT OF ODIE COLOGNIE FROM GATE TOWER. HE SPOTS ITCHY WITH HIS BINOCULARS, AND RAISES FREE ARM IN "UP" SIGNAL)

Odie: Guards! Raise the draw bridge! That's no loyal subject -- that's Itchy Brother ... and up to no good!

(DRAW BRIDGE GOES UP JUST BEFORE ITCHY GETS TO IT. ITCHY, WITH HIS SIGN MARCHES OFF BANK INTO AIR UNTIL HE REALIZES HIS PREDICAMENT)

Itchy: Man! Dig that crazy bridge! (THEN ITCHY CRASHES INTO THE MOAT AND UNDER THE WATER. COMES UP SHAKING AND BEDRAGGLED) Cool! Really cool! (SOUND: SPLASH) (SOUND: THRASHING IN WATER)

(NEXT SHOT, BIGGY IN A MOTHER HUBBARD DRESS IS DRESSING ITCHY AND THEY BOTH PUT THEIR WIGS ON)

BIGGY: Now get this, Itch -- we're mothers, see? We'll push these baby buggies straight to Kingsy.

Itchy: Great, Big -- let's scratch (AS HE SCRATCHES. THEY PUSH OFF WITH SIGNS HANGING FROM THEIR BACKS -- "MOTHERS AGAINST SPACE")

(SHOT TO KING LEONARDO WITH ODIE BY HIS SIDE)

KING: Confound it! What's going on around here?

Odie: They would have you believe they are mothers with their babes, oh Sire.

King: You know this isn't my day to kiss babies!

Biggy: Now look, Kingsy, -- we mothers don't like it, see?

King: Confound it! Don't like what?

Odie: Come! Come! Give his Majesty your message ...

Itchy: Oh, yeah, man! Like the message is don't let any mother's boy go up in the Whirl-a-scope! It's -- like not safe!

Biggy: It's like he- er- she says, Majesty. Even if you take the Whirl-a-scope up, with all your lion-like courage, let us not be -- shall we say -- foolish.

King: Ridiculous! I'm the king!
Curtsy

Odie: Bow to his Majesty! Your time is up.

(BIGGY AND ITCHY CURTSY AWKWARDLY. ITCHY LOSES BALANCE AND FALLS, WIG FALLS OFF)

Odie: Itchy Brother! Just as I thought, your Majesty! It's an ugly plot. Guards! Out with these imposters!

Itchy: Hey, Big! I flipped my wig! Let's roll!

Biggy:	(AS TWO GO HURTLING OUT OF PALACE IN THE BABY CARRIAGES) Stick with me, guy. When that Whirl-a-scope goes, Kingsy will be in it! We'll take this to the people! (SHOT TO ITCHY ON SOAP BOX INTRODUCING BIGGY ON LARGER BOX TO CROWD OF BONGO-ITES)
Itchy:	And now all you loyal subjects, dig this message from your friend and mine -- Biggy Rat!
Biggy:	Now, listen, you guys. Is the king a man or a mouse? If the Whirl-a-scope is safe, why doesn't the king go up in it, himself?
Itchy:	Yeah, if the king -- like doesn't fly, then no test!
Crowd:	Yes! Yes!' ~~If The king must fly or no test!~~ The King must fly! The King must fly! (SHOT TO KING PULLING CURTAIN BACK AND WATCHING CROWD SCENE FROM HIS WINDOW)
King:	Of course, I'll fly, confound it!
Odie:	Oh please, your Majesty! This takes months of training! Heed not the rabble crowd!
King:	Train -- my mane! Details--details!
Odie:	But, Sire, if you should go too high, you might not be be able to return to Bongo Congo!
Crowd:	Let the king fly! On with the countdown! We want a space ship!
King:	Well, what are we waiting for?
Odie:	(HEAD TO HANDS) Very well, Your Majesty. But I fear for your very throne! ~~Oh, would that I were wrong!~~

Narrator: And so ~~kixx~~ brave king Leonardo made the fateful decision to take the whirl-a-scope up, himself! All Bongo Congo waited breathlessly for the countdown to begin ...

Odie: (ON LAUNCHING STAND – WHIRL-A-SCOPE VIBRATES IN BACKGROUND TO BEAT OF SLOW, LOW BONGO DRUMS) ~~You~can~still~~ My king can still turn back! Oh let me tell the people you're not well!

King: Humpf! Never felt better!

Odie: As your Majesty commands. (HOLDS OUT HELMUT) Your space helmut, Sire.
(KING PUTS ON SPACE HELMUT. MANE IS PULLED DOWN OVER KING'S EYES, INSIDE HELMUT)

King: Confound it, turn the lights back on! (ACTS AS THOUGH HE CAN'T SEE)

Odie: It's your mane, Sire -- it's pulled down over your eyes!

King: Hmmm, so it is. Well, there's no time to fix that now.

Narrator: (ON LOW, TENSE TONE) Only the Bongo drums could be heard ~~between the counts~~ as loyal Odie Colognie ~~begins the countdown~~ guided ~~brave~~ King Leonardo in his blind bravery to the door of the Whirl-a-scope and helped him in. Then as the huge crowd of Bongo-ites silently watched and waited, Odie Colognie began the countdown...

Odie: Ten nine eight
~~one ... two ... three~~
(SHOT TO STOPWATCH IN BIGGY'S HAND)

Biggy: Well, see you around the world, kingsy! Everything's like I planned it. When Colognie gets to zero, you and I are in the driver's seat. (TO ITCHY)

ITCHY: Yeah, Big? Let's hurry or we'll - like miss it!
(ITCHY STARTS TO RUN OFF BUT BIGGY GRABS BINOCULAR BAND. AS ITCHY RUNS BAND STRETCHES, THEN ITCHY SPRINGS BACK AND BINOCULARS CRASH BACK INTO HIM) (SOUND: BAM)

King: Confound it, I'M not your king, and for the last time, which way is Mars?

Odie: (HEAD TO HANDS) Oh, my poor king! (THEN LOOKS UP WITH BRIGHT IDEA) (ASIDE) But, of course! ~~There is only one way!~~ (TO KING) Very well, Moon Man, follow my instructions, ~~and you'll be there in no time!~~

King: Humph, that's better.

Odie: (STANDS DUNGEON BENCH UP ON END) Climb up here and I'll help you spin off.

King: But, confound it, where's the whirl-a-scope?

Odie: No, No, your Maj -- I mean Moon Man. The Bongo Congo way we just use your tail. Start the countdown!

King: (AS ODIE WINDS THE KING'S TAIL AROUND THE KING) Ten -- eight -- six -- four -- two --

Odie: And ZERO! (AND GIVES A GREAT PULL OF KING'S TAIL. KING SPINS OFF END OF BENCH. BENCH AND ODIE COME CRASHING DOWN. (SOUND: Co) KING LOOKS DOWN AND SEES HE'S IN THIN AIR, HE FLIPS UPSIDE DOWN AND COMES CRASHING DOWN ON HIS HEAD) (SOUND: THUD)

Odie: Your majesty! Speak to me! Now can you remember?

King: Confound it, of course I can -- what am I doing in my own dungeon?

Odie: As your Majesty would guess, it's Biggy Rat and Itchy Brother.

King: Guard! (GUARD APPEARS) Confound it, open this gate! I'm the king!

Guard: King Leonardo! (RECOGNIZING HIM WITHOUT THE HELMUT). Yes, your Majesty! (SOUND: UNLOCKING Gate) (ODIE ABOUT TO LEAVE, REMEMBERS ROLLED-UP CARPET AND TAKES IT ALONG).

Narrator: And meanwhile, up in the throne room, Itchy and Biggy were having a quiet evening at home ... (SOUND: SWEET MUSIC)

(BIG EXPLOSION, THEN SILENCE FOLLOWED BY DISTANT SOUND OF BURSTING ROCKETS AND SUCH IN ALL DIRECTIONS WITH FADE IN OF BONGO DRUMS - GROWING SLOWLY TO FRENZY)

Narrator: What a terrific explosion! Will king Leonardo be saved? Will Biggy put Itchy on the throne? ... and what about Odie Colognie? Will he be left without a friend... or a country? ... We'll find out in our next exciting episode ... "The Man From the Moon"!

(BONGO DRUMS UP TO CRESCENDO - PULSATING - THEN OUT)

(DISSOLVE)

King And Odie - Episode # 10A (4:00)

"Royal Amnesia"

(MUSIC: AFRICAN DRUM BEATS OVER TITLE CARD)

Narrator: It was a great day in Bongo Congo. Not to be passed up by other countries, Bongo Congo entered the Space Race. For weeks citizens of Bongo Congo had worked on the great whirl-a-scope and now it would soon be time for the countdown. (UNDER NARRATION SHOT OF STRANGE LOOKING MACHINE - WHIRL-A-SCOPE - THEN SILHOUETTE OF BIGGY RAT BREAKING INTO MACHINE) But little did the king know that someone was breaking into the whirl-a-scope to cross its wires ... and now these traitors plotted to get the king, himself, to fly the broken space machine.

(CLOSEUP OF A PLACARD WITH ITCHY'S HAND POINTING OUT THE WORDS)

Itchy: (READING) "The - king - flys - or - no - test!" Gee! Big, that's a real cool sign!

Biggy: OK, now listen, guy -- cross the draw bridge and march up and down in front of the palace gates until they open up, see?

Itchy: Yeah, Big, I dig.

(AS ITCHY GOES TOWARD BRIDGE, SHOT OF ODIE COLOGNIE FROM GATE TOWER. HE SPOTS ITCHY WITH HIS BINOCULARS, HE RAISES FREE ARM IN "UP" SIGNAL)

Odie: Guards! Raise the draw bridge! That's no loyal subject -- that's Itchy Brother ... and up to no good!

- 2 -

              (DRAW BRIDGE GOES UP JUST BEFORE ITCHY GETS TO IT.
              ITCHY MARCHES WITH HIS SIGN OFF BANK INTO AIR UNTIL
              HE REALIZES HIS PREDICAMENT)

Itchy: Man! Dig that crazy bridge! (ITCHY PLUNGES INTO MOAT AND UNDER WATER)(SOUND: DIVING PLANE AND SPLASH) (COMES UP SHAKING AND BEDRAGGLED) (SOUND: THRASHING IN WATER) Cool! <u>Really</u> cool!

              (NEXT SHOT, BIGGY IN A MOTHER HUBBARD DRESS IS DRESSING ITCHY AND THEY BOTH PUT THEIR WIGS ON)

Biggy: Now get this, Itch -- we're mothers, see? We'll push these baby buggies straight to Kingsy.

Itchy: Great, Big -- let's scratch (AS HE SCRATCHES. THEY PUSH OFF WITH SIGNS HANGING FROM THEIR BACKS -- "MOTHERS AGAINST SPACE")

              (SHOT TO KING LEONARD) WITH ODIE BY HIS SIDE)

King: Confound it! What's going on around here?

Odie: They are mothers with their babes, oh Sire.

King: You know this isn't my day to kiss babies!

Biggy: Now look, Kingsy -- we mothers don't like it, see?

King: Confound it! Don't like what?

Odie: Come! Come! Give his Majesty your message ...

Itchy: Oh, yeah, man! Like the message is don't let any mother's boy go up in the whirl-a-scope! It's -- like not safe!

Biggy: It's what he - er - she says, Kingsy. This is no job for a boy. <u>You</u> should take the whirl-a-scope up.

King: Ridiculous! I'm the king!

Odie: Curtsy to his Majesty! Your time is up.

              (BIGGY AND ITCHY CURTSY AWKWARDLY. ITCHY LOSES BALANCE AND FALLS, WIG FALLS OFF)

-3-

Odie: Itchy Brother! Just as I thought, your Majesty!
It's an ugly plot. Guards! Out with these imposters!

Itchy: Hey, Big! I flipped my wig! Let's roll!

Biggy: (AS TWO GO HURTLING OUT OF PALACE IN THE BABY CARRIAGES)
Stick with me, guy. When that whirl-a-scope goes, Kingsy will be in it! We'll take this to the people!
(SHOT TO ITCHY ON SOAP BOX INTRODUCING BIGGY ON LARGER
BOX TO CROWD OF BONGO-ITES)

Itchy: And now all you loyal subjects, dig this message from your friend and mine -- Biggy Rat!

Biggy: Now, listen, you guys. Is the king a man or a mouse? If the whirl-a-scope is safe, why doesn't the king go up in it, himself?

Itchy: Yeah, if the king -- like doesn't fly, then no test!

Crowd: Yes! Yes! The king must fly! The king must fly!
(SHOT TO KING PULLING CURTAIN BACK AND WATCHING CROWD
SCENE FROM HIS WINDOW)

King: Of course, I'll fly, confound it!

Odie: Oh please, your Majesty! This takes months of training! Heed not the rabble crowd!

King: Train -- my mane! Details -- details!

Odie: But, Sire, if you should go too high, you might not be able to return to Bongo Congo!

Crowd: Let the king fly! On with the countdown! We want a space ship!

King: Well, what are we waiting for?

Odie: (HEAD TO HANDS) Very well, your Majesty. But I fear for your very throne!

- 4 -

Narrator: And so brave King Leonardo made the fateful decision to take the whirl-a-scope up, himself! All Bongo Congo waited breathlessly for the countdown to begin ...

Odie: (ON LAUNCHING STAND -- WHIRL-A-SCOPE VIBRATES IN BACKGROUND TO BEAT OF SLOW, LOW DRUMS) (SOUND: VIBRATING AND DRUMS) My king can still turn back! Oh let me tell the people you're not well!

King: Humpf! Never felt better!

Odie: As your Majesty commands. (HOLDS OUT HELMET) Your space helmut, Sire.
(KING PUTS ON SPACE HELMUT. MANE IS PULLED DOWN OVER KING'S EYES, INSIDE HELMUT)

King: Confound it, turn the lights back on! (ACTS AS THOUGH HE CAN'T SEE)

Odie: It's your mane, Sire -- it's pulled down over your eyes!

King: Hmmm, so it is. Well, there's no time to fix that now.

Narrator: (IN LOW, TENSE TONE) Only the Bongo drums could be heard (SOUND UNDER: DRUMS) as loyal Odie Colognie guided King Leonardo in his blind bravery to the door of the whirl-a-scope and helped him in. Then as the huge crowd silently watched and waited, Odie Colognie began the countdown ...
(SOUND OF DRUMS OUT)

Odie: Ten...nine...eight...

(SHOT TO STOPWATCH IN BIGGY'S HAND)

Biggy: Well, see you around the world, Kingsy! (TO ITCHY) Everything's like I planned it. When Colognie gets to zero, you and I are in the driver's seat.

Itchy: Yeah, Big? Let's hurry or we'll - like miss it!

- 5 -

(	(ITCHY STARTS TO RUN OFF BUT BIGGY GRABS BINOCULAR BAND. AS ITCHY RUNS BAND STRETCHES, THEN ITCHY SPRINGS BACK AND BINOCULARS CRASH BACK INTO HIM) (SOUND: BAM)
Biggy:	Not *that* seat, blockhead. The Throne! With Kingsy out of the picture, you fill the chair -- get it?
Itchy:	Yeah, Big -- crazy!
	(BACK TO ODIE ON LAUNCHING PLATFORM)
Odie:	Two ... one ... ZERO! (WHIRL-A-SCOPE GOES UP CRAZILY INTO SKY) (SOUND: FURIOUS DRUM BEATING AND WHOSH OF MACHINE) (SOUND: CROWD CHEER)
Narrator:	And the whirl-a-scope was off on its wild, zigzag course toward the planets. The crowd cheered, but Odie Colognie, knowing Biggy and Itchy had been plotting against the king, was worried. Now Odie's radar picked up the space machine's strange course ...
	(CLOSEUP OF RADAR RECORDER SHOWING WILDLY FLASHING LIGHTS AND LINES CLIMBING AND FALLING AND TYING IN AND OUT OF THE GRAPH)
Odie:	(GRABBING A WALKIE TALKIE) This is Odie to his Majesty, this is Odie to his Majesty, come in, your Majesty! (ONLY MORE WILDNESS FROM THE SPACE RADAR RECORDER) (HEAD TO HANDS) Oh, your Majesty! I fear the worst! (SHOT TO BIGGY AND ITCHY TAKING TURNS FOLLOWING COURSE WITH A LONG SPY GLASS)
Biggy:	(AS HE GRADUALLY RAISES GLASS) It's like I said, see? Kingsy's in real trouble. He's going right out of this world!
Itchy:	(TAKING TURN AT GLASS) Hey, Big, my royal relative is like changing his course! (SIGHT THROUGH GLASS SHOWS

- 6 -

WHIRL-A-SCOPE SPECK STOP AND BEGIN FALLING)

Biggy: What'da you mean! (GRABS GLASS AND WATCHES SCOPE GET CLOSER) (SOUND: SCREAM OF DIVING PLANE) (SHOT TO ODIE FRANTICALLY WORKING INSTRUMENTS AND CALLING ON WALKIE-TALKIE)

Odie: Come in, your Majesty, come in, your Majesty! (SOUND: SCREAMING DIVE REACHING CRESCENDO AND THEN CRASH) (THEN BIG EXPLOSION. THEN SILENCE FOLLOWED BY DISTANT SOUND OF BURSTING ROCKETS AND SUCH IN ALL DIRECTIONS WITH FADE IN OF BONGO DRUMS - GROWING SLOWLY TO FRENZY)

Narrator: What a terrific explosion! Will King Leonardo be saved? Will Biggy put Itchy on the throne? ... and what about Odie Colognie? Will he be left without a friend? ... We'll find out in our next exciting episode, "The Man From The Moon"! (MUSIC: DRUMS UP TO PULSATING CRESCENDO AND OUT)

King And Odie - Episode # 10B (3:30)
"The Man From The Moon"

Narrator: Biggy Rat and Itchy Brother moved into the palace and things looked bad for King Leonardo's loyal servant, Odie Colognie. (UNDER NARRATION, FLAG WITH LEONARDO'S PICTURE IS PULLED DOWN FROM TOP OF PALACE, ITCHY'S PICTURE GOES UP IN ITS PLACE. SHOT TO THRONE ROOM WITH ITCHY SPRAWLED AND SCRATCHING ON THRONE -- BIGGY SMOKING CIGAR AND PACING) (ODIE BURSTS INTO THRONE ROOM) (SOUND: DOORS THROWN OPEN)

- 7 -

Odie:	Ah hah! Just where I thought I'd find you scoundrels!
Biggy:	Not so fast, big shot. Who let you in, anyway?
Odie:	Imposters! My king will have your heads for this!
Itchy:	Gee, Odie -- don't be square. Your king is like nowhere!
Odie:	My duty is clear -- I must drag you from the throne. (ODIE CHARGES THE THRONE ONLY TO BE PLUCKED UP BY BIGGY, WHIRLED AND TOSSED LIGHTLY INTO THE CHANDELIER ABOVE THEM) (SOUND: SCUFFLING -- THEN TINKLE OF CHANDELIER)
Biggy:	Now listen, guys -- you're both wrong. Look, Colognie, your king's right here. With Kingsy gone, his loyal brother is just doing his duty, see?
Odie:	Traitors! My king lives and I shall find him! But first ... (ODIE SWINGS ON CHANDELIER AND LEAPS ON ITCHY SENDING HIM CRASHING THROUGH THE THRONE) (SOUND: CRASH) (BIGGY CALMLY PINS ODIE BY HOLDING HIM DOWN WITH HIS FOOT)
Biggy:	Now, look, Colognie -- don't get tough, see! (TAKES TOE AND GIVES COLOGNIE A PUSH -- HE ROLLS TO OTHER END OF THRONE ROOM BEING WRAPPED UP IN ROYAL RED CARPET AS HE ROLLS) (SOUND: THUMP DOWN STAIRS AND ROLL)
Itchy:	So long, Odie, hit the roadie!
Narrator:	And at this very moment as Odie Colognie struggled to free himself from the royal carpet, a strange sight was seen in a far-away part of Bongo Congo ... THE WHIRL-A-SCOPE HAS LANDED IN ONE PIECE AND A CROWD HAS GATHERED) (SOUND: MACHINE HISSING AND SPUTTERING) (MAN FROM CROWD BOLDLY GOES UP AND PULLS DOOR OPEN) (SOUND: DOOR PULLED OPEN)
King:	(STAGGERING OUT, STILL WEARING SPACE HELMUT WITH MANE OVER HIS EYES, LOOKING VERY BATTERED) Confound it! Can't see a thing! Where am I anyway?

- 8 -

Crowd voices:	Bongo Congo -- the earth -- our country --
King:	Bongo Congo, eh? Well who am I?
Man:	Why you must be the man from the moon!
King:	The Moon! Of course, that's it! But you don't fool me -- you're no Earthlings!
Crowd:	Yes! Yes! This is Bongo Congo!
King:	Ridiculous! If you were Earthlings you couldn't speak my language.
Crowd:	But you're speaking our language!
King:	I'll settle this, confound it! Take me to your leader.
Crowd:	Yes, yes! To King Leonardo!
King:	Leonardo, huh? Sounds more like a moon name to me ... well, let's go. (STARTS WALKING AND GOES BLINDLY INTO SIDE OF WHIRL-A-SCOPE) (SOUND: THUMP)
Crowd:	No, Moon Man, this way.
King:	(BEING LED AWAY) Confound it, don't you Earthlings ever have any daylight?
Narrator:	And so King Leonardo had returned -- but had been so shaken up he'd lost his memory. In his space helmut, his people didn't know him from the man in the moon and went off with him to meet their leader, King Leonardo! But another king was on the throne ... (THRONE ROOM - ITCHY IN SAME POSITION AS EARLIER - SPRAWLING AND SCRATCHING ON THRONE, BIGGY WITH A CIGAR AND PACING)
Itchy:	(AS KING ENTERS THRONE ROOM AND HEADS FOR WRONG DIRECTION UNTIL GUARD TURNS HIM AND LEADS HIM TO ITCHY) Man! Dig that crazy face from outer space!
Biggy:	Watch it, King -- this may be a plot! Guard, who is this guy?

- 9 -

King:	I'm the man from the moon, of course -- and who are you?
Biggy:	I'm the king's friend, see? And here's the king ... (YANKS ITCHY FROM DOZING INTO REGULAR POSITION ON THRONE)
Itchy:	(STARTLED FROM SLEEP) Er- what? Oh, yeah! I am like the royal leader and all that jazz.
King:	So you're Leonardo, huh? (ASIDE) These Earthlings look sick!
Itchy:	Like no, Moon Man -- you're not hep with the latest!
Biggy:	Meaning Kingsy blew up in the whirl-a-scope, and this is his loyal brother and next man on the throne, see?
King:	(AS ODIE STRUGGLES TO FREE HIMSELF FROM ROLLED UP CARPET IN THRONE ROOM CORNER) Well, I'm a busy man. Just point me toward Mars and I'll be on my way!
Odie:	(BURSTING FREE FROM THE CARPET) Wait! Wait, your Majesty! This is all a dreadful mistake! (RUSHES TO KING AND TUGS AT HELMUT)
Biggy:	Now look, Colognie, don't be a trouble-maker, see? (PLUCKS AT ODIE TO PULL HIM AWAY FROM KING -- YANK PULLS HELMUT FROM KING) (SOUND: CORK OUT OF BOTTLE)
Itchy:	Dig that crazy resemblance! Haven't we -- like met before?
Odie:	Yes, traitor! This is your brother, the King!
King:	Ridiculous! I'm the man from the moon. Who are you?
Odie:	Never fear, your Majesty. You'll soon remember everything!
Biggy:	(SUDDENLY TURNING ON KING AND ODIE) All right you guys -- don't anyone move! (BIGGY SLAMS HELMUT BACK DOWN ON KING) (SOUND: SQUSH) (ITCHY PUSHES ODIE BACK INTO ROLLED-UP CARPET) (SOUND: PLOP)
King:	Confound it, dark again! Turn on those lights!
Itchy:	Like right away, Moon Man. Hey, guards, like lead these two cats to the cooler!

- 10 -

Biggy:	Meaning the dungeon, see? (PUFFS CIGAR WITH VICTORY GLEAM)
Odie:	(FROM CARPET) You've gone too far, Biggy Rat! You'll pay for this! Your heads will (BIGGY AGAIN KICKS CARPET WITH HIS TOE AND IT ROLLS OUT ROOM) (SOUND: BUMPING AND ROLLING) r - o - l - l - l - l - l! (GUARDS TAKE KING OUT AS ITCHY PLAYS BONGO BEAT) (SOUND: BONGOS)
Narrator:	We'll be right back to this exciting story!

King And Odie - Episode 10C (1:30)

Narrator:	Deep in the dungeon, time was running out ... (SHOT OF ALARM CLOCK RUNNING OUT OF DUNGEON ONLY TO BE KICKED BACK IN BY GUARD) (SOUND: RUNNING, THEN KICK AND CLANK OF CLOCK) (CLOCK BOUNCES AND STOPS AT ODIE WHERE HE IS TALKING TO THE KING AFTER PULLING KING's HELMUT OFF)
Odie:	Now that your Majesty can see, again, surely you recognize your loyal servant!
King:	Confound it, I'm not your king, and for the last time, which way is Mars?
Odie:	(HEAD TO HANDS) Oh, my poor king! (THEN LOOKS UP WITH BRIGHT IDEA) (ASIDE) But, of course! When he hit his head in the whirl-a-scope, he lost his memory...if his head gets hit again, his memory may come back! (TO KING) Very well, Moon Man, follow my instructions!
King:	Humph, that's better.
Odie:	(STANDS DUNGEON BENCH UP ON END) Climb up here and I'll help you spin off.

- 11 -

King: But, confound it, where's the whirl-a-scope?

Odie: No, No, your Maj -- I mean Moon Man. The Bongo Congo way, we just use your tail. Start the countdown!

King: (AS ODIE WINDS THE KING'S TAIL AROUND THE KING) Ten -- eight -- six -- four -- two --

Odie: And ZERO! (GIVES A GREAT PULL TO KING'S TAIL. KING SPINS OFF END OF BENCH. BENCH AND ODIE COME CRASHING DOWN) (SOUND: CRASH) (KING LOOKS DOWN AND SEES HE'S IN THIN AIR, HE FLIPS UPSIDE DOWN AND COMES CRASHING DOWN ON HIS HEAD) (SOUND: THUD)

Odie: Your Majesty! Speak to me! Now can you remember?

King: Confound it, of course I can -- what am I doing in my own dungeon?

Odie: As your Majesty would guess, it's Biggy Rat and Itchy Brother.

King: Guard! (GUARD APPEARS) Confound it, open this gate! I'm the king!

Guard: King Leonardo! (RECOGNIZING HIM WITHOUT THE HELMET) Yes, your Majesty! (SOUND: UNLOCKING OF GATE)(ODIE, ABOUT TO LEAVE ALSO, REMEMBERS ROLLED-UP CARPET AND TAKES IT ALONG)

Narrator: And meanwhile, up in the throne room, Itchy and Biggy were having a quiet evening at home ... (SOUND: SWEET MUSIC)(SCENE SHOWS ITCHY LAZILY PLAYING BONGO DRUMS WHILE BIGGY EMPTIES THE ROYAL SAFE OF ITS GOLD) (DOORS BURST OPEN) (SOUND: DOORS THROWN OPEN, MUSIC OUT) (KING ENTERS WITH ODIE AND GUARDS)

Biggy: All right, you guys, do some fast talking. Nobody gets out of that dungeon, see?

- 12 -

Itchy:	Yeah, like how, Moon Man?
King:	Moon Man? Ridiculous! I'm the king.
Odie:	There, your Majesty! The two traitors -- on your throne and stealing your gold!
King:	Guards! Get those theives. (KING LEAPS ON BYCYCLE AND SPEEDS TO THRONE)
Itchy:	Gee, Big! It's my royal relative, all right! Let's cut out of here! (SOUND: SCREECH OF BICYCLE BRAKES) (GUARDS THROW ITCH AND BIG AT KING'S FEET. ODIE UNFURLS CARPET FROM DOOR, RIDING IT ALL THE WAY TO THRONE LIKE A LOG. WHEN CARPET REACHES THRONE ODIE HOPS OFF AND KING GIVES ONE KICK TO BIGGY AND ITCHY WITH HIS ROYAL TOE. THE TWO GO ROLLING UP IN CARPET AND OUT THE ROOM. ODIE AND KING SHAKE HANDS) (SOUND: SWISH OF CARPET, CARPET BUMPING AND ROLLING AND CRASHING OUT ROOM)

###

CHAPTER 3

"I AM THE HUNTER!"

Other *Short Subjects* to appear on the show included *The Hunter*, a dog detective pursuing a fox character appropriately named The Fox. The Hunter worked for a human being cop, Officer Flim Flanagan. Each episode follows a similar theme: The Fox steals some outlandish product and goes into business for himself reselling whatever he has stolen as it is now a rare commodity. Usually, Officer Flanagan puts the Hunter on the case and the Hunter gets the Fox either intentionally or by dumb luck, more often dumb luck. His business card reads: "Have Nose, Will Hunt." 65 episodes were produced and new episodes aired not only on *King Leonardo*, but on *Tennessee Tuxedo* and *Underdog* as well.

Covington confirms, "We had another episode within the half hour called *The Hunter*, and this had a private-eye detective hound dog character. Buck and Chet said that they had in mind the character of the senator that Kenny Delmar did on Allen's Alley on *The Fred Allen Show* — Senator Claghorn."

Biggers remembers the story of how they got voice actor Kenny Delmar to portray the Hunter. "We were so used to using imitators that when we dreamed up the Hunter, we were going to use a Kenny Delmar impersonator. It was Tread who said, 'Why don't we call Kenny Delmar?' And we called him and he leaped at it. In the movies they always did a chicken of him [Foghorn Leghorn] and always had some imitator's voice [Mel Blanc]. He always got sick of that. So, we used Kenny Delmar and he became a voice of other characters as well."

Adds Covington, "They said, 'Let's have a voice that sounds sort of the way Kenny Delmar did Senator Claghorn.' I said, 'Why don't I see if I can get in touch with Kenny Delmar?' and they laughed and said, 'Just get someone who sounds like him.'

"I was determined to find out if Kenny was still around and kicking. I guess you might say I was too naïve to think this couldn't possibly work. I just went into the Manhattan phone book, and there was Kenny Delmar listed. I called him and told him about our show and how we'd like The Hunter to sound like Senator Claghorn. I must have reached him at a good time. And I said, 'If you are interested, let's get together and talk more about it,' and he said, 'Yes, I think that would be terrific.' So I said, "Would you like to meet for lunch at '21'?' 'That would be just fine,' Kenny suggested.

"I knew that they wouldn't know me from Adam so I said, 'I'm calling for Mr. Kenny Delmar. He and Tread Covington would like to have lunch. You know Kenny loves the Bar Room, it has model airplanes.' They promptly gave me a very nice table, and that was the way we met. He was terrific. We became great personal friends, and I'm still in touch with one of his sons who is now a New York real-estate lawyer. So that was a sample of our finding voices we like for our shows."

Delmar was born September 5, 1910, in Boston, and died on July 14, 1984.

The Fox and Officer Flim Flanagan were the first of many TTV characters portrayed by voice actor Ben Stone. Not much is known about Stone, and in preparing this book, not much further information was given other than he also portrayed Rocky Monanoff, Cad Lackey and Cauliflower Cabby/The Champion for TTV in succeeding years. Prior to TTV, Stone portrayed Major "Blast-Off" Connel in the 1950 live-action TV series *Tom Corbett: Space Cadet*.

George S. Irving portrayed virtually all of the other male characters on *King Leonardo* and especially in *The Hunter*. He was born George Irving Shelasky, in Springfield, Massachusetts, on November 1, 1922. His biggest claim to fame at TTV was the narrator for *Underdog*, but he always seemed to be lurking in the background on other TTV shows.

Outside of TTV, Irving is a noted actor/comedian from the Broadway stage, a career that landed him a 1973 Tony for Outstanding Supporting Actor in *Irene*. He also had a role on the short-lived 1976 sitcom *The Dumplings*, and is probably best known for his portrayal of the temperamental Heat Miser in the 1974 Rankin-Bass holiday classic *The Year Without a Santa Claus*, which also features fellow TTV voice alumnus Bradley Bolke. Irving still appears occasionally on the New York stage to this day.

Little is also known about voice actress Delo States, who portrayed all other female characters on this and every TTV show, except for Sweet Polly Purebred. States is an accomplished New York voice actress and more misinformation has been given about her than accurate information. Claims that she was the original voice of the Trix Rabbit or Stanley Livingston on *Tennessee Tuxedo* are erroneous, yet they appear in a number of references. Both characters were actually portrayed by Mort Marshall.

Biggers comments on how many of their characters got their names. "We found that when kids read about a hunter, they thought about *The Hunter*. That's where Tennessee Tuxedo got his name. Every time they saw Tennessee in the books or in school or heard about it on the radio, they thought about our character. That's called 'top spin' and that's how Underdog got his name. America loves an underdog. It's hard to read a sports section of a newspaper without seeing the word 'underdog.' You hear it on the news all the time."

The cast of *The Hunter* segment of *King Leonardo and his Short Subjects* included The Hunter, Officer Flim Flanagan, and The Fox. The Hunter's nephew, Horrors Hunter, did not appear until the later episodes that originally aired during *Tennessee Tuxedo*.

The complete rough draft, complete second draft and complete final script for *The Hunter*, episode #2, entitled "Counterfeit Wants." The rough draft script is in brittle shape. SCRIPTS COURTESY OF TREAD COVINGTON.

Narrator:	Well, it started out to be a Monday just like any other Monday in Spring, except that it was raining. BUCKETS of water. The Hunter -- on the prowl for a desperate criminal -- decided to stop for a cup of tea ... (UNDER NARRATION BUCKETS OF WATER FALLING ON THE HUNTER WHO DUCKS INTO A TEA SHOP)
Hunter:	(AS WAITRESS BRINGS CUP OF TEA, HE UNFURLS A WANTED POSTER AND STUDIES IT) (READING) "Wanted -- Kindly old grandmother for peddling HOT TEA!" Hmmmm -- That kindly, crooked face -- Ah say ah'd know it anywhere! (IN OLD LADY VOICE)
Waitress:	(WHO'S PICTURE IS ON THE POSTER) Here's your hot tea, Mr. Hunter-- (THEN LOOKS AT PICTURE) My! What a pretty girl -- and looks so familiar!
Hunter:	My very words, fair lady -- ah say ah'd know it anywhere!
Waitress:	(CACKLING) Why I do believe it's me! Imagine you carrying my picture!
Hunter:	(LEAPS UP TURNING TABLE OVER WHICH THROWS TEA CUP INTO WAITRESS'S HAND) Ah hah! Just as I thought -- and everything fits -- even the hot tea!
Waitress:	Pity sakes! What do you mean?
Hunter:	(PUTTING HANDCUFFS ON WAITRESS) Come quietly, fair lady --you're the kindly crooked old grandmother and ah'm takin' you in! (DISSOLVE WITH DUM-DE-DUM-DUM MUSIC TO POLICE STATION WHERE OFFICER FLIM FLANAGAN IS STUDYING WANTED POSTERS AND LOOKS UP AS HE HEARS THE COMMOTION OF VOICES AS HUNTER AND WAITRESS ENTER)
Waitress:	I'll tell your mother, Sonny, treatin' an old lady like this!
Hunter:	Ah hah! Just what a kindly old grandmother would say! ITS FLANAGAN!
Flanagan:	Sure an I mighta' known it would be the Hunter! It's a regular flood I'm havin' of false arrests, and you had to go and add on

Hunter: False arrest? Folderol! Ah say, son, it's right here in black and white!

Flanagan: Sure, sure. And look at all the others right here on me desk! (SHOTS OF WANTED POSTERS AS FLANAGAN CALLS THEM OUT) The mayor -- the banker -- the nursmaid -- the teacher -- and on an' on!

Hunter: Don't worry, son -- ah say ah'll bring 'em all in or my name isn't --- THE HUNTER! (WHIPS OUT HORN AND BLASTS) (FLANNAGAN AND WAITRESS COVER EARS IN PAIN)

Flanagan: No, no, Hunter! It's all a mistake! We haven't got a thing on these people -- but sure as me name's Flim Flanagan, someone's up to no good!

Hunter: Hmmmm -- (TO WAITRESS) Very well, fair lady -- (REMOVING HANDCUFF) you're free. (SHE CLAMPS HER OPENED HAND-CUFF ON HUNTER'S OTHER HAND SO THAT HE'S HANDCUFFED TO HIMSELF)

Waitress: (AS SHE EXITS) There! That'll keep you from harming old ladies!

Hunter: Trapped by my own handcuffs! That's a mean practical joke, son!

Flanagan: Wrong again, Hunter -- with you it's just practical! Now listen closely ... (THE HUDDLE IN CONFIDENCE)

Narrator: Little do Flanagan and the Hunter know that someone watches from a room nearby -- (SHOT TO SMALL LIGHT IN WINDOW THEN TELESCOPE AND FOLLOWING IT TO IT'S END, IT IS THE FOX)

Fox: So they're planing to get me, huh? (PUTS TELESCOPE DOWN AND GOES OVER TO CAMERA, WHERE HE'S COPYING PICTURES ON WANTED POSTERS) Well, looks like this little poster is just in time -- (SHOT OF THE HUNTER, HIMSELF, AS FOX READS MESSAGE) "Wanted -- dead or alive -- suggest immediate hanging without trial!" ... Poetry! Sheer poetry! Guess that'll fix the long nose of the law!

+ Whoever is behind this is makin' countafit postera to arrest people for other people — for a price. — 'an I say, surer 'n sure — it's the fox!

(PHONE RINGS AND FOX ANSWERS)

FOX: FOX studios -- your face is xxxx my -- er your fortune" -- can I help you?

Voice: Pick a pack of posters ...

Fox: Hmmm -- the passwords! Friend! You've come to the right place-- I'll get your man -- just name the face!

Voice: You make phony wanted posters, right?

Fox: Please, please! watch your language! (IN MOCK HURT)

Voice: I want my wife arrested -- can you fix it?

Fox: Fix it! My good man, her poster will be my masterpiece -- just send money ... I'll take care of the rest! -- In the park in ten minutes! (FOX GRABS CAMERA, LOWERS HIMSELF DOWN ROPE OUT WINDOW TO WAITING BICYCLE AND DASHES OFF TO PARK) (DISSOLVE TO PARK -- HUNTER HALF DOZES ON BENCH, PORTABLE RADIO PLAYS NEWS BESIDE HIM)

Radio news: Brought in for kidnapping babies, the suspect turned out to be a little girl xxx with her doll -- but -- and get this -- her picture was on wanted posters all over town. This makes the tenth false arrest. The xxwxrdxx city is losing all it's money on rewards, alone, and it looks like officer Flim Flannagan's job unless he gets to the bottom of this !"

Fox: (Slams on brakes in front of the Hunter) and flips radio dial to music) You poor old man trying to sleep with all that noise! Ah, music! Music will soothe!

Hunter: Ah'll thank you suh, to unhand my radio -- ah'm on a case, son!

Fox: (LEAPING ON BICYCLE) Yes, friend, you are a case, and that's the truth! (AS FOX DASHES AWAY, A FRESH POSTER FALLS FROM HIS COAT TO THE FEET OF THE HUNTER -- THE POSTER OF THE HUNTER)

Hunter: (PICKS UP POSTER) Hmmm ... another crooked face. Ah say the woods are full of'em. And ah need all the help ah can get -- ah'll just tack this poster up where everyone can see it -- (BEGINS TACKING POSTER TO A TREE. NIXXX ON OTHER SIDE OF THE

	(MAN AND WIFE TALK TO FOX WHO IS UNDER HIS PHOTO CLOTH)
Man:	Are you from Fox Studios?
Fox:	That's the place, friend -- "your face is your fortune" -- how about shooting the little lady?
Man:	Just a picture, please. This is my wife.
Fox:	Oh, yes, your wife. (TO WIFE) My; you're the lucky one -- it's my special this week. Now watch the birdie -- (GRABS BIRD FROM TREE) (FLASH AND PICTURE IS TAKEN) That's a beauty! Fifty greenbacks, thank you!
Wife:	Fifty dollars! Herbert!
Fox:	I know what you're thinking, but don't force more money on me. People will talk about this picture everywhere! It'll be ready tomorrow -- pick it up at the post office! (AND ON OTHER SIDE OF TREE, HUNTER HAS TACKED HIS POSTER UP AND STANDS BACK TO TAKE LONG LOOK)
Hunter:	Public enemy number one! He'll never escape me! Ah say ah know that face like my own! (FOX SLYLY WATCHING FROM AROUND TREE QUICKLY CHANGES INTO POLICE UNIFORM AND STEPS UP TO HUNTER)
Fox:	Hey, you with the nose, what's goin' on here?
Hunter:	My card, suh -- I am the hunter!
Fox:	Hunter, eh? A likely story. I'm taking you in.
Hunter:	Now wait a minute, son -- ah say, who do you think ah am?
Fox:	(WHIPPING OUT MIRROR AND POINTING TO POSTER) See for yourself!
Hunter:	Why -- why that's me! An' a mighty good likeness at that!
Fox:	(ASIDE) Thanks, it was nothing! (TO HUNTER) Well, sorry, old man, but like the sign says --"suggest immediate hanging without trial!" (FOX THROWS ROPE AROUND TREE BRANCH AND BEGINS TO TIE LO AROUND HUNTER'S NECK)

(SOUND OF SIREN GROWS LOUDER AS PATROL WAGON RUSHES UP WITH FLANAGAN AND WOMAN WHOM FOX PHOTOGRAPHED IN PARK. FOX TURNS TO LOOK AND HUNTER INNOCENTLY PUTS NOOSE AROUND FOX)

Hunter: Now just hold it a minute boy, you tie a no-count knot -- here, ah'll show you how.

(FLANAGAN RACING FROM PATROL WAGON WITH WOMAN RUNNING ALONG)

Woman: THat's the crook, officer -- the one tied up!

Flanagan: Sure ' an it's the fox, for all his hidin' in a police uniform!

Hunter: The fox, eh? Well, boy, looks like the ropes on you! that's a joke, son -- get it!

Fox: Very funny. Very funny. Ok, Flanagan -- so I make a few posters, and you wanna make a federal case out of it!

Flanagan: (TAKING ROPE OFF FOX AND PUTTING HIM IN WAGON) Tell it to the judge, Fox.

Woman: (TO FLANAGAN AND LOOKING TOWARD HUNTER) Officer, thank goodness that man was handy with a rope! Who is he?

Flanagan: Handy with a rope, you say? Why that's (LOOKS AT HUNTER WHO STEPS INTO NOOSE AND IS SWUNG UPSIDE DOWN TO HANG FROM TREE BRANCH BY HIS FOOT. UNDAUNTED, HUNTER BLASTS HIS HUNTING HORN) the HUNTER!

(DISSOLVE)

Hunter - Episode # 2 (4:00)
"Counterfeit Wants"

Narrator: Well, it started out to be a Monday just like any other Monday in spring, except that it was raining buckets of water. The Hunter -- on the prowl for a desperate criminal -- decided to stop for a cup of tea ... (UNDER NARRATION BUCKETS OF WATER FALL ON THE HUNTER WHO DUCKS INTO TEA SHOP) (SOUND: BUCKETS AND WATER CRASHING)

Hunter: (AS WAITRESS BRINGS CUP OF TEA, HE UNFURLS A WANTED POSTER AND STUDIES IT) (READING) "Wanted -- kindly old grandmother for peddling HOT TEA!" Hmmm -- that kindly, crooked face -- I say, I'd know it anywhere!

Waitress: (WHO'S PICTURE IS ON THE POSTER) (IN OLD LADY VOICE) Here's your hot tea, Mr. Hunter -- (LOOKS AT PICTURE) My! What a pretty girl -- and looks so familiar!

Hunter: My very words, fair lady -- I say I'd know it anywhere!

Waitress: (CACKLING) Why, I do believe it's me! Imagine you carrying my picture!

Hunter: (LEAPS UP TURNING TABLE OVER WHICH THROWS TEA CUP INTO WAITRESS'S HAND) (SOUND: CRASH OF TABLE) Ah huh! Just as I thought -- and everything fits -- even the hot tea!

Waitress: Pity sakes! What do you mean?

Hunter: (PUTTING HANDCUFFS ON WAITRESS) (SOUND: CLANK) Come quietly, fair lady -- you're the kindly crooked old grandmother and I'm takin' you in! (DISSOLVE WITH DUM-DE-DUM-DUM MUSIC TO POLICE STATION WHERE OFFICER FLIM FLANAGAN IS STUDYING WANTED POSTERS AND LOOKS UP AS HE HEARS THE COMMOTION OF VOICES AS HUNTER AND WAITRESS ENTER) (MUSIC OUT UNDER VOICES)

- 2 -

Waitress: I'll tell your mother, Sonny, treatin' an old lady like this!

Hunter: Ah hah! Just what a kindly old grandmother would say!

Flanagan: Sure an' I mighta' known it would be the Hunter! It's a regular flood I'm havin' of false arrests -- sure an' you're not adding another?!

Hunter: False arrest? Folderol! I say, son, it's right here in black and white!

Flanagan: Sure, sure. And look at all the others right here on me desk! (SHOTS OF WANTED POSTERS AS FLANAGAN CALLS THEM OUT) The mayor -- the banker -- the nursemaid -- the teacher -- and on an' on!

Hunter: Don't worry, son -- I -- I say I'll bring 'em all in or my name isn't -- THE HUNTER! (WHIPS OUT HORN AND BLASTS) (SOUND: HORN) (FLANAGAN AND WAITRESS COVER EARS IN PAIN)

Flanagan: No, no, Hunter! It's all a mistake! We haven't got a thing on these people -- but sure as me name's Flim Flanagan, someone's up to no good!

Hunter: Hmmm -- (TO WAITRESS) Very well, fair lady -- (REMOVING HANDCUFF) you're free! (SHE CLAMPS HER OPENED HANDCUFF ON POLE IN OFFICE) (SOUND: CLANK)

Waitress: (SAYS TO HERSELF AS SHE EXITS) There! That'll keep him from harming old ladies!

Flanagan: Now come here an' look at these, close, Hunter. (POINTING TO POSTERS) (HUNTER STARTS IN RUSH TO FLANAGAN'S DESK, IS JERKED BACK BY HANDCUFF AND SLAMS HEAD ON POLE)

Hunter: Caught by my own cuffs! That's a mean joke, son! (UNLOCKS HANDCUFFS AND GOES TO DESK)

- 3 -

Flanagan: Whoever is behind this is makin' counterfeit posters to arrest people for other people -- for a _price_ -- an' I say, surer 'n sure -- it's the fox!

Narrator: Little do Flanagan and the Hunter know that someone watches from a room nearby --
(SHOT TO SMALL LIGHT IN WINDOW, THEN TELESCOPE AND FOLLOWING IT TO ITS END, IT IS THE FOX)

Fox: So they're after me, huh? (PUTS TELESCOPE DOWN AND GOES OVER TO CAMERA WHERE HE'S COPYING PICTURES ON WANTED POSTERS) Well, looks like this little poster is just in time -- (SHOT OF THE HUNTER, HIMSELF, AS FOX READS MESSAGE) "Wanted -- dead or alive -- suggest immediate hanging without trial!" ... Poetry! Sheer poetry! Guess that'll fix the long nose of the law!
(SOUND: PHONE RING) (FOX ANSWERS)

Fox: Fox studios -- "your face is my -- er _your_ fortune" -- can I help you?

Voice: Pick a peck of posters ...

Fox: Hmmm -- the passwords! Friend! You've come to the right place -- I'll get your man -- just name the face!

Voice: You make phony wanted posters, right?

Fox: Please, please! Watch your language! (MOCK HURT)

Voice: I want my wife arrested -- can you fix it?

Fox: Fix it! My good man, her poster will be my masterpiece -- just send money ... I'll take care of the rest! -- In the park in ten minutes! (FOX GRABS CAMERA, LOWERS HIMSELF DOWN ROPE OUT WINDOW TO WAITING BICYCLE AND DASHES OFF TO PARK)

- 4 -

               (DISSOLVE TO PARK -- HUNTER WALKING ALONG PATH
               AND LISTENING INTENTLY TO PORTABLE RADIO)

Radio: "...brought in for kidnapping babies, the suspect turned out to be a little girl with her doll -- but -- and get this -- her picture was on wanted posters all over town. This makes the tenth false arrest. The city is losing all its money on rewards, alone, and it looks like Officer Flim Flanagan's job unless he gets to the bottom of this!"

               (SOUND: CRASH) (FOX WHIPS AROUND CORNER ON BICYCLE, SLAMS INTO HUNTER WHO FLIES INTO AIR AND LANDS IN TREE, HANGS FROM LIMB BY ONE FOOT)

Fox: Looks like somebody's got you up a tree, Friend!

Hunter: Listen, Son -- I ... am ... THE HUNTER, and I'm on a big case! Get me outa this tree!

Fox: Happy to oblige! (SHAKES LIMB AND HUNTER SLAMS TO GROUND ON HIS HEAD) (SOUND: THUD) (FOX DASHES AWAY ON BICYCLE, BUT A FRESH POSTER FALLS FROM HIS COAT TO THE FEET OF THE HUNTER -- THE POSTER OF THE HUNTER)

Hunter: (PICKS UP POSTER) Hmmm ... another crooked face. I say the woods are full of 'em. And I need all the help I can get -- I'll just tack this poster up where everyone can see it -- (BEGINS TACKING POSTER TO A TREE) (SOUND: TACKING) (ON OTHER SIDE OF TREE MAN AND WIFE TALK TO FOX WHO IS UNDER HIS PHOTO CLOTH)

Man: Are you from Fox Studios?

Fox: That's the place, Friend -- "your face is your fortune" -- how about shooting the little lady?

- 5 -

Man: Just a picture, please. This is my wife.

Fox: Oh, yes, your wife. (TO WIFE) My! you're the lucky one -- it's my special this week. Now watch the birdie -- (GRABS BIRD FROM TREE) (SOUND: SQUAWK) (FLASH AND PICTURE IS TAKEN) (SOUND: POP) That's a beauty! Fifty greenbacks, thank you!

Wife: Fifty dollars! Herbert!

Fox: I know what you're thinking, but don't force more money on me. People will talk about this picture everywhere! It'll be ready tomorrow -- pick it up at the post office! (AND ON OTHER SIDE OF TREE, HUNTER, TACKING UP HIS POSTER, NAILS EAR TO TREE. MOVES TO STAND BACK TO LOOK AT POSTER AND REALIZES EAR IS NAILED. EAR STRETCHES AS HUNTER PUTS BOTH FEET ON TREE, BOTH HANDS ON NAIL TO PULL HIMSELF LOOSE)

Hunter: (MUMBLING TO HIMSELF) Ear so close, I say I can hear the tree bark. (STRUGGLING) This nail is hard as nails! Can't even ... (SOUND: THUD) (NAIL PULLS OUT. HUNTER FALLS TO THE GROUND. RISES, GRUMBLING, AND LOOKS AT POSTER ON TREE) Public enemy number one! He'll never escape me! I say I know that face like my own! (FOX SLYLY WATCHING FROM AROUND TREE QUICKLY CHANGES INTO POLICE UNIFORM AND STEPS UP TO HUNTER)

Fox: Hey, you with the nose, what's goin' on here?

Hunter: My card, Sir -- I am the Hunter!

Fox: Hunter, eh? A likely story. I'm taking you in.

Hunter: Now wait a minute, Son -- I say, who do you think I am?

Fox: (WHIPPING OUT MIRROR AND POINTING TO POSTER) See for yourself!

- 6 -

Hunter: Why -- why that's me! An' a mighty good likeness at that!
Fox: (ASIDE) Thanks, it was nothing! (TO HUNTER) Well, sorry, old man, but like the sign says -- "suggest immediate hanging without trial!" (FOX THROWS ROPE AROUND TREE BRANCH AND BEGINS TO TIE LOOP AROUND HUNTER'S NECK) (SOUND: SIREN GROWING LOUDER) (PATROL WAGON RUSHES UP WITH FLANAGAN AND WOMAN WHOM FOX PHOTOGRAPHED IN PARK. FOX TURNS TO LOOK AND HUNTER INNOCENTLY PUTS NOOSE AROUND FOX)
Hunter: Now just hold it a minute, boy, you tie a no-count knot -- here, I'll show you how.
(FLANAGAN RACES FROM PATROL WAGON WITH WOMAN RUNNING ALONG)
Woman: That's the crook, officer -- the one tied up!
Flanagan: (SEEING HUNTER) And you, Hunter! Thanks to you we've got him. Sure an' it's the Fox, for all his hidin' in a police uniform!
Hunter: The Fox, eh? Well, boy, looks like the rope's on you! That's a joke, Son -- get it!
Fox: Very funny. Very funny. (A BATCH OF POSTERS FALLS FROM FOX'S DISGUISE)
Flanagan: An' begorra, all the evidence on him!
Fox: OK, Flanagan -- so I make a few posters, and already you wanna make a federal case out of it!
Flanagan: (TAKING ROPE OFF FOX AND PUTTING HIM IN WAGON) Tell it to the judge, Fox. (TO HUNTER) Sure an' you've done it, again! How can we thank ya'?
Hunter: Just money, Son -- I say, a big reward is enough for me!
Woman: (TO FLANAGAN AND LOOKING TOWARD HUNTER) Officer, thank goodness that man was handy with a rope! Who is he?

Flanagan: Handy with a rope, you say? Why that's (LOOKS AT HUNTER WHO STEPS INTO NOOSE AND IS SWUNG UPSIDE DOWN TO HANG FROM TREE BRANCH BY HIS FOOT. UNDAUNTED, HUNTER BLASTS HIS HUNTING HORN) (SOUND: HORN) the HUNTER!

Hunter – Episode # 2 (4:00)
"Counterfeit Wants"

Narrator: Well, it started out to be a Monday just like any other Monday in spring, except that it was raining buckets of water. The Hunter -- on the prowl for a desperate criminal -- decided to stop for a cup of tea ...
(UNDER NARRATION BUCKETS OF WATER FALL ON THE HUNTER WHO DUCKS INTO TEA SHOP) (SOUND: BUCKETS AND WATER CRASHING)

Hunter: (AS WAITRESS BRINGS CUP OF TEA, HE UNFURLS A WANTED POSTER AND STUDIES IT) (READING) "Wanted -- kindly old grandmother for peddling HOT TEA!" Hmmm -- that kindly, crooked face -- Ah say Ah'd know it anywhere!

Waitress: (WHO'S PICTURE IS ON THE POSTER) (IN OLD LADY VOICE) Here's your hot tea, Mr. Hunter -- (LOOKS AT PICTURE) My! What a pretty girl -- and looks so familiar!

Hunter: My very words, fair lady -- Ah say Ah'd know it anywhere!

Waitress: (CACKLING) Why, I do believe it's me! Imagine you carrying my picture!

Hunter: (LEAPS UP TURNING TABLE OVER WHICH THROWS TEA CUP INTO WAITRESS'S HAND) (SOUND: CRASH OF TABLE) Ah ha!! Just as Ah thought -- and everything fits -- even the hot tea!

Waitress: Pity sakes! What do you mean?

Hunter: (PUTTING HANDCUFFS ON WAITRESS) (SOUND: CLANK) Come quietly, fair lady -- you're the kindly crooked old grandmother and Ah'm takin' you in!
(DISSOLVE WITH DUM-DE-DUM-DUM MUSIC TO POLICE STATION WHERE OFFICER FLIM FLANAGAN IS STUDYING WANTED POSTERS AND LOOKS UP AS HE HEARS THE COMMOTION OF VOICES AS HUNTER AND WAITRESS ENTER) (MUSIC OUT UNDER VOICES)

- 2 -

Waitress:	I'll tell your mother, Sonny, treatin' an old lady like this!
Hunter:	Ah hah! Just what a kindly old grandmother would say!
Flanagan:	Sure an' I mighta' known it would be the Hunter! It's a regular flood I'm havin' of false arrests -- sure an' you're not adding another!
Hunter:	False arrest? Folderol! Ah say, son, it's right here in black and white!
Flanagan:	Sure, sure. And look at all the others right here on me desk! (SHOTS OF WANTED POSTERS AS FLANAGAN CALLS THEM OUT) The mayor -- the banker -- the nursmaid -- the teacher -- and on an' on!
Hunter:	Don't worry, son -- Ah say Ah'll bring 'em all in or my name isn't -- THE HUNTER! (WHIPS OUT HORN AND BLASTS) (SOUND: HORN) (FLANAGAN AND WAITRESS COVER EARS IN PAIN)
Flanagan:	No, no, Hunter! It's all a mistake! We haven't got a thing on these people -- but sure as me name's Flim Flanagan, someone's up to no good!
Hunter:	Hmmm -- (TO WAITRESS) Very well, fair lady -- (REMOVING HANDCUFF) you're free! (SHE CLAMPS HER OPENED HANDCUFF ON HUNTER'S OTHER HAND SO THAT HE'S HANDCUFFED TO HIMSELF) (SOUND: CLANK)
Waitress:	(AS SHE EXITS) There! That'll keep you from harming old ladies!
Hunter:	Trapped by my own handcuffs! That's a mean practical joke, son!
Flanagan:	Now listen closely ...(THEY HUDDLE IN CONFIDENCE) Whoever is behind this is makin' counterfeit posters to arrest people for other people -- for a price --

- 3 -

'an I say, surer 'n sure -- it's the fox!
(SOUND: PLOT-THICKENS-TYPE MUSIC UP AND OUT)

Narrator: Little do Flanagan and the Hunter know that someone watches from a room nearby --
(SHOT TO SMALL LIGHT IN WINDOW, THEN TELESCOPE AND FOLLOWING IT TO ITS END, IT IS THE FOX)

Fox: So they're after me, huh? (PUTS TELESCOPE DOWN AND GOES OVER TO CAMERA WHERE HE'S COPYING PICTURES ON WANTED POSTERS) Well, looks like this little poster is just in time -- (SHOT OF THE HUNTER, HIMSELF, AS FOX READS MESSAGE) "Wanted -- dead or alive -- suggest immediate hanging without trial!" ...Poetry! Sheer poetry! Guess that'll fix the long nose of the law!
(SOUND: PHONE RING) (FOX ANSWERS)

Fox: Fox studios -- "your face is my -- er your fortune" -- can I help you?

Voice: Pick a pack of posters ...

Fox: Hmmm -- the passwords! Friend! You've come to the right place -- I'll get your man -- just name the face!

Voice: You make phony wanted posters, right?

Fox: Please, please! Watch your language! (IN MOCK HURT)

Voice: I want my wife arrested -- can you fix it?

Fox: Fix it! My good man, her poster will be my masterpiece -- just send money ... I'll take care of the rest! -- In the park in ten minutes! (FOX GRABS CAMERA, LOWERS HIMSELF DOWN ROPE OUT WINDOW TO WAITING BICYCLE AND DASHES OFF TO PARK)

- 4 -

(DISSOLVE TO PARK -- HUNTER HALF DOZES ON BENCH, PORTABLE RADIO PLAYS NEWS BESIDE HIM)

Radio: "..brought in for kidnapping babies, the suspect turned out to be a little girl with her doll -- but -- and get this -- her picture was on wanted posters all over town. This makes the tenth false arrest. The city is losing all it's money on rewards, alone, and it looks like Officer Flim Flanagan's job unless he gets to the bottom of this!"

(SOUND: BRAKES SLAMMING) (AS FOX STOPS IN FRONT OF HUNTER AND FLIPS RADIO DIAL TO MUSIC) (SOUND: MUSIC)

Fox: You poor old man trying to sleep with all that noise! Ah, music! Music will soothe!

Hunter: Ah'll thank you, Suh, to unhand my radio -- Ah'm on a case, son!

Fox: (LEAPING ON BICYCLE) Yes, friend, you are a case, and that's the truth! (AS FOX DASHES AWAY A FRESH POSTER FALLS FROM HIS COAT TO THE FEET OF THE HUNTER -- THE POSTER OF THE HUNTER)

Hunter: (PICKS UP POSTER) Hmmm ...another crooked face. Ah say the woods are full of 'em. And Ah need all the help Ah can get -- Ah'll just tack this poster up where everyone can see it -- (BEGINS TACKING POSTER TO A TREE) (SOUND: TACKING) (ON OTHER SIDE OF TREE MAN AND WIFE TALK TO FOX WHO IS UNDER HIS PHOTO CLOTH)

Man: Are you from Fox Studios?

Fox: That's the place, friend -- "your face is your fortune" -- how about shooting the little lady?

- 5 -

Man:	Just a picture, please. This is my <u>wife</u>.
Fox:	Oh, yes, your <u>wife</u>. (TO WIFE) My! you're the lucky one -- it's my special this week. Now watch the birdie -- (GRABS BIRD FROM TREE) (SOUND: SQUAWK) (FLASH AND PICTURE IS TAKEN) (SOUND: POP) That's a beauty! Fifty greenbacks, thank you!
Wife:	Fifty dollars! Herbert!
Fox:	I know what you're thinking, but don't force more money on me. People will talk about this picture everywhere! It'll be ready tomorrow -- pick it up at the post office! (AND ON OTHER SIDE OF TREE, HUNTER HAS TACKED HIS POSTER UP AND STANDS BACK TO TAKE LONG LOOK)
Hunter:	Public enemy number one! He'll never escape me! Ah say Ah know that face like my own! (FOX SLYLY WATCHING FROM AROUND TREE QUICKLY CHANGES INTO POLICE UNIFORM AND STEPS UP TO HUNTER)
Fox:	Hey, you with the nose, what's goin' on here?
Hunter:	My card, Suh -- I am the Hunter!
Fox:	Hunter, eh? A likely story. I'm taking you in.
Hunter:	Now wait a minute, son -- Ah say, who do you think Ah am?
Fox:	(WHIPPING OUT MIRROR AND POINTING TO POSTER) See for yourself!
Hunter:	Why -- why that's me! An' a mighty good likeness at that!
Fox:	(ASIDE) Thanks, it was nothing! (TO HUNTER) Well, sorry, old man, but like the sign says -- "suggest immediate hanging without trial!" (FOX THROWS ROPE AROUND TREE BRANCH AND BEGINS TO TIE LOOP AROUND HUNTER'S NECK)

- 6 -

(SOUND: SIREN GROWING LOUDER) (PATROL WAGON RUSHES UP WITH FLANAGAN AND WOMAN WHOM FOX PHOTOGRAPHED IN PARK. FOX TURNS TO LOOK AND HUNTER INNOCENTLY PUTS NOOSE AROUND FOX)

Hunter: Now just hold it a minute, boy, you tie a no-count knot -- here, Ah'll show you how.

(FLANAGAN RACES FROM PATROL WAGON WITH WOMAN RUNNING ALONG)

Woman: That's the crook, officer -- the one tied up!

Flanagan: (SEEING HUNTER) And *you*, Hunter! Thanks to you we've got him. Sure 'an it's the fox, for all his hidin' in a police uniform!

Hunter: The fox, eh? Well, boy, looks like the rope's on you! That's a joke, son -- get it!

Fox: Very funny. Very funny. (A BATCH OF POSTERS FALLS FROM FOX'S DISGUISE)

Flanagan: An' begorra, all the evidence on him!

Fox: OK, Flanagan -- so I make a few posters, and already you wanna make a federal case out of it!

Flanagan: (TAKING ROPE OFF FOX AND PUTTING HIM IN WAGON) Tell it to the judge, Fox. (TO HUNTER) Sure an' you've done it, again! How can we thank ye'?

Hunter: Just send money, son -- Ah say, a big reward is enough for me!

Woman: (TO FLANAGAN AND LOOKING TOWARD HUNTER) Officer, thank goodness that man was handy with a rope! Who is he?

Flanagan: Handy with a rope, you say? Why that's (LOOKS AT HUNTER WHO STEPS INTO NOOSE AND IS SWUNG UPSIDE DOWN TO HANG FROM TREE BRANCH BY HIS FOOT. UNDAUNTED, HUNTER BLASTS HIS HUNTING HORN) (SOUND: BLAST OF HORN) the HUNTER!

CREATED AND PRODUCED BY TOTAL TELEVISION PRODUCTIONS

CHAPTER 4

"HELP, MR. WIZARD!"

There was also *Tooter the Turtle*, a daydreamer boy turtle who consistently went to see his friend Mr. Wizard the Lizard, in order to transform him into a new occupation or role. By the end of the episode, due to some hardship, Tooter finally accepts who he really is and asked to be changed back. 39 episodes were produced.

Originally Tooter was conceived as Toonerville Turtle, but worries about the similarity in name to the old comic strip called *Toonerville Trolley* hastened a name change to simply Tooter.

For voices, no celebrities were intentionally imitated, but Tooter's dumb guy voice, as portrayed by Allen Swift, reminds one of Mortimer Snerd.

Mr. Wizard the Lizard, as portrayed by Sandy Becker, is strongly reminiscent of any generic German scientist from the movies, or, more specifically, Albert Einstein. "Sandy Becker was a very popular local personality in New York. Sandy did the voice of Wizard the Lizard," Covington adds. Various sources claim that an actor named Frank Milano portrayed Wizard the Lizard, but this fact is also erroneous.

Sandy Becker was born Sanford George Becker, on February 19, 1922, in New York City, where he eventually became an icon of New York children's television, performing on his own *Sandy Becker Show* in 1953, and *Wonderama* in 1955. He also did many other voices for the various TTV shows in the succeeding years. Becker died on April 9, 1996.

With the success of these three segments of *King Leonardo and his Short Subjects*, Biggers and Stover both resigned DFS for "personal reasons" and moved to Cape Cod, Massachusetts, and Litchfield, Connecticut, respectively.

Many products featuring *King Leonardo* appeared, including a seven-issue comic book series from Dell and Gold Key Comics and a book, entitled *King Leonardo and the Royal Contest* (1962), and various toys and games. Most of these products featured The Hunter, The Fox, Tooter Turtle and Mr. Wizard in fleeting appearances.

It wasn't until the days of videotape that a product starring Tooter Turtle appeared.

The cast of the *Tooter Turtle* segment of *King Leonardo and his Short Subjects* included Tooter Turtle and Mr. Wizard the Lizard. PHOTOS COURTESY OF TREAD COVINGTON.

Toonerville -- Episode # 13, "Lossie -- doggone dog"

(AFTER STANDARD OPENING -- WIZARD AND TOONERVILLE AT WIZARD'S)

Wizard: Vell, vat iss you feeling like, today, mine boy -- a chiant, maybe?

Tooner: Naw, Mister Wizard. Ah just been a'wishin' I could have me a dog like that famous dog, Lossie.

Wizard: Lossie? Vot dog iss dat?

Tooner: You know, that good and brave dog that has so many adventures and all that.

Wizard: Ach, but yes! I know dat dog --and I'm tellink you, mine boy -- hit's a dog's life -- but, see for yourself!

Tooher: Gosh, thanks, Mister Wizard! This time, I _know_ I'll be all right!

Wizard: (RUBBING MAGIC STICK) Vee see, vee see!
(TOONER PROCEEDS DOWN MAGIC CORRIDOR CHANGING INTO A LANKY BOY. THEN DISSOLVE TO BOY WALKING ALONG PATH TOWARD CABIN.)
Vell, dis iss de vay it vas mit Lossie's friend, Dimmy. Effry morning, Dimmy shhtart de day by vashing his vace in de brook. Den his dog, Lossie vould greet him on de path home ...
(LOSSIE, A BIG SAINT BERNARD TYPE DOG BOUNDS UP TO DIMMY AND KNOCKS HIM DOWN. DIMMY'S FACE COMES UP COVERED WITH MUD)
Den, de mudder vould call sveetly to her boy an hiss dog...

Mother: (HAGGISH WOMAN CALLING FROM CABIN DOOR WITH ANGRY SHRIEK)
Dim - **MY**! Los-**SIE**! Vittels!

Wizard: Alvays, dey come bounding in, eager for de breakfast...
(SHOT OF MOTHER PUTTING PLATES ON TABLE AS SCREECHING SKID AND CRASH IS HEARD AS DIMMY AND LOSSIE COLLIDE AT DOOR, FALLING INTO ROOM AND KNOCKING OVER TABLE)

The complete rough draft and complete final script for *Tooter Turtle*, episode #13, entitled "Lossie — Doggone Dope." Note that Tooter is still referred to as Toonerville or Tooner in these scripts. Following that is the complete shooting script for *Tooter Turtle*, episode #24, entitled "Jerky Jockey or Kenducky Derby." SCRIPTS COURTESY OF TREAD COVINGTON.

2

Mother: Drat that dog! Look here, Dimmy! It's him or you! I can't wait on the both of you!

Dimmy: All right, Ma, I'll go. Take good care of Lossie. (STARTS LEAVING CABIN)

MOTHER: Los-SIE! Get that boy! (LOSSIE OBLIGINGLY PINS DIMMY TO FLOOR WITH ONE PAW)

Dimmy: Aw, Lossie! Lemme up!

Mother: Good dog, Lossie. All right, now -- Dimmy, you an' Lossie act like a boy an' his dog should and take this rent money to mean old farmer Brown before we get put out of our house at sun down.

Dimmy: Through the woods, Ma!?

Mother: And why not?

Dimmy: Lossie'll get lost!

Mother: Hits all right-- you'll be with him. Now git! (SHE SENDS DIMMY AND LOSSIE HURTLING OUT THE DOOR. DIMMY LANDS FIRST AND LOSSIE LANDS ON TOP OF HIM IN HORSEBACK RIDING POSITION. DIMMY GETS UP AND STARTS OFF WITH LOSSIE ON HIS BACK)

Wizard: And so, boy and his faithful, protecting friend, vere off on dere adventhure. Little did dey know dat up ahead vas dancher! (SHOT OF WOLF BUSY CHANGING SIGNS AT FORK IN WOODS -- ONE SIGN READS "FARMER BROWN'S" AND THE OTHER READS "QUICK SAND". BEFORE SLINKING INTO THE TREES, WOLF HOWLS) (SOUND: WOLF CALL) (SHOT TO DIMMY AND LOSSIE. LOSSIE JUMPS BEHIND DIMMY AND COWS)

Dimmy: Could a' swore I heard a wolf! How 'bout you, Lossie? (LOSSIE SHAKES HEAD TO SAY NO, AND THEY WALK ALONG TO FORK IN PATH) (READING SIGNS) Hmmm -- Farmer Brown's thisaway -- and QUICK SAND thataway! Wow! Lucky I read those signs ... (DIMMY NOTICES LOSSIE STARTS GOING DOWN THE "QUICK SAND" PATH) -- Hey, Lossie! (LOSSIE SLAMS ON BRAKES) (SOUND: SCREE

#3

```
              Not that way -- you'll get drownd in quick sand!
              (LOSSIE SHRUGS AND FOLLOWS DIMMY)
    Wizard:   Vel, Lossie had tried to show de vey, but Dimmy vouldn't lissen.
              Meanvile -- de wolff vas still scheeming...
              (WOLF LOOKS BACK OVER SHOLDER IN DIRECTION OF DIMMY AND LOSSIE,
              THEN SPEEDS ALONG PATH ON MOTORCYCLE TO THE QUICK SAND, BRINGS
              MOTORCYCLE TO SCREECHING STOP JUST IN TIME) (SOUND: BRAKES OF
              MOTORCYCLE) ( WOLF LEAPS OFF AND QUICKLY PUTS UP ANOTHER SIGN
              READING "MUD BATH FOR ACHING FEET")
              And as if dat vasn't bad enough...
    Dimmy:    (CARRYING EXHAUSTED LOSSIE ON HIS BACK) Lossie, you are just
              plain heavy! If your feet hurt, how about mine! (THEY COME
              TO QUICK SAND AND DIMMY DOESN'T SEE SIGN) And now look! Mud!
              I'll just go around through these trees.
              (LOSSIE LEAPS DOWN, RUNS TO SIGN AND PULLS IT UP, TAKES SIGN
              TO DIMMY)
    Dimmy:    (READING) "MUD BaTh for aching feet"! Well, good just what I
              need. Good dog, Lossie! (DIMMY PATS LOSSIE, AND LOSSIE WAGS
              TAIL AND WHIMPERS) Oh, boy! Here goes ...
              (SHOT TO WOLF COVERING HIS EYES)
    WOLF:     I just can't look!
    Wizard:   Yes, de vorst had happened -- but ven a boy is vith his dog,
              protection iss alvays dere ...
              (SHOT TO LOSSIE FLOUNDERING IN THE QUICK SAND, WITH DIMMY
              CALLING FROM THE BANK)
    Dimmy:    Lossie! Quit rollin' in all that mud -- hits just for your feet!
              (LOSSIE SINKS DEEPER)
    Dimmy:    Lossie! Come out of there!
              (ONLY LOSSIE'S NOSE IS OUT OF MUD)
    Dimmy:    Hold on, Lossie! You must be in quick sand -- I'll run for help!
```

4

(SHOT TO WOLF WHO QUICKLY ERECTS A FIRST AID STAND)

Dimmy: Help! Help! My dog Lossie is drowning in quick sand!

Wolf: Quick sand? Impossible! This is the way to Farmer Brown's.

Dimmy: Please, mister! Hurry, or Lossie will be lost!

Wolf: (GATHERING ELABORATE FIRST AID KIT) All right. Follow my instructions. (SPREADS OUT MAP AND GOES TO WORK WITH PENCIL AND COMPASS, ETC) Now, as I see it, your dog should be about there. (MARKS WITH X)

Dimmy: That's right!

Wolf: (CONTINUING TO MAKE ELABORATE MARKS): And we'll throw a line from here (ANOTHER X)

Dimmy: That's right!

Wolf: Then we'll take it around that tree (ANOTHER X)

Dimmy: That's right!

Wolf: No, that's wrong. I've tried that before -- I've lost more dogs, that way ...

(SOUND: LOSSIE BARKING)

Dimmy: Hurry, mister! Lossie can't last long!

Wolf: Ok, here we go -- (THROWS LASSO AROUND LOSSIE'S SNOUT) Now, take this end around that tree and pull! (DIMMY RUSHES AROUND TREE, PULLS ON LINE. THEN SHOT TO WOLF, ONE HAND WITH SCISSORS ABOUT TO CUT LINE LEADING FROM LOSSIE TO TREE, OTHER HAND COVERING HIS EYES)

Wolf: I just can't look!

(WHEN LINE IS CUT, DIMMY STAGGERS BACKWARDS INTO QUICK SAND, RUNNING INTO WOLF'S MOTORCYCLE ON THE WAY. MOTORCYCLE STARTS AND RUNS CRAZILY OFF -- RIGHT THROUGH WOLF'S LEGS, CARRYING WOLF ALSO INTO QUICK SAND)

Wizard: And so chuss ven everyvon vas in de drink, who should be co... (UNDER NARRATION, THE THREE BUBBLE AND BEGIN SINKING IN SAN...

	an olt farmer Brown mit de sherriff...
Brown:	That wolf can't be far -- saw him after my sheep, just this afternoon!
Sherriff:	Wait! Look up the path! There's something moving in all that mud!
Wolf:	Help! help! save this poor little sheep!
Lossie:	(SOUND: BARKS)
Dimmy:	Glub! Glub!
Sheriff:	(THROWING LINES WITH LASSOES OUT) You get that one. I'll get t'other.
Brown:	(PULLS LOSSIE OUT) Why, tarnation, that's no sheep -- that's that dopey dog Lossie!
Sheriff:	(PULLS WOLF OUT) An here's your wolf. I'm takin' you in ... thanks to Lossie!
Wolf:	(HANDS OVER EYES) I just can't look!
Browne	Well I guess you're right, Sheriff! I won't be mean old farmer brown any more! Come on, Lossie! Come home, Lossie!
Lossie:	(WHIMPERS, WAGS TAIL AND FOLLOWS BROWN HAPPILY AWAY AS END-OF-PERFECT-DAY MUSIC RISES UP AND OUT)
	(SOUND: MUSIC)
	(SHOT TO DIMMY COMING UP FOR THIRD TIME IN QUICK SAND)
Dimmy:	Help! Glub! I don't want that dog or his adventures -- it's me, Toonerville, Mister Wizard -- bring me home, glub!
Wizard:	Vel, here I go again -- drizzle, drazzle, druzzle drome... time for dis von to come home!

Toonerville -- Episode # 13 (4:30)

"Lossie -- doggone dope"

(AFTER STANDARD OPENING -- WIZARD AND TOONERVILLE AT WIZARD'S)

Wizard: Vell, vat iss you feeling like, today, mine boy -- a chiant, maybe?

Tooner: Naw, Mister Wizard. Ah just been a'wishin' I could have me a dawg like that famous dawg, Lossie!

Wizard: Lossie? Vot dog iss dat?

Tooner: You know, that good an' brave dawg that has so many adventures an' all that.

Wizard: Ach, but yes! I know dat dog -- and I'm tellink you, mine boy -- it iss a dog's life -- but, see for yourself!

Tooner: Gosh, thanks, Mister Wizard! This time I reckon' ah'll be all right for sure!

Wizard: (TOUCHING TOONER WITH MAGIC STICK) Vee see, vee see! (TOONER GOES DOWN MAGIC CORRIDOR CHANGING INTO FARMER-BOY CLOTHES MUCH TOOSMALL FOR HIM. THEN DISSOLVE TO TOONER WALKING ALONG PATH TOWARD CABIN) Vell, dis iss de vay it vas mit Lossie's friend, Dimmy. Effry morning, Dimmy shhtart de day by vashing his vace in de brook. Den his dog, Lossie vould greet him on de path home ... (LOSSIE, A BIG SAINT BERNARD TYPE DOG BOUNDS UP TO DIMMY AND KNOCKS HIM DOWN, BARKING PLAYFULLY. DIMMY'S FACE COMES UP COVERED WITH MUD)

	- 2 -
	Den, de mudder vould call sveetly to her boy and his dog ...
Mother:	(HAGGISH WOMAN CALLING FROM CABIN DOOR WITH ANGRY SHRIEK) Dim - MY! Los - SIE! Vittels!
Wizard:	Alvays, dey come bounding in, eager for de breakfast ... (SHOT OF MOTHER PUTTING PLATES ON TABLE AS SCREECHING SKID AND CRASH IS HEARD AS DIMMY AND LOSSIE COLLIDE AT DOOR, FALLING INTO ROOM AND KNOCKING OVER TABLE) (SOUND: SCREECHING SKID AND CRASH)
Mother:	Drat that dawg! Look here, Dimmy! It's him or you! I can't wait on the both of you!
Dimmy:	All right, Ma, I'll go. Take good care of Lossie. (STARTS TO LEAVE CABIN)
Mother:	Los - SIE! Get that boy! (LOSSIE OBLIGINGLY PINS DIMMY TO FLOOR WITH ONE PAW)
Dimmy:	Aw, Lossie! Lemme up!
Mother:	Good dawg, Lossie. (LOSSIE WHIMPERS AND WAGS) All right, now -- Dimmy, you an' Lossie act like a boy an' his dog should and take this rent money to mean old farmer Brown a'fore we gets put out of our house at sundown.
Dimmy:	Through the woods, Ma?
Mother:	An' why not?
Dimmy:	Lossie'll get lost!
Mother:	Hits all right -- you'll be with him. Now git! (SHE SENDS DIMMY AND LOSSIE HURTLING OUT THE DOOR) (SOUND: CRASH AND THUD) (DIMMY LANDS FIRST AND LOSSIE LANDS ON TOP OF HIM. DIMMY GETS UP AND STARTS OFF WITH LOSSIE ON HIS BACK)
Wizard:	And so, Dimmy and his faithful, protecting friend, vere

- 6 -

off on dere advenchure. Little did dey know dat up ahead vas dancher! (SHOT OF "VILLAIN" FARMER BROWN BUSY CHANGING SIGNS AT FORK IN WOODS -- ONE SIGN READS "FARMER BROWN'S" AND THE OTHER READS "QUICK SAND". BEFORE SLINKING INTO THE TREES, BROWN SPEAKS)

BROWN: Think they'll get to my house before sundown, do they? I'll show them! (VILLAINOUS LAUGHTER)
(SHOT TO DIMMY AND LOSSIE. LOSSIE JUMPS BEHIND DIMMY AND COWS DOWN BEHIND HIM)

Dimmy: Could a' swore I heard a laffin' Hyena! How 'bout you, Lossie? (LOSSIE BARKS AND SHAKES HEAD TO SAY NO. THEY STOP AT FORK IN PATH) (READING SIGNS) Hmmm -- Farmer Brown's thisaway -- and QUICK SAND thataway! Wow! Lucky I read those signs ... (DIMMY NOTICES LOSSIE STARTING DOWN THE "QUICK SAND" PATH) -- Hey, Lossie! (LOSSIE SLAMS ON BRAKES) (SOUND: BRAKES) Not _that_ way -- you'll get drowned in quick sand! (LOSSIE SHRUGS, WHIMPERS, AND FOLLOWS DIMMY)

Wizard: Vell, Lossie had tried to show de vey, but Dimmy vouldn't lissen. Meanvile -- mean farmer Brown vas still schmeming... (BROWN LOOKS BACK OVER SHOULDER IN DIRECTION OF DIMMY AND LOSSIE, THEN SPEEDS ALONG PATH ON MOTORCYCLE TO THE QUICK SAND -- BRINGS MOTORCYCLE TO SCREECHING STOP JUST IN TIME) (SOUND: MOTORCYCLE) (BROWN LEAPS OFF AND QUICKLY PUTS UP ANOTHER SIGN)

Brown: (READING) "Mud bath for aching feet" -- Ha, ha! This is where I'll get the money and his ma'll never know what happened! (VILLIANOUS LAUGH)

- 4 -

Wizard: And as if dat vasn't bad enough ...

Dimmy: (CARRYING EXHAUSTED LOSSIE ON HIS BACK) Lossie, you is just plain heavy! (LOSSIE WHIMPERS) If *your* feet hurt, how 'bout *mine*! (THEY COME TO QUICK SAND AND DIMMY DOESN'T SEE SIGN) An' now look! Mud! I'll just go around through these trees.
(LOSSIE LEAPS DOWN, BARKS AND RUNS TO SIGN AND PULLS IT UP, TAKES SIGN TO DIMMY) (LOSSIE WAGS TAIL)
(DIMMY READS) "Mud bath for aching feet!" Well, just what ah needs! Good dawg, Lossie! (LOSSIE WHIMPERS AND WAGS TAIL WHEN DIMMY PATS) Oh boy! Here goes ...
(SHOT TO BROWN LEERING THROUGH TREES)

Brown: Now I have him!

Wizard: Yes, de vorst had happened -- but ven a boy is vith his dog, protection iss alvays dere ...
(SHOT TO LOSSIE FLOUNDERING IN THE QUICK SAND AFTER BIG SPLASH) (SOUND: SPLAT)

Dimmy: Lossie! Quit rollin' in all that mud -- hits just for your feet! (LOSSIE SINKS DEEPER) Lossie! Come outta' thar! (ONLY LOSSIE'S NOSE IS OUT OF MUD) Hold on, Lossie! You must be in quick sand -- I'll run for help!
(SHOT TO BROWN WHO QUICKLY ERECTS A FIRST AID STAND AND DISGUISE AS AID MAN)

Dimmy: Help! help! My dawg Lossie is drowning in quick sand!

Brown: Quick sand? Impossible! This is the way to farmer Brown's.

Dimmy: Please, mister! Hurry, or Lossie will be lost!
(GATHERING ELABORATE FIRST AID KIT) All right. Follow my instructions. (SPREADS OUT MAP AND GOES TO WORK WITH

                                                                    E-5-

            PENCIL, COMPASS, ETC.) Now, as I see it, your dog
            should be about there. (MARKS WITH X)
Dimmy: Thass right!
Brown: (CONTINUING TO MAKE ELABORATE MARKS) And we'll throw
            a line from here (ANOTHER X)
Dimmy: Thass right!
Brown: Then we'll take it around that tree (ANOTHER X)
Dimmy: Thass right!
Brown: No, that's wrong. I've tried that before -- I've lost
            more dogs, that way . ..
            (SOUND: LOSSIE BARKING)
Dimmy: Hurry, mister! Lossie can't last long!
Brown: OK, here we go -- (THROWS LASSO AROUND LOSSIE'S NOSE)
            Now, take this end around that tree and pull! (DIMMY
            RUSHES AROUND TREE, PULLS ON LINE. SHOT TO BROWN,
            ONE HAND WITH SCISSORS ABOUT TO CUT LINE LEADING FROM
            LOSSIE TO TREE, OTHER HAND COVERING HIS EYES)
Brown: This way, I won't be a witness! (ASIDE)
            (WHEN LINE IS CUT, DIMMY STAGGERS BACKWARDS INTO QUICK
            SAND, RUNNING INTO BROWN'S MOTORCYCLE ON THE WAY.
            MOTORCYCLE STARTS AND RUNS CRAZILY OFF) (SOUND: SNAP OF
            CUT ROPE, THEN MOTORCYCLE, THEN DIMMY FALLING IN QUICK
            SAND) (MOTORCYCLE RUNS RIGHT BETWEEN BROWN'S LEGS,
            CARRYING HIM ALS INTO THE QUICK SAND)
Wizard: And so chuss ven everyvon vas in de drink, who should
            be coming (UNDER NARRATION, THE THREE BUBBLE AND BEGIN
            SINKING IN SAND) But Dimmy's mudder mit de sheriff ...

TOOTER TURTLE

#24 - "Jerky Jockey" (Or "Kenducky Derby")

TITLE CARD: JERKY JOCKEY (OR KENDUCKY DERBY)		(MUSICAL INTRO :05)
OPEN ON WIZARD'S LIVING ROOM, WIZARD REMONSTRATING AS TOOTER HANGS ON FOR DEAR LIFE TO A VIOLENTLY MOVING MECHANICAL EXERCISE HORSE	WIZARD:	But Tooter! You are chuss not meant to be a horseback riding chocky!
ECU TOOTER GOING UP AND DOWN	TOOTER:	Why there's nothin' to this ridin' stuff! I'm ridin' hi-i-i-i-g-g-g-h-h-h!
TOOTER IS THROWN SPINNING OFF		
CUT TO TOOTER IN HEAP ON FLOOR WIZARD CUTS OFF MACHINE		(SOUND: CRASH)
	WIZARD:	Tch, tch, tch! If you can't stay on my exercise machine, how you effer can race on a real life horse?
TOOTER GETS UP DAZED	TOOTER:	Aw shucks, Mr. Wizard -- I just didn't get on right! Please let me be a horse racer!
WIZARD TOUCHES TOOTER WITH MAGIC STICK	WIZARD:	All right, Tooter! Iss very dangerous, but I giff you your wish! ...
SPIN EFFECT BEGINS		(EFFECT MUSIC BEGINS)
DISSOLVE TO RACETRACK PANORAMA AND COME IN TO ECU OF SIGN OF FLYING DUCK AND NAME "KENDUCKY DOWNS"		A real race horse chocky! ...Vonce every year at da famous Kenducky Downs - the race track with the duck pond in the middle - there
LONGSHOT OF CROWD CHEERING AND WAVING		iss da big championship horse race. Da crowd is very excited when da announcer calls the line-up... (SOUND: CROWD NOISE)
CUT TO CU OF HORSES GOING TO POST, ONE BY ONE	ANNCR:	(V.O.) ... and in number three position = Orange Juice... and

#24   - 2 -

	ANNCR:	(CONT.) there's the champion jockey Blacky Bark on number four - Marmalade ... now that new jockey Tooter Turtle on number five - Taffy. (SOUND: BUGLE)
DISSOLVE TO BUGLER BLOWING BEGINNING OF RACE. CUT TO DUCK IN CENTER OF TRACK POND PUTTING FINGER IN EARS AND GRIMACING	WIZARD:	(V.O.) Den da bugler blows da horn and the horses iss all ready at the starting gate... ...as I was saying...<u>almost</u> all the horses iss ready!
CUT TO TOOTER IN "READY" POSITION ON TAFFY BUT TAFFY IS BACKWARD IN STARTING SLOT		
CU TOOTER OBSERVING HIS POSITION	TOOTER:	I just can't help but win this race - specially with all them other horses ready to run the wrong way ...
CUT TO LOUDSPEAKER FROM STANDS AND SHOW SOUND WAVES	ANNCR:	(VO) Turn around, dopey - <u>you're</u> headed the wrong way!
LONGSHOT OF SILHOUETTE OF TOOTER TURNING HORSE AROUND	WIZARD:	(VO) And so da chocky chockeyed his horse into position and dey was all ready to go -
CUT TO BLACKY ON MARMALADE IN SLOT NEXT TO TOOTER AND TAFFY	BARK:	Psst! Hey, Buddy! Take a tip from Blacky for a fast start!
CUT TO CU TOOTER	TOOTER:	Why you must be Blacky Bark! (ASIDE) That's down right neighborly wantin' to help me!
CUT TO BARK WHO TAKES TOOTER'S STIRRUPS AND FASTENS THEM TO STARTING GATE APPARATUS	BARK:	Take your stirrups and hook 'em up here, like this --- Now! They won't be in your way and you'll really take off!

#24   - 3 -

CUT TO CU TOOTER	TOOTER:	(ASIDE) That's what I call friendly!
CUT TO DUCK IN POND. WHEN SIGNAL SHOT IS HEARD, DUCK REACTS AND TAKES OFF.	ANNCR:	(VO) They're off!
CUT TO TOOTER AND TAFFY HANGING FROM STARTING GATE AND IN THE AIR WITH DUST OF OTHER HORSES WHICH HAVE TAKEN OFF	WIZARD:	(VO) And so Tooter was off to a flying start!
CUT TO LONGSHOT OF SILHOUETTE HORSES IN RACE	ANNCR:	(VO) There they go, folks, Orange Juice squeezed out ... but Marmalade is sticking...and Taffy's - pulling up!
BARK SEES TOOTER COMING UP FROM BEHIND. BARK SPEEDS AHEAD, STICKING ROADSIGNS ALONG THE WAY. CUT TO TOOTER AS HE RIDES PAST SIGNS	TOOTER:	(READING) "Be smart - retape every 500 yards!" Oh, ho! So that's what them horses socks is all about!
CUT TO CU TOOTER READING		
CUT TO SAME SIGN SHOT AGAIN, NEW SIGN	TOOTER:	(READING) "Retape at Bark's - fast and friendly!"
CUT TO BARK STEPPING OUT INTO FRAME AND HOLDING UP HAND. TAFFY PUTS ON BRAKES AND TOOTER GOES SPINNING OFF.		(SOUND: SCREECH OF BRAKES)
CUT TO BARK WHO WRAPS TAPE AROUND TAFFY'S LEGS TAPING FRONT TWO TOGETHER AND HIND LEGS TOGETHER.		(SOUND: THUD OF TOOTER'S FALL OFF SCREEN)
CUT TO TOOTER AND BARK. TOOTER IS PICKING HIMSELF UP FROM GROUND	BARK:	You're all set, Buddy! That tape ought to hold just fine!
CU BARK GRINNING EVILLY		
CUT TO BARK BOUNDING AWAY ON HORSE		See ya' down the home stretch!
CUT TO TOOTER BY HIS HORSE	TOOTER:	Guess I'll show 'em a thing or two! It's tricks like this that make the difference!
TOOTER GETS ON HORSE AND TRIES TO GO. TAFFY MAKES REPEATED ROCKING HORSE MOTION BECAUSE OF TIED LEGS	WIZARD:	(VO) Taffy didn't seem to be running so fast but maybe de smart chocky was saving his horse for later!
CUT TO BARK RIDING UP TO		(SOUND: BRAKES)

#24   - 4 -

                             BARK: Say, Buddy - you got a slow starter -
                                      what you need is a riding crop! A
                                      little tap and you're off!

CUT CU TOOTER   TOOTER: Gosh, Blacky, thanks a lot!
                                      (ASIDE) Fair sport if I ever saw
TOOTER TAKES FIREWORKS ROCKET   one!
WHICH BARK HAS LIT AND GIVEN HIM
FOR A RIDING CROP. TOOTER HOLDS   High-ho, Taffy ... Away-y-y-y-y...
ROCKET UP AND COMES DOWN WITH IT   yeeeeeoooooooowwwwwww!
ON TAFFY

FULL SCREEN EXPLOSION   (SOUND: EXPLOSION)

CUT TO TOOTER RIDING SKYWARD
ON NOSE OF ROCKET AND PASSES
STARTLED DUCK

DISSOLVE TO RACE AGAIN. SAME
REPEATED RACING SHOT SHOWING
TOOTER AGAIN COMING UP TO A ANNCR: Now Orange Juice looks fresher than
LEAD ON TAFFY   ever ... here comes Taffy, stretch-
                                      ing ahead, with Marmalade sticking
                                      close!

CUT TO CU BARK   BARK: Psst! Buddy - your horse is runnin'
                                      zigzag!

CUT TO TOOTER   TOOTER: Well no wonder I've been all mixed
                                      up with them other horses!

CUT TO BARK   BARK: Right, Mack - here - these blinders
BARK SLAPS BLINDERS ON   will straighten her out!
TAFFY SO HORSE CAN'T SEE
CUT TO TOOTER   TOOTER: (TO HIMSELF) Blinders, huh?
                                      These here race people think of
DISSOLVE TO LONGSHOT OF   everything!
HORSE RUNNING CRAZILY AND
WRONG WAY. REPEAT SEVERAL   WIZARD: With the blinders the horse could
TIMES AROUND TRACK   only see straight ahead which is
                                      sometimes verry helpful. Tooter now

#24   - 5 -

	WIZARD:	(CONT.) let Taffy haff her head. She shot past effry odder horse... and passed them...again...and again... and again!
DISSOLVE TO USUAL RACE SHOT AGAIN. HORSES RUNNING WITH TOOTER COMING UP FAST ON TAFFY TO A LEAD	ANNCR:	(VO) ...Looks like Orange Juice is running out ... with Marmalade spreading ahead – and here comes Taffy in a long stretch!
BARK, PASSED BY TOOTER, LEAPS FROM HORSE TO MOTORCYCLE AND SPEEDS AHEAD. STOPS AND TAKES RAIL OPEN TO MAKE NEW DIRECTION FOR RACE TRACK. TOOTER ON TAFFY RACES AHEAD AND COMES TO BARK IN POLICE UNIFORM DIRECTING "TRAFFIC" AT NEW INTERSEPTION BARK HAS MADE. BARK SIGNALS FOR TAFFY TO GO OUT NEW DIRECTION THROUGH OPEN RAIL.	WIZARD:	Yes, now was Tooter's big chance to push for the finish line first! (SOUND: MOTORCYCLE)
TOOTER AND TAFFY GO PLUNGING INTO DUCK POND. DUCK TAKES OFF AGAIN.	TOOTER:	Say! This must be a short cut! I'm just lucky, I guess!
CUT TO TOOTER AND TAFFY ALMOST UNDER		--hmmm, this is about the muddiest track I ever saw! ... Hey, what's happening to the track - I'm sinking! Mister Wizard! Mister Wizard! Help!
TOOTER GOES UNDER AND COMES UP GASPING		Get me outa here! I've had enough of this horse racin' stuff! Glub! Bring me home! Blurb!
BEGIN SPIN DISSOLVE	WIZARD:	Vell, enuf iss too much! -- Drizzle, Drazzle, Druzzle, Drome, Time for dis von to come home!

(DISSOLVE)

TOOTER TURTLE 39 Episodes
STORYLINES   4 ½ min.

ode #	Title	Storylines
	Two-Gun Turtle or (Fast on the Flaw)	Tooter Turtle, aided by Wizard the Lizard, tries life in the Old West as Sheriff Two-Gun in this episode.
	Tailspin Tooter	Tooter Turtle becomes a World War I flying ace until his target turns on him and Wizard has to come to the rescue.
X	Sea Haunt or (Follow the Fish)	Tooter Turtle becomes a deep sea diver and is torpedoed while trying to rescue a youth playing "submarine."
	Highway Petrol-Man	Tooter Turtle, aided by old Wizard the Lizard, becomes a "Highway Petrol'man" who loses his man every time and finally must be resuced by the Wizard.
	Knight Of The Square Table or (The Joust and The Unjoust)	Tooter Turtle, aided by the Wizard, goes back to the days of old when knights were bold to become Sir Laffalot.
	Mish-Mash-Mush or (Panting for Gold)	Gold Rush days in the klondike appeal to Tooter Turtle until he gets the bum's rush from claim jumpers.
X	The Unteachables or (The Lawless Fears)	Tooter Turtle has the Wizard turn him into a "FBY Unteachable" and Tooter sets out to get Black Bark and his gang in the roaring Twenties in this episode.
	Kink of Swat or (Babe Rube)	Tooter Turtle, with an assist from the Wizard takes a swing at baseball as "Babe Rube" only to strike out.
	One Trillion B.C. or (Dinosour Dope)	Tooter Turtle goes back into the Stone Age, but as he faces the hazards of the cave man, he calls on the Wizard to rescue him in this episode.
	Olimping Champion or (Weak Greek)	Tooter Turtle goes back to ancient Greece and has to be rescued by the Wizard when he gets into trouble.

A folder containing character descriptions, episode titles and storylines for the Tooter Turtle series. Note that although 43 episodes are mentioned, only 39 episodes were produced. The missing episodes bearing the mysterious legend "Not Accepted."
COURTESY OF TREAD COVINGTON.

TURTLE STORYLINES (Page 2)

e #	Title	Storylines
	Buffaloed Bill	As "Buffaloed Bill", Tooter Turtle shows General Custard how to fight Indians.
	Not Accepted	
	Moon Goon or (Space Head)	Tooter blasts off as the first explorer to the moon and makes an important discovery.
	Robin Hoodwink	Tooter Turtle goes back to the days of "Robin Hoodwink" and clashes with the sheriff of Nuttyham.
	Steamboat Stupe	Life on the river appeals to Tooter Turtle and he challenges Blackie Bark to a big river boat race.
	Souse Painter or (Brush Boob)	Tooter finds that there's more to decorating and painting than meets the brush.
	Not Accepted	
	Railroad Engineer	Tooter Turtle has Wizard the Lizard whisk him back to the early days of railroading where, as Stupefied Jones, the engineer, he is challenged by Black Bark to race a stagecoach.
	Quarterback Hack	Fight, team, fight! as Tooter Turtle gets his wish to play professional football.
	Overwhere	Black Bark is the "fatherly" Sergeant and Tooter Turtle is the private when the Wizard gives him a hitch in the army.
	Lumberquack	Tooter Turtle becomes a lumberquack and gets into a logjam with the toughest lumberman of the Northwest.
	Not Accepted	
	Jerky Jockey	Blacky Bark is out to beat Tooter, foul or fair, when Tooter sets his cap to win the big race at "Kentucky Downs".
	Fired Fireman	Tooter Turtle to the rescue on a four alarm fire. Thanks to Wizard, the Lizard, Tooter is also rescued.

TURTLE STORYLINES (Page 3)

de #	Title	Storylines
	Sky Diver	Tooter flys high as a Sky Diver until a doting mother Eagle gives him the bird.
	Tuesday Turtle	Tooter Turtle becomes Tuesday Turtle, private eye, and goes after hot pies -- but gets the raspberry.
	Snafu Safari	Tooter Turtle makes a real "snafu" out of a jungle safari which only Wizard, the Lizard, can untangle.
	Anti-Arctic	The North Pole gives Tooter Turtle a chilly reception complete with a shaky kayak, thin ice, and a polar bear.
	Master Builder	Tooter Turtle decides to give up his dreams of glory and be a construction worker, but Lizard, the Wizard, has to come to the rescue more than ever.
	Taxi Turtle	Lizard, the Wizard, grants Tooter Turtle's wish to be a taxi driver, and all his passengers wish they had walked.
	Canned Camera	All of Tooter's tricks backfire on him when he tries his skill at producing his own "Canned Camera" show.

Not Accepted

	Slowshoe Mountie	As a Royal Mounted Policeman, Tooter Turtle tracks down Big Black Bark until tooter gets trapped and has to call for Lizard the Wizard.
	Duck Haunter	"Field and Scream" magazine gives Tooter Turtle the idea of being a duck hunter, but the ducks decoy Tooter right into the water.
	Bull Fright	"Oley!" and Tooter Turtle's in the arena as the dashing bull fighter who really has to dash when the brave bull has ideas of his own.
	News Nuisance	As a star newspaper reporter, Tooter Turtle gets all the big stories -- completely mixed up, and he's about to go to jail when Lizard, the Wizard, steps in.

TOOTER TURTLE STORYLINES (Page 4)

Episode #	Title	Storylines
38	Foreign Fleegion	The French Foreign Legion looks exciting to Tooter Turtle until he's captured by unfriendly Arabs in the desert and needs Lizard, the Wizard's, magic in a hurry.
39	Waggin' Train	Tooter Turtle is sure he can lead a "waggin'" train" to California but winds up taking the great circle route back to Chicago.
40	Anchors Away	Life on the high seas is what Tooter Turtle thinks he wants, but the sample that Lizard, the Wizard, gives him makes "Mutiny on the Bounty" look like a picnic.
41	Vaudevillain	As a "Vaudevillain," Tooter Turtle, in the hands of a W.C. Fields-type agent, turns out to be a real "song and dance man."
42	Rod & Reeling	Tooter Turtle is totally "miscast" as a big time fisherman and Lizard, the Wizard, has to reel him in.
43	Man In The Blue Denim Suit	As a farm hand, Tooter Turtle soon learns the hard way why they won't keep him down on the farm, and between the farmer and the cow it's a rescue job for Lizard, the Wizard.

CREATED AND PRODUCED BY TOTAL TELEVISION PRODUCTIONS

CHAPTER 5

ALL ABOUT GAMMA

By *King Leonardo's* second season (1961-1962), animation for TTV was no longer done at TV Spots but done completely at Gamma, the animation studio controlled by General Mills. Gamma had disappointed Jay Ward. Biggers agrees, to a point. "There were a couple of major occasions where we were [too], but I think the difference is that Jay Ward had had hit series before he ever got to *Bullwinkle*, before he had ever got to Gamma, so he had done all different kinds of animation. He knew what he wanted and he knew what he liked. We only knew Gamma animation. I had been the one responsible for getting the *Rocky and Bullwinkle* shows ready for the network. That's the kind of animation I looked at and realized that's the kind of animation we would have to work with if we were to do anything, so we got what we expected."

Harris offers his opinion about the rumors that Gamma didn't really know what they were doing. "Well, they're probably true, but they never missed a deadline, and neither did I, and neither did any of us. We had some problems with one scene or another and I would just simply redraw or tell them what to do down in Mexico, but I frankly, because we were turning out 18 minutes of animation every week, don't think they could afford to say we don't want that, or else we would have interrupted the whole schedule. It was based on absolute timing. We had to get out 18 minutes a week, and that for me meant every 4½ minutes of the 18 was anywhere from 160 to 300 panels of storyboard." He also mentions in an interview on the *Underdog Collectors Edition* DVD that Gamma used house enamel for painting the cels and this created the most vibrant looking cels that didn't chip, even after 20 years.

Biggers continues, "We didn't have any choice. We came up with the series to sell to General Mills and that meant you had to use Gamma. They had put them in business. That was what we were created for. In other words, Ward and Scott were giving General Mills trouble or Gamma trouble and so we actually came into being because we could be somebody to keep Ward and Scott from doing so many dirty jokes for kids." TV Spots also did other animation for Dancer-

Fitzgerald-Sample [DFS] and for General Mills, which is how they were initially involved with Jay Ward and TTV.

Most of the horror stories about Gamma are detailed in great length in *The Moose That Roared*. In it, Keith Scott claims that "Ward was strongly opposed to the Mexican farm-out from the start."

In reality, most animation improves with time. For a more recent example, check out the first season of *The Simpsons* or the episodes done for *The Tracey Ullman Show*, and compare it to what was being done 20 years later. So, like Gracie did for *The Simpsons*, Gamma did for Jay Ward and TTV.

Gamma was originally called Val-Mar Productions. It was supposed to be a cost-saving measure to use Val-Mar and it was estimated that DFS and General Mills could save around $500,000 a year utilizing the Mexican studios. Len Key recalled, "I don't think Gordon Johnson or the client knew what the hell was happening."

Roman Arambula was born September 18, 1935, in Guadalajara, Mexico, and grew up in Mexico City. He worked for Gamma from roughly June 1960 to March 1967. He defends Gamma as being a quality outfit after having a bumpy beginning as Val-Mar.

Arambula takes up the story: "Ever since my early youth, I've had a fascination with drawing. I always viewed copying or tracing from photos or the drawings of others as cheating, in a sense. As a youngster, I would always strive to come up with my own original characters and designs.

"From an early age, I was attracted to figures in action, from the dynamics of athletes in motion to the fluidity and power of animals in their stride. I'm sure my early attempts at trying to capture the essence of man and beast in motion led me on my destined path to the field of animation, the ultimate *'Illusion Of Life'!*

"Growing up in Mexico, my friends and I would often go to a local movie house that ran animated films, almost exclusively. We revel in the zany antics of the now-vintage cartoons of MGM, Terry-Toons, Walter Lantz and Walt Disney. Another neighborhood theater specialized in action/adventure-type films which fed our minds with concepts for character and plot development. Viewing and discussing movies with my friends was an exciting and rewarding chapter in my life.

"I studied art at the Academia de San Carlos School of Fine Arts. Upon graduation, I entered the field of ceramics, where my job was to paint picturesque landscapes on large plates and bowls, in the style of the French Impressionists. This enterprise lasted almost a year.

"I met an old friend from art school who invited me to drop by the animation studio where he was employed as an animator. I checked it out, although I was not seriously looking for a job; however, the studio's art director was curious about my abilities and asked if I would do some drawings. The director came over and collected my array of drawings to show to a few of his animators. He returned and, to my amazement, offered me a job with the studio! 'We'll teach you and pay you,' he added.

"I took the job, working primarily on animated TV commercials, as an animator, character designer and storyboards. After roughly one year under my belt at the studio, I heard rumors that Gamma Productions was hiring. This was the summer of 1960, initiating a seven-year run at the studio, ending in March of 1967. The studio folded due to lack of work.

"At Gamma, I put in a regular 40-hour work week, and would often take work home on weekends to bring in some extra income.

"The shows I worked on were *King Leonardo, Tennessee Tuxedo, Commander McBragg, Hoppity Hooper, Mr. Peabody and Sherman, Fractured Fairy Tales, Aesop and Son, Go Go Gophers, Rocky and Bullwinkle, Dudley Do-Right* and *Underdog.*

"I did some commercials with Gamma Productions, but I don't recall working on any Bullwinkle projects. I do remember doing animation on a few Trix cereal spots.

"Gamma was a fun place to work, with jovial camaraderie and shared humor; caricatures of one another and practical jokes were commonplace. We got to know each other's backgrounds and families. It was a very relaxed and compatible group.

"I started in the layout department (character posing and background design) and after two years segued into animation.

"The studio was situated in a nice Mexico City neighborhood, with three public parks in the area and a wide variety of fine eateries close by."

Arambula reflects on his many Gamma co-workers. "I knew Jesus Martinez. He was the studio's Operations Manager. He had glasses and was a very nice person. He never acted like the owner. He was just one of the guys. He worked at the office taking care of the business and that's it.

"Ernesto Terrazas was Animation Supervisor. Ernie worked at Walt Disney Productions before he came to Mexico. He worked on the 'Posades' segment in *The Three Caballeros*. It comes from a tradition where Jesus goes through town in the procession in the Catholic tradition.

"Carlos Manriquez was the head of the background painting department. He came from Los Angeles. Ernie was also from Los Angeles, but [he was] born in Chihuahua.

"Bob Schleh worked a short time at Gamma (five months). He was an animator. He was Argentinean, but he got the name Bob Schleh. He could speak both English and Spanish. He was a peculiar person ... [but he] was a very nice person.

"Harvey Siegel was the head of layouts. Harvey was the one that hired me. I couldn't speak more than two words in English, and he could hardly speak anything in Spanish, so we communicated with drawings. So he saw me and said, 'Can you do this character in many sizes, many scales and poses and this and that?' and I did and he liked my drawings.

"Jaime Torres was Second Operations Manager under Jesus Martinez. Rodolfo Gonzara was a layout man. Sergio de la Torre was a layout man. Eduardo Olivares was a layout man. Daniel Burgos was an animator. Cesar Canton was an animator. Angel Canton was an animator. Julio Guerrero was an animator. Tex Hansen was an animator.

"After Gamma I went to work in comics in Mexico City until I moved to the US in August 1967 to work on animated commercials in Dallas, Texas. I did this until 1970 when I moved to Los Angeles, California, to work for Hanna-Barbera. In April 1975, I joined the Walt Disney Studios and in October of that year, my first Mickey Mouse comic-strip dailies week was published.

"In 1982, I began doing the Sunday strip as well. I did this until November 1989, when the strip was no longer published.

"Since then I have kept myself busy working with different animation studios, like Marvel Productions, Warner Bros. and Hyperion Productions. Then I went to teach animation in a local college until my retirement."

American animators Bob Schleh and Harvey Siegel were sent to Mexico by DFS. They also sent Bud Gourley, a production manager with live-television experience. But it apparently wasn't enough talent to shape up Val-Mar, which was now a disaster lacking basic organization within the studio. Other problems included budget, quality and professionalism, and the fact that Val-Mar was simply too slow in turning out product.

Glen Glenn Sound's James G. Stewart visited Mexico to check out the audio problems that Val-Mar was having and as a result, a new German sound system was installed, removing the inferior sound equipment that they had. This proved to be very helpful for TTV later on as all of the original theme songs were recorded in Mexico, including the entire "Beagles" album.

Bill Hurtz recommended that Val-Mar employ a full-time Spanish-speaking animation supervisor to help straighten the problems out and increase output. DFS hired the highly skilled Mexican animator Rudy Zamora to fulfill this role, but Zamora left after six months due to Gordon Johnson's constant badgering about the lack of significant improvements in output.

At this point, Schleh took over as Production Manager and got things organized and hired another Mexican animator named Sandoval to be the Animation Supervisor. Sandoval was stricter in his approach, but this was necessary to shape up the staff. Siegel, meanwhile, was Layout Supervisor.

Sal Faillace arrived in August 1960 to help the animators with character poses, and was eventually promoted to be Animation Coordinator, replacing Ernie Terrazas, who in turn, was promoted to Director in November of that year.

It was around this point, at the one-year mark, that the studios changed their name from Val-Mar to Gamma (or officially Producciones Animades Gamma SA).

Schleh eventually left *Rocky and his Friends* and the Ward shows to accept the position of Director on *King Leonardo* and the TTV shows on February 3, 1961.

In 1964 Harvey Siegel became co-owner of Gamma, with Jaime Torres Vasquez, and was the head of Gamma until in closed in 1970. Some confusion has arisen about when Gamma officially closed (1967 or 1970), but Arambula sets the record straight. "In Mexico, the labor laws demand that if you own a business and if you fire somebody, you have to pay him three months of salary and 20 days for every year that he worked at your company, so it was very difficult to fire people in Mexico. So, in the case of Gamma Productions, they leased all the equipment and couldn't afford to pay everybody, so they leased all the equipment to the two animation cameras and also the building, so it was a committee to continue doing animation through the head of Carlos Manriquez. I didn't like the idea, so I didn't participate. So I didn't like the idea to be in a partnership with my co-workers. I didn't see a future of it running that way. It would be like a Communist place. I mean, everyone would share if we made $1,000. We were 1,000 people. Everyone would get $1. It didn't make sense to me. I didn't want a part of it, and I wanted out of it. Just give me my pay now, so that was it. So they stayed in business, so to speak, until, I don't know, maybe '70, but at that time I was no longer in Mexico."

The Mexican cartoon outfit existed from 1959 to 1970. The final assignments were for *Go Go Gophers* and *Klondike Kat*. Piech recalls in an interview for *The Moose That Roared*, that when Gamma ceased operations, "Seven and a half cameras, and some other equipment, purchased originally for Val-Mar from as far away as New York and Japan, were donated to the Cartoonists Guild."

Arambula claims he never went to the US during the Gamma years, but General Mills did visit Gamma once and gave everyone "Big G" cufflinks!

The animators at Gamma worked with a base salary and a quota of footage per week. If you did more than your quota, then you were paid a bonus. Salary was about 700 pesos per week, but, with the quota, animators could earn three or four times that.

CREATED AND PRODUCED BY TOTAL TELEVISION PRODUCTIONS

CHAPTER 6

"TODAY OUR STORY IS ABOUT...TWINKLES"

According to *How Underdog Was Born,* Twinkles was what Biggers and Stover chose to talk about while Covington was giving the initial TTV presentation to Gordon Johnson. In that conversation, Biggers and Stover discussed obtaining a pink elephant to represent Twinkles in the upcoming Macy's Thanksgiving Day Parade as a promotional stunt. They were worried what people would think, if people would feel they were harming the elephant, but as they spoke, the conversation gradually drifted back to King Leonardo, even though they had both promised each other not to discuss TTV at DFS during business hours. Ultimately, Covington sold the show, and although Twinkles was a regular part of each King Leonardo show, it was not truly a TTV segment and as a result Biggers and company had virtually nothing to do with it.

Comments Biggers, "I wish we had. I was an account executive and one of my brands was 'Twinkles,' a cereal that no longer exists, and Chet was the creative director on all of the cereals, but we didn't have anything to do with the development of the characters." It is assumed that the limited animation of the segment was also done by TV Spots but Biggers could not recall for certain as "it was just different people, different guys. That stuff was mostly farmed out by General Mills. What happened was, cartoons were mushrooming on TV at that time, so all of that did happen all at the same time."

The Twinkles segment remained in syndicated packages of *King Leonardo* (rechristened *The King and Odie* in syndication) until FCC rules changed in the early 1970s prohibiting characters on children's shows from promoting products during the show. (Twinkles episodes aired as late as the 1980s, but with all cereal references removed.) Biggers agrees, "Yeah, they wouldn't allow anything like that anymore ..."

The 52 segments produced featured very limited animation of Twinkles the pink elephant and his various animal pals as they were involved in very simplistic adventures. The entire segment was narrated by George S. Irving.

Harris comments on his involvement with the Twinkles segments. "That was an add-on and I think it was one of those inspirations by General Mills. I don't know if there's a strict prohibition or simply a tradition of not combining entertainment with advertising. I think that was sort of a no-no. I think it was probably formed about then. I was kind of surprised at the time, but I thought maybe the restrictions were eased or maybe General Mills said, 'We're big enough to get away with this.' but I did the storyboards on that - Twinkles - and we produced it, and I don't remember much about it. It was of those little things where they say, 'Can you do this? Fine,' and that was that, and I don't remember what happened after that. I always wondered whatever did happen to Twinkles. I don't know if it's still being made by General Mills.

"I hired a guy by the name of Ernie Bart to do some storyboards for me, because I was going under, and he did the original Twinkles storyboards, and then I picked it up from there. I don't remember where that was at. That's a blank spot in my mind. It was one of several. I know that we did the storyboards; I know that we got them produced, and I don't remember what happened after that. It was one of those things that weren't important. General Mills wanted us to do them a favor. So, I did it and then said, 'Thanks. I've got to get back to work.'"

Eventually, Twinkles dropped the elephant character and was renamed "Sugar Frosted Twinkles" with no particular mascot by 1964. The cereal was dropped for good shortly thereafter; however, the cereal design made a comeback in 2007 as "Dora the Explorer" cereal, featuring the same star-shaped puffs with a center hole. A few toys were made of Twinkles, including a storybook called *Twinkles and Sanford's Boat* (1962), a Halloween costume and, of course, numerous stories on the backs of the cereal boxes with a fold-out back.

As stated before, Twinkles is not an official segment in the TTV canon, but its regular appearances and limited involvement by TTV warrant its inclusion here.

Twinkles was merchandised almost as much as King Leonardo. He appeared in his own 1962 storybook entitled *Twinkles and Sanford's Boat.* FROM THE AUTHOR'S COLLECTION.

128   CREATED AND PRODUCED BY TOTAL TELEVISION PRODUCTIONS

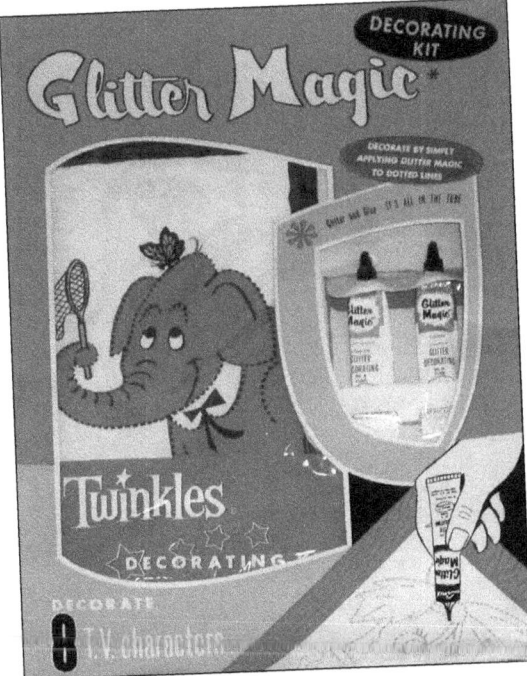

Various other merchandise featuring Twinkles, which included a glitter magic kit which featured images from *King Leonardo* as well as Jay Ward's *Rocky and his Friends* and *The Bullwinkle Show*, as well as an obscure live-action show called *Pip the Piper* and, of course, the "Twinkles" cereal box which featured a fold-out story flap.

"TWINKLES" STORYLINES

Episode 1: TWINKLES AND THE SAILBOAT

Sanford, the parrot, takes Twinkles for a boat ride and uses an umbrella for a sail.

Episode 2: TWINKLES AND THE TRIP TO CHINA

Wilbur, the monkey, and Sanford, the parrot, run into trouble digging to China.

Episode 3: TWINKLES AND THE BULL FIGHT

On Twinkles' picnic, the Bull in the pasture meets El Sanfordo, the great Matadoro.

Episode 4: TWINKLES AND THE AIRPLANE

Sanford boasts to Twinkles and Wilbur that he can fly a plane, and Wilbur puts him to the test.

Episode 5: TWINKLES AND THE HONEY BEES

Fulton, the camel, shows Twinkles his new invention for taking honey from the bees.

Episode 6: TWINKLES AND THE BIG FAN

Fulton's new invention for beating the heat causes unexpected trouble, with Twinkles to the rescue.

Episode 7: TWINKLES AND THE FISHING TRIP

Wilbur gets a head start on Twinkles so that he can catch all the fish, but he runs into thin ice.

Episode 8: TWINKLES AND THE ROLLER SKATES

Fulton thinks his jet skates are just what he needs to win the race against Harley, the horse.

Episode 9: TWINKLES AND THE CARNIVAL

Sanford, "the lone parrot", gets thrown by the electric bucking horse, and the ferris-wheel makes matters worse.

Episode 10: TWINKLES AND THE BANANAS

Wilbur and Twinkles visit Terrible Mike, the gorilla, who is captain of the banana tugboat.

A folder containing character descriptions, episode titles and storylines for the Twinkles segments. COURTESY OF TREAD COVINGTON.

Episode 11: TWINKLES AND THE MOUNTAIN CLIMB

Twinkles, Sanford, and Wilbur get into trouble when Wilbur's trick starts an avalanche.

Episode 12: TWINKLES AND THE PARADE

Fulton's invention for seeing parades over other people's heads has surprising results.

Episode 13: TWINKLES AND THE HAUNTED HOUSE

Twinkles, Wilbur, and Sanford explore an old house and meet an unexpected "ghost."

Episode 14: TWINKLES AND THE HORSE SHOW

Jimmy, the zebra, can't enter the horse show until Wilbur thinks of a monkey trick.

Episode 15: TWINKLES AND THE SNOW SHOVEL

Wilbur volunteers to clear Twinkles' walk of snow with Fulton's new invention.

Episode 16: TWINKLES AND THE RUBBER RAFT

Sanford and Wilbur have a race with rubber rafts and who should turn up but Mr. Whale.

Episode 17: TWINKLES AND THE DESERT RESCUE

Twinkles tells how Fulton started making inventions, even though they never work.

Episode 18: TWINKLES AND THE HOUSE BOAT

Sanford and Wilbur think Twinkles does things the hard way but a storm helps change their minds.

Episode 19: TWINKLES AND THE LEAPING ROBBER

Twinkles and Fulton go to see Twinkles' uncle Jumbo and meet a train robber on the way.

Episode 20: TWINKLES AND THE FLYING SAUCER

"Sharp-eye" Sanford is sure he's seen a flying saucer and rushes out to tell all his friends.

Episode 21: TWINKLES AND THE LITTLE BOY

Twinkles and Sanford, out for a walk, help Little Boy Blue who has lost his horn.

Episode 22: TWINKLES AND THE BIG FISH

Sanford, "the world's greatest fisherman", catches a big one, and he swims right over the dam.

Episode 23: TWINKLES AND THE SWIMMING POOL

Wilbur decides to make a swimming pool, but half way through the digging, the steam-shovel breaks.

Episode 24: TWINKLES AND THE TUBE BALLOON

Fulton takes Twinkles for a ride in his strange new invention, but doesn't know how to come down again.

Episode 25: TWINKLES AND THE MUSICAL BAND

Twinkles and Sanford form a band, and Thomas, the octopus, proves to be quite a musician.

Episode 26: TWINKLES AND THE AMATEUR SHOW

Twinkles shows Fulton, and Wilbur and Sanford how teamwork can win.

Episode 27: TWINKLES AND THE RODEO

"Never-Fall Sanford, the Bronco King" is in for a surprise when Wilbur plays a monkey trick.

Episode 28: TWINKLES AND THE SHOW BOAT

Twinkles hates to miss the show but when the big paddle wheels break, the show must go on.

Episode 29: TWINKLES AND THE BOAT RIDE

Wilbur, Sanford, and Twinkles try out Wilbur's boat, but Wilbur makes it go too fast.

Episode 30: TWINKLES AND THE CLIMBING SHOES

Wilbur thinks Fulton's unfinished invention is just what he needs to get to the best coconuts.

isode:
    Falling Leaves
    The faster Sanford rakes leaves, the faster they fall, until
    Twinkles discovers Wilbur is up to monkey tricks.

    Big Storm
    A rain storm almost ruins the picnic until Twinkles puts his
    magic trunk to work to prove that every cloud has a silver
    lining.

    Trailer
    Fulton, the camel, invents a motor made of soap for his boat.
    The motor works just fine until it gets suds in Fulton's eyes.

    Bird Cage
    Sanford decides that the life of a pet parrot is best, but he
    soon discovers he's only a bird in a little wire cage.

    Soap Boat
    Sanford thinks he's the greatest driver in the world and takes
    Twinkles and Wilbur for a wild ride in a trailer.

    The Game
    Twinkles and his friends play "hide and seek". Twinkles finds
    everyone but Jimmy the Zibra who hides himself in a funny way.

    Parachute
    Fulton, the camel, makes a parachute out of feathers, and he
    figures if one feather floats to the ground, a hundred would
    work even better.

    Lawn Mower
    Sanford's lawn mower breaks down, and he's out of a job until
    Twinkles comes along and thinks of a strange way to make the
    lawn mower work.

    Baby Sitter
    Twinkles and his friends start a baby sitting business, and
    just when everything is going wrong, Twinkle's gets an idea to
    make the children behave.

    Lemonade Stand
    Sanford and Wilbur have a lemonade stand but no customers-
    until they decide to take the lemonade to the customers.

    Tractor
    Wilbur and Sanford become farmers and all goes well until
    Sanford wrecks the tractor.

    Nite
    Fulton invents a "camel-carrying Kite" and when he tries it out
    he runs into trouble because Wilbur has played a monkey trick.

    Little Girl
    Twinkles and Sanford, out for a walk, meet Miss Muffet, who
    tells them about a huge spider that has just frightened her.

Gold Mine
Sanford and Wilbur explore an old lost gold mine in search of treasure, but part of the ceiling falls down and they can't get out.

Mechanical Man
Fulton, the camel, invents a mechanical man that works but won't do anything right, and Twinkles discovers that the mechanical man has a tail that looks like a monkey's.

Volunteer Fireman
Mrs. Horse's house is on fire and Wilbur and Sanford, the volunteer firemen, go to her rescue. Luckily they take Twinkles with them.

Sportscar
Sanford takes Twinkles for a fast ride in his sports car, but the car runs out of gas in the middle of heavy traffic.

Missing Fish
Twinkles and Fulton go fishing and have wonderful luck, but then they discover that their fish are gone... and they also discover why.

Birthday Party
Twinkles is sad because he thinks he's being left out of a birthday party for someone special -- then he gets a big surprise.

Toboggan
Sanford, Wilbur, and Twinkles go to the top of Slippery Hill to slide down on their toboggan. On their way down they run into trouble.

Sheep
Coming home from a picnic, Twinkles and Sanford meet Little Bo Peep who has lost her sheep. Twinkles thinks of a way to help her.

Carousel
Wilbur and Sanford and Twinkles go to the Carousel in the park. Sanford boasts that he can catch the brass ring but he reaches out too far.

"TODAY OUR STORY IS ABOUT...TWINKLES"

CREATED AND PRODUCED BY TOTAL TELEVISION PRODUCTIONS

CHAPTER 7

"TENNESSEE TUXEDO WILL NOT FAIL!"

TTV-Leonardo's next series was called *Tennessee Tuxedo and his Tales*, which debuted on CBS at 9:30 a.m. on September 28, 1963, ironically the same day that *King Leonardo and his Short Subjects* had its last network run on NBC. Veteran stand-up comic Don Adams was recruited to lend his unique voice and speaking style to the always-confident penguin. Harris continues, "*King Leonardo* was followed by *Tennessee Tuxedo and his Tales*. Both of these were ideas of Chet's. Chet was the idea man."

One reason a second series was created is that both Biggers and Stover knew that once General Mills got the allotment of episodes they needed for *King Leonardo* production would stop, so the need to create a new series was of the essence. Biggers and Stover's initial idea was to be a show called *Parrot Playhouse*, but this idea only went as far as the planning stages. Biggers contacted Eli Feldman, still at Pelican Films, and discussed the idea, which was basically a format where each episode would parody a different TV show, the first one being a parody of *Gunsmoke* with an episode called "Spoofs 'n' Saddles," with a completed script and a 10-minute pilot made.

Unfortunately for Biggers and Stover, although the presentation for *Parrot Playhouse* went over extremely well at ABC, the series ultimately did not sell. This was primarily due to a change in power at ABC between the time of the presentation and closing the final deal. The other networks were approached, but ABC's abrupt turndown ruined those chances. Fortunately, *Tennessee Tuxedo* sold, but even it wasn't completely an easy sell. The education idea went from hot to cold to hot again, but barely made it onto the schedule. It ended up being TTV's second most successful series.

New supporting segments were created for this new show, including new episodes of *King and Odie* and *The Hunter*, as well as a new segment called

The World of Commander McBragg — more on this segment later. Strangely, no new segments of *Tooter Turtle* were made.

Tennessee Tuxedo and its new components were the first to be animated by the Mexican animation studio Gamma Productions. Here is where the confusion begins. Gamma was also the animation studio that animated the various *Rocky and Bullwinkle* incarnations and its other components, as well as Jay Ward's follow-up series, *Hoppity Hooper*. When these series ended up in syndication, many components from TTV series ended up in Jay Ward series, especially *Tooter the Turtle* and *Commander McBragg*.

To add insult to injury, when the "Bullwinkle's" restaurant chain debuted in the '80s, Underdog, Tennessee Tuxedo, Tooter, Baldy and others TTV characters were there alongside Rocky and Bullwinkle and all of the other Jay Ward characters to create a "Gamma mish-mash." And, now, both Jay Ward and TTV's assets are owned by Classic Media, so the separation is blurred even more.

One could argue that if the series is funny, then it is a Jay Ward one, but TTV had a charm all its own. Whereas a Jay Ward series might stoop to cheap belly laughs from corny puns, a TTV series would compensate with good storytelling. Granted, TTV series could be considered highly repetitive, but that could be said about countless animated cartoon series.

As far as *Tennessee Tuxedo* goes, a viewer could receive a fairly decent education from the factual information that was presented every time Tennessee and Chumley escaped from the zoo to visit their friend Mr. Whoopee, who discussed many a topic via the 3DBB (3-dimensional blackboard). *Tennessee Tuxedo* ran on CBS until September 3, 1966. Covington comments, "[Buck and Chet] really did their research. They didn't make statements that they didn't check with a college textbook or an encyclopedia.

"When we'd start work on a new series, I think as far as the voice tracks are concerned, we really concentrated more on the sound, and the type of voice that we had in mind. Obviously, all of the actors that were involved with our series eventually had seen them on the air and the new ones and the characters they were doing. I wouldn't say that we were not trying to have them visualize themselves as a lion or cartoon skunk. The penguin that is Tennessee Tuxedo obviously got his name from being a penguin. The personality is essentially one of Don Adams' character who is sort of a know-it-all and smartass who gets caught up on points along the way. Bradley Bolke did his sidekick, Chumley the Walrus, and he was a comic relief sidekick. Adams was the know-it-all and his sidekick was sort of the 'duh' character. Then they would go to Mr. Whoopee for information to help them solve whatever predicament they would be in."

Bradley Bolke, the voice of Chumley, comments, "You see, that was the gimmick of that show. The gimmick was that it had an educational twist. Tennessee and Chumley would go through their antics and they were sort of like Laurel &

Hardy, and then they'd have a problem and then go to Mr. Whoopee with the 3DBB and he'd come up with some very specific, scientific answer to whatever the problem was. This was their selling point - and it worked!"

Strangely, even though there was a *King Leonardo* comic book series, there never was a *Tennessee Tuxedo* comic book series. This is true to this day. There wasn't even an *Underdog* comic book series until long after the program was in reruns. A new comic book series was not tried again until 1969 and this one featured an unsold pilot called *The Colossal Show*.

In fact, *Tennessee Tuxedo* is one of the most popular yet least merchandized cartoon characters in the history of animation. The total merchandise amounts produced during the series original run amounts to a Soaky bottle, a Halloween costume, a couple of children's books, a couple of coloring books, and a "FrostyO's" box that featured Chumley.

The succeeding years have not been much kinder to the stalwart penguin, yet his popularity has never waned. One mention of "Total TeleVision" to a casual cartoon fan receives blank stares, yet mention *Underdog* or *Tennessee Tuxedo* and the eyes light up, and fond nostalgic memories burst forth.

Of all the shows Total TeleVision produced, *Tennessee Tuxedo* is one of the most realized and holds up best to repeat viewings, partially due to the variety of plots. It is also the most dated of the TTV series, as much of the technology discussed has been updated or replaced. For example, in the episode entitled "Telephone Terrors or Dial 'M' For Mayhem," Tennessee solves the problem of running around the zoo delivering the news by developing his own phone system using the wires from Stanley Livingstone's piano. Nowadays, the problem could be solved with the purchase of a simple cell phone.

Although the main plot exists where Tennessee and Chumley escape the zoo to solve a problem with Mr. Whoopee, how this occurs is a different matter altogether, and in at least one episode, "Helicopter Hi-Jinx," Tennessee and Chumley do not even leave the zoo, and instead Tennessee relays information from a previous Whoopee visit, implying that the duo had left the premises on occasions not previously televised.

What makes *Tennessee Tuxedo* truly engaging is the educational angle. While that may seem to be the death knell in any other children's series, *TT* was able to disguise the fact that it was teaching anything under the guise of a plot device.

George W. Woolery points out what inspired the educational idea of *Tennessee Tuxedo* in *Children's Television: The First 35 Years*: "*Tennessee Tuxedo and his Tales* was one of the first humorous educational cartoons introduced in the wake of FCC Chairman Newton R. Minow's 1961 'vast wasteland' speech." Minow delivered this speech at the 39th Annual Convention of the National Association of Broadcasters in Washington, D.C., on May 9, 1961. Minow's name was also immortalized as the name of the three-hour tour boat on *Gilligan's Island* in

1964, though it was modified slightly to read "Minnow." With this educational requirement, *Tennessee Tuxedo* got the go-ahead and *Parrot Playhouse* was put on the shelf, ultimately permanently.

Another strong point for *Tennessee Tuxedo and his Tales* was the use of strong character voices. In this case, stand-up comedian and television personality Don Adams was recruited for the role. Not yet known for *Get Smart*, Adams based his stage persona on an exaggerated imitation of *The Thin Man's* William Powell. This, by Adams own admission on his *A&E Biography* special, allowed him to make even the most mundane lines of dialogue funny. Adams also (according to Biggers and Stover), resembled a penguin. Adams was apparently signed late in the game as it was always assumed that if Adams refused to do the role, someone like Allen Swift or Jackson Beck could easily take on the part.

Adams was born Donald James Yarmy, on April 13, 1926, in New York City. He began his career as a nightclub comedian in Miami, and also was a commercial artist and draftsman. In 1954, Adams auditioned for *Arthur Godfrey's Talent Scouts* and, according to *A&E Biography*, changed his last name to Adams in order to appear first on the name roster.

Adams won the competition and soon teamed up with fellow comedian Bill Dana and appeared with and without him on various TV shows during the 1950s, including *The Steve Allen Show*, *The Ed Sullivan Show* and *The Garry Moore Show*. His early shtick was to appear as a bumbling detective with the voice that soon became his trademark.

Bolke comments on his soon-to-be-famous co-star, "Don Adams, his character with that clipped voice that he had. He said that this was sort of a take-off on William Powell, so when you had to do an impersonation of William Powell, all you had to do was an impersonation of Don Adams.

"Well, I'll be honest with you, with Don Adams; he was a very strange duck. I'm serious! You know, a very talented guy, but I'd say in the three years that we worked, aside from dialogue between Tennessee and Chumley, he never had two words to say to me. Yeah, very strange, very strange, unfriendly guy. I don't know why. He did *Get Smart* after *Tennessee Tuxedo*. Of course, it was very successful."

Covington remembers, "I first knew Don Adams when he did a series where he was a bumbling detective. It was called *The Bill Dana Show*. Don had some sort of routine where there was a trial and he was a defense attorney and he said, 'Your honor, the prosecuting attorney can say that, and why? Because he's got proof.' And, of course, it was that kind of personality; an idiotic smartass know-it-all who really didn't know, and that was the type of character that Don did so well.

"Well, I think Don Adams was pretty involved with his career and he was on the way up getting more and more successful. We were quite lucky to get him, because he might not have even done it once he did *Get Smart*. I think he was particularly ambitious. Bradley Bolke was a perfectly good voice actor and he filled the role as sidekick for Don Adams the way we wanted. But he was really not in the same league with Adams.

"I think Don Adams, with his particular talents, was really more in a straight line for big-time success and I think he probably viewed Bradley as sort of an 'extra,' while he was headed for stardom. And, of course, Wally Cox had been successful and Kenny Delmar had done a lot of things and knew everyone."

Adams went on to star in other TV series, including *The Don Adams Screen Test*, *Check it Out*, and *The Partners*, and even voiced another popular cartoon character, Inspector Gadget. He died on September 25, 2005, in Beverly Hills, CA, of a pulmonary infection.

Bolke comments on the rest of the *Tennessee Tuxedo* cast: "Now, on the other hand, Larry Storch, very, very pleasant guy, and the rest of them, Kenny Delmar, Mort Marshall and who else? I guess that was about it. Mort Marshall was a nice fellow. A really nice guy. He was not too tall, but he had a BIG VOICE!" Marshall was born August 17, 1918, in New York City. Among his other projects, he appeared on the short-lived sitcom *The Dumplings* in 1976, which also featured fellow TTV alumnus George S. Irving.

Covington remembers Marshall, as "one of our terrific voice actors. He was a very funny person. Unfortunately, he's dead [Marshall died February 1, 1979]. He was Stanley Livingstone in *Tennessee Tuxedo* as well as a lead in *Go Go Gophers* and *The Beagles*, and did many other voice parts." Marshall's Stanley Livingstone was an imitation of character actor Franklin Pangborn. Marshall also portrayed Baldy the Eagle, a characterization based upon character actor Ned Sparks.

Bolke continues, "Very interesting and small world that it is, my brother and Kenny Delmar wrote a play together many, many years ago in the early '40s. They kind of collaborated on something and one of the characters in the play, according to my brother, he felt was the Senator Claghorn-type character and he felt that Kenny sort of plagiarized it and my brother felt that he should have gotten some sort of compensation for it, and he subsequently sued Kenny for it, and it went to arbitration and my brother lost. This was back about 60 years ago, when he was on *The Fred Allen Show* doing this character of Senator Claghorn of 'Allen's Alley.' We worked together. He was the narrator for *Tennessee Tuxedo*. Delmar performed the voices for Flunky, Stanley Livingstone's zoo assistant; Yak, one of Tennessee, Chumley and Baldy's zoo animal friends; Sergeant Badge, the generic policeman role based upon character actor Edgar Kennedy; and also handled the narration for the episodes."

Another strong and versatile voice added to the cast was that of Larry Storch for his Phineas J. Whoopee character. Sort of an imitation of Frank Morgan (the Wizard in 1939's *The Wizard of Oz*), Storch brought in elements of excitement to the learning process. Nothing seemed to upset the brilliant Whoopee, save for Tennessee's proclamations that he received all the information he needed on a particular topic, regardless if he had or hadn't, prompting an occasional, "But wait…" from Whoopee as Tennessee and Chumley scooted out the door.

Storch was born January 8, 1923, in New York City, and began his career like fellow cast mate Adams as a stand-up comic and impressionist. He received his first big break on the *Kraft Music Hall* doing an apparently hilarious impression of ailing actor Frank Morgan, whom Storch was replacing on the show that week. This impression was the basis for Mr. Whoopee a decade or so later.

Bolke comments on his other co-star, "I think I saw Larry Storch many, many years ago at an audition. I imagine he's still around and he's a nice guy. The funny thing is that the only guy Don talked to was Larry, 'cause I understand that they knew each other as kids. I think they grew up in New York City on the West Side together. I don't know if they were roommates or not, but they knew each other as kids."

Covington adds, "Larry Storch did Mr. Whoopee. I feel like Larry had big plans. I think he had already done pretty successful work in radio and television. I don't remember personally knowing about him as a performer at the time that we got involved with him. At any rate, things I've read later, such as *Conversations with Woody Allen*, have mentioned Larry favorably."

Storch indeed grew up in the Bronx with Adams and they were lifelong friends. He even appeared on an episode of *Get Smart* as the Groovy Guru, and went on to star in such TV series as *F Troop* and *The Ghost Busters* and many films, including *Airport 1975* and *The Great Race*, and did many other cartoon voices, including The Joker, Koko the Clown and Cool Cat, though strangely, no others for TTV. He currently lives in New York City and makes regular convention appearances.

A few commercials were made at the time featuring Bolke as the dimwitted walrus. "That's right. It was for 'FrostyO's.' For some reason or other they had some problems with Don [Adams] or something. There was some contractual problem so I think Chuck McCann did the character. I know he went into the studio and we did the 'FrostyO's' commercial [actually they did three], which turned out to be very lucrative. General Mills was the sponsor for the original run of *Tennessee Tuxedo* and we did a 'FrostyO's' commercial and we did it a couple of times, but not with Don. It was some sort of contractual problem there. The character of Chumley became a minor star in his own right, and even appeared solo on a 'FrostyO's' box during the mid-'60s."

The role of Chumley was originally voiced by an actor who didn't work out. Voiceover actor Bradley Bolke (brother of Dayton Allen) was brought in after six episodes were completed to "loop" the lines of the dimwitted walrus. If you listen closely to one of these early episodes (#3, "The Lamplighters"), you can hear the original voice as Bolke's voice was inadvertently left off. Even before that, the original concept of Chumley was that he was to mumble and speak unintelligibly. This idea proved to be limiting, and so Chumley got his voice. (The idea was never completely discarded and the unintelligible voice idea was later resurrected for *Go Go Gophers*.)

Bolke relates the story of how he got the role of Chumley. "Apparently, they had done three or four shows and for some reason or other they weren't happy with the voice of Chumley, so they auditioned a few people, and someone gave them my name as somebody who does voices."

Covington concurs, "That *is* possible. I don't remember that we had a different voice, once we started actually recording. He may have a better memory than I do. I only remember the voice as done by him. That's the way the stories could mesh, that we had not gone on the air yet."

Bolke continues, "I got there and they said, 'What we're looking for is a character…' There was a radio show called *Duffy's Tavern* and on *Duffy's Tavern* was a character called Clifton Finnegan, played by a guy by the name of Charlie Cantor, and the guy said [in Chumley's voice], 'Duh, the way he talked, he was a real moron.' What they said they were looking for was someone who could sound like Finnegan. Covington said, 'Whoever comes closest to Finnegan at the audition today, we're going to record today, and we're going to record the first four or five shows.' So, about a half a dozen of us auditioned, we're waiting outside, and they came out and they said, 'All right, Bradley, you're the one we want. You're the one that sounds like Finnegan.' So, what we did was just wild lines. At that particular time I didn't work with anyone else.

"At that time, these were the lines for the first four or five shows, and they had to come in at a certain time like two seconds, three seconds … at that time I was pretty good, I had a built-in timer. So we did that and that was it and after that they said, 'We'll be getting back to you. We're going to be doing more shows.' We recorded over three years, '62-'65.

"The only show I did was *Tennessee Tuxedo*; Chumley the Walrus and Jerboa Jump. He didn't come in too often, though. That was it, just those two characters. The only thing I did for Total TeleVision was *Tennessee Tuxedo*.

"We did 70 shows, and how they used them I don't know. So, they had all these shows in the can and we got some residuals and then they paid off on the basis of six showings. So, we got the original session fees, and then our residuals quarterly, then after six showings, under the SAG contract at that time, it was theirs in perpetuity. Most of the time we all recorded together, but if somebody like Don Adams or Larry Storch was on the road or something, they would go to a local studio, do the copy and then mail it into the producers and then Ben Stern would put it all together."

Bolke ("[It's pronounced] Bowl-kee") was born October 1, 1925, in New York City, and "I was always kind of a performer. I started doing voices, I suppose, when I was a kid. I found out that I could do impersonations. Maybe in seventh grade, I remember one night I was lying in bed talking to myself and I was doing impersonations. I remember my first three impersonations were President [Franklin D.] Roosevelt, Boake Carter, who was a news commentator, and Ed Wynn, who was a comedian.

"I found out it worked and my brother was also an actor and this gave me a segue into performing. When I was in school I was always involved in athletics and performing and was always in plays and shows and from there I decided that I wanted to get into broadcasting. Back then, when I finished high school, you could major in Radio, which I did. I majored in Radio and minored in Speech and English at New York University back in the dark ages. Those programs changed from Radio to Television to Film. All those programs were amalgamated into Dramatic Arts, all amalgamated into this Tisch School of Arts of New York University, which was formed many, many years after my graduation. It's one of the most prestigious schools in the country today. Some very famous people have come out of it. I think Martin Scorsese and Spike Lee are among them, and Alec Baldwin, and the girl who played the lead in *Will and Grace* [Debra Messing], I think she's a graduate. From there I went on to college and while I was still in college I started knocking around in business and doing radio work and getting a little bit of work here and when I finished, I did some television. In fact, I did television back when I was still in college back in 1945. It was live television and it was nothing to be nervous about because there was exactly about 1,000 sets back in the New York metropolitan area. It was experimental television.

"From there I went on just knocking around for a long time before I made a living for myself. I did radio, television, films, commercials, and for what I did for many years I did mostly commercials. This was the bulk of my work. It was on camera, off camera, side of camera, and this was the bulk of my work and it was very good and it was very lucrative, but it made me a lazy actor. I should have being going out doing more 'legitimate' stuff. You know, when you go into a studio, you record something and then residuals come in and you wait and go to the mailbox and it was like hitting the slot machine. It spoils you. Anyway, I did that and then I did voices for cartoons. I did a lot of things like and I did a lot of voices and then I had to stop doing them because I started *hearing* voices," Bolke said with a laugh.

"Once in a while I would double up as an announcer, too, but more often than not, it was character voices. You go in there and they show you a storyboard and you look at the character and you figure well, give 'em a few different voices. I found out afterwards that if you give them too many, it kind of confuses them.

So you give them about three or four different character voices and approaches and if it works, it works. If it doesn't, you go on to the next audition. That's the name of the game. You win some, you lose some.

"In some cases, yes, but in some cases just characters I made up out of my head, and in some cases, people I knew. There were some people I knew that had funny characteristics in their voice and I made mental notes and when I went into an audition or went to do a character, I would write this down so I'd remember. There were a lot of people I knew who had funny characteristic voices.

"People like me; I'm what they call in the industry, a middle-class journeyman actor. The stars that do the voices for these feature animation movies, they're stars. They're playing themselves."

Due to Don Adams' and Larry Storch's frequent absences due to their extensive touring schedules, a compromise was made. Covington explains, "This was a long time ago and there was technology that people think nothing of anymore. All kinds of digital things you can do and all kinds of tricks of different studios and things like that and it's nothing to work things out so that it matches as if done at one time and one place. For instance, we could tape Don in California and blend it with the other voice track in our NY studio; at the time this was quite innovative. We were trying to be efficient and save money and make it work. If we couldn't schedule our voice people to act in the same recording sessions, and it looked like it would hold up our cartoon schedule, we simply had to figure another way of doing it. So, sometimes we had tapes coming in from Chicago where one was, and another coming from California where another was, and our actors who were in New York would record their parts in New York, and then we put it all together in the editing."

Covington reflects on the recording sessions, in general, "I worked with Ben Stern at Aura Recording Studios. It was a great outfit and we were fond of them and I think they were fond of us. It was sort of fun for them. I think we were the first network continuing cartoon series that had decided to make them our regular studio. I didn't know that Ben's son is the famous Howard Stern. I guess Howard Stern was a child at the time. Ben Stern was our basic studio producer/director and I worked with him the whole time. It was with Ben Stern that I did most of the editing. [Howard] may have [come to the studio at one time]. He must have been so young at the time. Ben probably would pat him on the head and say, 'Ok, run along now, Daddy has to work.'

"[Recording sessions] were very professional. We would do some retakes, occasionally for technical reasons with the equipment, but then we would do some things — for instance — if something concerned one of the actors, or bothered me, because that was about the degree of my directing. If it didn't seem like it was coming off the way we hoped it would, then we would all listen to it. Ben would play it for us and then we'd talk it over, and then we'd try a different approach and do another take. As a rule, our actors were so professional and did their parts so well, that it went pretty smoothly."

Bolke recalls working with Stern as well. "They call you for an audition and, you know, more often than not, they knew my work, and they'd call me in and more or less ask what characters I was going to do and we'd agree on the characters and then we'd set up a recording date. It was a very funny thing. I was working for Rankin-Bass, and this was at Aura Recording and Aura Recording, one of the partners was Ben Stern, Howard Stern's father. We were there recording one of the Rankin-Bass shows, which took quite a bit of time because they were hour shows. We would be there for maybe four or five hours or something and we'd take a break and I went down the hall to go to the men's room and a producer from BBD&O comes out and he says, 'Where are you going?' 'I gotta go to the men's room. We're taking a break next door here.' He said, 'You got five minutes?' I said, 'Yeah. All right.' I'll tell you how far back this was; they were still doing cigarette commercials. He said, 'We just did a Lucky Strike commercial where one of the lines got screwed up and the actor has already left. We're trying to get him to come back here, but if he can't get back in time, do you want to do this one line?' I said, 'Sure, why not?' I went in and it took me two minutes. I did the line, I filled out a W-4, and I figured that was it. It turned out I made more money on that than I did working for Rankin-Bass that day. They used what they called the unlimited network run. The first time I heard that commercial was one day I had a recording job and set the radio alarm to get up on time and it was my voice that woke me up, on that commercial! But it was very weird. I remember taking a little time to go to the bathroom and stopping along the way."

Though Bolke's brother, Dayton Allen, never worked for TTV, he was a significant voice artist in his own right, creating the voice of Terry-Toon's Deputy

Dawg. "My brother, he did a lot of work, and it's just a shame he wasn't too well. He died about three years ago, and he wasn't too well for a couple of years before that, but if he were up in this neck of the woods, and was feeling well, he could have done a lot of that stuff. He did a lot of stuff. He could have done a lot of these autograph sessions and he would have been paid well for it. I'm amazed that people remember all of the things that he did. Well, he was on the original *Howdy Doody Show* from '49-'53 as Phineas T. Bluster.

"You know, when he left the show, interestingly enough, to show you what a small world this is, Allen Swift replaced him. They had some contractual difficulties. When he left the show, he and a few other people had some contractual difficulties and differences and they left the show; my brother and the others. They were all talented people. They figured they'd get other work. There was one guy on the show that played Clarabelle the clown. The guy didn't have any talent. He couldn't sing, dance, act or anything and they said, 'What's going to happen to Bobby?' Bobby Keeshan went on to become Captain Kangaroo, an American Icon, and a millionaire."

Bolke continued voice acting after his short but memorable tenure at TTV. "I did a lot of stuff for Rankin-Bass, but the one that I think stands out is *The Year Without a Santa Claus*. We did that in 1974. They did *Frosty the Snowman* and *Rudolph, the Red-Nosed Reindeer* and they go back to the '60s, but *The Year Without a Santa Claus* we did in '74." But, most of all, Bolke remembers fondly his years with TTV and working with Covington. "He was a nice guy. He was a very nice fellow to work with. He was very easygoing."

Another little segment of *Tennessee Tuxedo* was the quick-riddle segment. Bolke seems to remember that they did a riddle for every show, but that may be too many, as only 31 have been confirmed by the time of this writing.

The cast of the *Tennessee Tuxedo* segment of *Tennessee Tuxedo and his Tales* included Tennessee Tuxedo, Chumley, Yak, Baldy and Phineas J. Whoopee, the man with all the answers.

And, finally, another "star" of *Tennessee Tuxedo* was Mr. Whoopee's closet, in which he retrieved his three-dimensional blackboard, after causing all kinds of commotion and mess by opening his closet door, an idea borrowed from the old *Fibber McGee and Molly* radio show.

Tread Covington contributed this damaged Tennessee Tuxedo production photo.

Two *Tennessee Tuxedo* children's books from 1964: *Tennessee Tuxedo and Old '97* and *Tennessee Tuxedo and the Sailboat Race*. FROM THE AUTHOR'S COLLECTION.

CREATED AND PRODUCED BY TOTAL TELEVISION PRODUCTIONS

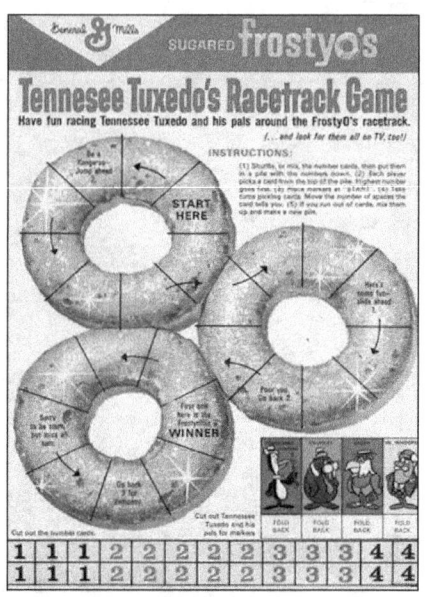

Various merchandise featuring *Tennessee Tuxedo*.

The original art for the *Tennessee Tuxedo* coloring book.

Original storyboard art and production background art from *Tennessee Tuxedo*.
ARTWORK COURTESY OF THE COLLECTION OF JOHN BRUSZEWSKI.

CREATED AND PRODUCED BY TOTAL TELEVISION PRODUCTIONS

Above: Howard Stern's father, Ben Stern, was the sound engineer for the various TTV voice sessions. *Below:* Bradley Bolke signed this photo for the author after being interviewed for this book.

Don Adams (pictured here with Barbara Feldon) is best known for his portrayal of Maxwell Smart on TV's *Get Smart*.

A rare set of TTV playing cards.

CREATED AND PRODUCED BY TOTAL TELEVISION PRODUCTIONS

CHAPTER 8

"THERE'S NO NEED TO FEAR, UNDERDOG IS HERE!"

TTV's next series was definitely their *piece de resistance*. *The Underdog Show* debuted at 10 a.m., on October 3, 1964, and ran on NBC while *Tennessee Tuxedo and his Tales* continued concurrently on CBS. When *Tennessee Tuxedo* ended its network run on September 3, 1966, *The Underdog Show* switched networks and replaced the show on CBS from September 10, 1966 through September 1, 1968. It then returned to NBC from September 7, 1968 through September 5, 1970 and again from September 9, 1972 through September 1, 1973, ending an incredible nine-year network run (save for a two-year break), although production of new episodes ceased in March 1967.

The show almost didn't happen — a common theme of TTV. *Tennessee Tuxedo* had had the success of *King Leonardo* to give it the green light. When the presentations for *Underdog* were being given, *Tennessee Tuxedo* hadn't even been on the air yet, and had *Tennessee Tuxedo* failed, it is highly unlikely that General Mills would have wanted to press on with *Underdog*, but as the character says, "Tennessee Tuxedo will not fail," and so begat *Underdog*.

Much has been written about the unlikely canine superhero, much more than any other TTV creation. It is without a doubt the one series and character that will be remembered long after the name TTV is forgotten. So great was Underdog's popularity, that the character debuted as a balloon in the Macy's Thanksgiving Day Parade, only one year after Underdog's debut. To honor this event, TTV prepared a special episode to air right after the parade. NBC aired the parade at 10 a.m., on November 25, 1965, Thanksgiving Day. An all-new episode of *The Underdog Show*, entitled "No Thanksgiving," aired immediately following the parade at noon, which was also released as a small 7" record with picture sleeve soon after. (A year later, the Underdog balloon appeared in cartoon form on the cover of the November 26, 1966, issue of *The New Yorker*, behind Bullwinkle's feet.)

As a postscript, people to this day still believe that the original Underdog balloon still appears in the Macy's Thanksgiving Day Parade, but its last appearance was in 1984. In fact, an entire episode of *Friends* is based on Underdog's inclusion, literally titled "The One Where Underdog Gets Away," which originally aired in 1994. In it, the characters run to the rooftop to witness the runaway balloon.

There have, however, been other Underdog balloons in other parades, since, but the Underdog balloon still exists in commercials as recently as a 2008 Coke ad.

Harris says, "Chet came up with an idea – and I think this is a story you've heard before, about him watching television? It was *I Love Lucy*."

Harris continues, from an interview by Paulington James Christensen III, "Where did Underdog come from? My partner Chet was watching television one night. *I Love Lucy* was on. And Desi Arnaz had just told Lucy that he was inviting George Reeves over for dinner. And George Reeves was the man who did *Adventures of Superman* on television. So, Lucy said, 'Oh, my God!' She went and immediately made a Superman costume. Then she walked out on the fire escape so that she could come back in through the window and surprise George Reeves. But she never got in because the window was locked. And she was out there all night. As I said, my friend and partner Chet saw this episode. He never watches television, but he just happened to watch it that night. The next day he said, 'We've just got to create a superhero. A dog. And we have to animate him in these stories. It's the perfect idea.' So, he conceptualized the idea for Underdog. We all loved it, and we started doing the production. And that's where the idea originated."

Another item of note is the great lengths that TTV went to avoid using a frog character, mainly due to the fact that Jay Ward's *Rocky and Bullwinkle* follow-up animated series was to star a frog (and ultimately be called *Hoppity Hooper*, ironically, the one Ward show — in this author's opinion — that most closely resembles a TTV show), and Johnson's plea to "stay away from frogs" and that the show that they came up with had to be "super." Johnson was referring to the show being better than anything on television, but Biggers and Stover honed in on the superhero idea.

As a footnote, a *Hoppity Hooper* reference was added to *Underdog* in a clever bit of subtle wit. At the close of every four-part episode, a crowd would gather and shout, "Look, up in the sky. It's a bird. It's a plane. It's a frog! A frog?" to which Underdog would reply, "Not plane, nor bird, nor even frog, it's just little ol' me, Underdog." This frog reference was more than just a simple rhyme for "dog."

New backup segments were introduced into *Underdog*, including *Klondike Kat*, *Go Go Gophers*, and *The Sing-a-Long Family*. Repeat segments of *The Hunter* were added to the mix, though originally a *Hunter* episode spinning off Underdog as a pilot was wanted by General Mills. Fortunately, wiser minds prevailed and Underdog first appeared solo in a single-part episode called "Safe Waif."

To add to the confusion detailed previously, sometimes Jay Ward's *Fractured Fairy Tales* and *Bullwinkle's Corner* segments were spliced into *The Underdog Show*, although this occurred more after the series went into syndication. "Not originally, but later on in years since then, they did just about anything they wanted to. I don't remember seeing any combined, but I've heard people say that they were. And, you know, General Mills owned them outright and they could do any damn thing they wanted. I don't think any of our shows would have had Jay Ward material in them as much as their shows might have had ours because more of our shows were ordered than theirs," states Biggers on the confusion.

Underdog was a humble lovable character named Shoeshine Boy, who became Underdog by eating an energy vitamin pill. There was little protest made about this when *Underdog* originally aired, censorship occurred in the '80s and '90s by removing scenes where he eats the energy vitamin pill for fear of teaching kids about drugs.

Comments Biggers, "At the book signing on Tuesday, a guy who asked us to sign a book for him said, 'I probably shouldn't have loved *Underdog* as much as I did. It made me very sick. I had to have my stomach pumped because I ate a whole bottle of aspirin.' He used them to put in his ring. So, mothers wrote in about that and I suppose, all things considered, we probably wouldn't have put that in, but it was a great gimmick because we were looking for an 'Achilles Heel.' Underdog was too damn perfect! And just like Superman has his Kryptonite or something. No, it didn't bother us. What they did was just drop those episodes."

The incomparable Wally Cox, who had quite a history by the time he worked for TTV, voiced Underdog. "He'd been Mr. Peepers and Hiram Holiday, so he'd been on TV a lot. His voice was well known to a lot of people," recalls Biggers. Originally, actor Don Knotts was considered for the role of Underdog, but Biggers and Stover agreed that he would probably have been too similar to Don Adams, and they wanted to stay from a character that would look too much like Tennessee Tuxedo.

Covington confirms, "We were delighted to get Wally Cox. We wanted a shy, timid character and he had been on a successful series for a while, and wanted that kind of personality for Underdog. By that time, we were established. I called Wally Cox's agent, and we got together."

Cox was born December 6, 1924, in Detroit. According to his pseudo-autobiography, *My Life as a Small Boy*, published in 1961, "I come from many places, but the only place I like to think of myself as coming from is a northerly part of Michigan, itself a northerly state, where snow that fell in the middle of the winter fell upon snow that was already there, so that the depth of it merely varied and never ended until spring showed up."

Prior to becoming a successful actor, Cox worked a variety of odd jobs in New York City – among them shoe weaver, puppeteer apprentice, dance instructor and silversmith – to support his sister and mother, but it was Marlon Brando, a childhood friend from Evanston, IL, turned Greenwich Village roommate, who encouraged his show-business career. Cox then developed his droll observations into a nightclub act.

Covington continues, "It brings up the really strange background note on Wally Cox and Marlon Brando. They were roommates. They would ride around on motorcycles. One became the great Marlon Brando and one became (at least for a while), the great Wally Cox. He was around, and I had never known what happened to his money, but he was lively and quite pleasant. We enjoyed having him work for us very much. He was very friendly and nice and easy to work with. I think he was sort of typecast in his personality. We told him at the outset, we wanted Underdog to be a nerd-like character. I don't know if nerd was a word then – a nerd-type character that would come to the rescue at the last minute and do heroic things. If he were aiming for a perfect landing, he'd hit the wall instead. Anyway, everything always worked out. Then he was sort of authoritative in spite of all the screw-ups along the way. So a lot of it really was the way Wally was and his interpretation was one that we liked. We thought it was right. In that sense, I think I could honestly, on a modest level, compare some of my work with Woody Allen only in this respect. (It's what I read about him in the *Conversations* book.) Woody tried very hard to hire really fine actors and actresses. He said that he hired actors that were good enough that most of the time he'd just let 'em go, and that was the way I felt. Most of the time, I'd just let him go because I knew he'd done this voice and that voice, and I think that the goal for me was to just guide him along with a little for emphasis on a line here and there which would help the situation. Our four partners could honestly agree that when we did get together and start this, we wanted it to be fun for us, and I think that's why it worked, because we were having fun."

Cox's fame actually rose after voicing Underdog, and soon he became a regular in the upper left spot on TV's *Hollywood Squares* from its debut show on October 17, 1966, a spot he maintained until his untimely death from a heart attack on February 15, 1973, at the age of 48. He also appeared in several Disney movies during this same period and hosted three episodes of Disney's *Mouse Factory*.

Underdog's girlfriend was Sweet Polly Purebred, a news reporter for TTV, portrayed by voice actress Norma MacMillan. Born September 15, 1921, in Vancouver, she recalls that she started acting in her teens. She interjects, "My family tells me [it was] when I was a baby!" It was while she was a stage actress that she met her future husband, Thor Arngrim.

Later on, she started doing cartoon voices, including Casper the Friendly Ghost (with Bradley Bolke) on *The New Casper Cartoon Show* in 1963, and a few of the Casper theatrical shorts of the 1950s. She also worked with Bolke on the Kennedy parody album *The First Family*. Though she and Bolke both worked for Total TeleVision, they did not work on the same series or at the same time. (MacMillan was on *Underdog*, while Bolke was on *Tennessee Tuxedo*.) Another memorable turn was portraying both Davey *and* Sally Hanson on the Claymation show *Davey and Goliath*.

During the time of *Underdog*, MacMillan gave birth to a daughter, Alison, in 1964. Alison grew up to become Nellie Olson on the popular *Little House on the Prairie* TV series in the 1970s and '80s.

Covington remembers, "Norma was a very important actress who did a lot of commercials. She was very nice to work with and very good and I think that the voice was good and she had the talent and the ability to do Polly Purebread the way we thought it should be done."

She continued to do TV appearances and voices into the 1990s and passed away at the age of 79, on March 16, 2001.

There were many villains on *Underdog*, but the most recurring were Simon Bar Sinister, who used the phrase "Simon Says" in order to do some dastardly deed, and Riff Raff the wolf, a typical gangster type. Both were voiced by TTV mainstay Allen Swift. Bar Sinister was based on Lionel Barrymore and Riff Raff on George Raft. Simon's assistant, Cad Lackey, was based upon Humphrey Bogart, and he was voiced by another TTV regular, Ben Stone.

Biggers comments on how characters they designed were continually patterned after real-life personalities, "No, it wasn't [a fluke]. Actually, Riff Raff started out with a last name that was originally R-A-F-T after George Raft, the old gangster character in Hollywood. It was from him that we started and then we had worked on super characters and had a wolf in there and Joe drew that and Riff Raff just kind of grew out of that."

Harris adds, "So [Chet] came up with the idea of a little dog, that became Underdog and he said, 'Ok, now draw that.' Actually, he drew a dog and said, 'There, that's what I want him to look like.' Ok, fine. So I took his dog and designed it, if you know what I mean. Chet did the best thing he could do and put it down what he wanted on the paper, but it needed animation, so I did an animated dog and that was the beginning of Underdog. We put it together and we had already had two successes. Both of our earlier shows were great successes, and good ratings and all that.

"I don't know — somebody else could probably tell you that — there were 124 episodes? I tell you, I have no idea, I never made a count when I was working on the storyboards for the simple reason that working on the storyboards and then doing all the preproduction meetings with the animators was all that I could possibly handle, and so to this day, people will come up to me and say, 'You did the Marble Heads. God, I loved that thing, and Zot, how did you come up with the idea for that? You know, with the three eyes and everything.' And I say, 'Yeah, that was really fun.' But the honest truth is, I don't remember them.

"I just put them down on paper and then I had too many other things to do. I couldn't even think about it, and during that time, and even 'til today, I never saw a thing on television – saw any of our stuff on television during that whole period."

Arambula and the other Gamma animators enjoyed doing *Underdog*. "Every episode started with about 100 feet of repeating footage from the end of the previous episode, so all of the different animators were asking for that particular section because it was something free! You can charge money and it already was done. You have to expose it, but that was something very peculiar about that show."

Biggers and Stover discuss a rejected *Underdog* story in their book regarding Simon Bar Sinister's invention of truth paste. Both General Mills and DFS rejected the idea for reasons such as the story presumed that telling the truth was a bad thing and it also showed the characters tampering with products on the shelves. The characters did appear in a "Cheerios" commercial in 1964, in which Simon Bar Sinister changes Cheerios into tiddlywinks. The commercial was animated by Gamma, and features Cox, MacMillan and Swift reprising their usual roles.

Above: Simon Bar Sinister appears in a "Cheerios" commercial in 1964. *Below:* The cast of *The Underdog Show* — Underdog, Sweet Polly Purebread, Riff Raff, and Simon Bar Sinister.

168   CREATED AND PRODUCED BY TOTAL TELEVISION PRODUCTIONS

UNDERDOG
SHOW FORMAT
Effective September, 1967
CBS-TV

CODE	TIMING	CUME	ELEMENT
1	:10		"Dial Stopper"
2	:35		Action Cut
3	:15		Show Billboard (Neutral)
4	:10		Commercial Billboard
5	:30		Underdog Open (Shoeshine)
6	1:00	2:40	Commercial #1
7	4:30		Underdog Episode (Part I)
8	1:00	8:10	Commercial #2
9	:07		Underdog Lead-in
10	4:30		Underdog Episode (Part II)
11	:30		Stay Tuned
12	1:00	14:17	Commercial #3
13	:07		Underdog Lead-In
14	4:30		Underdog Episode (Part III)
15	1:00	19:54	Commercial #4
16	:35		Underdog Lead-In (Show Type)
17	4:30		Underdog Episode (Part IV)
18	1:00	25:59	Commercial #5
19	:15		Lead-In to Action to Come
20	:35		Action Cut- Next week's show
21	1:00	27:49	Commercial #6
22	:10		Show Closing Billboard
23	:10		Commercial Billboard
24	:20	28:29	Credits

Original

7/25/67

February 28, 1966

TO: Gamma Productions
    Pro-Directors
    Boardmen
    cc: Peter Piech
        TTV Partners

FROM: Joe Harris

RE: Openings and closings on current shows

KLONDIKE KAT episodes always open on a fade-in after the episode title, and close on an iris in.

GO GO GOPHERS episodes open on a fade in after episode title and close on a straight fade-out.

UNDERDOG episodes go thusly:
#1. opening:
   Episode title is supered over a freeze frame. Title is faded out and animation starts. There may or may not be a truck back or other camera action depending on the board instructions.

#1. closing:
   Freeze frame on last panel (usually selected to leave Underdog or Sweet Polly in a predicament). Truck in to CU of some pertinent part of the frame. Then fade out.

#2. opening:
   Episode title is supered over CU freeze frame from end of episode #1. Fade-out title, truck back to full scene, start animation.

#2. closing:
   same as no. 1

#3. opening:
   same as no. 2

#3. closing:
   same as no. 2

#4. opening:
   same as no. 2

#4. closing:
   straight fade out on animation.

Note that sometimes the video starting an episode may be different from the video closing the previous episode. At times the script calls for a different situation and the video has to go along. In spite of this, however, the camera movements and animation follow the pattern above.

When the *Underdog* episode "Simon Says... No Thanksgiving" aired on Thanksgiving Day 1965, a small 45RPM record was also issued to commemorate the occasion featuring the theme song and original vocal track from the episodes. FROM THE AUTHOR'S COLLECTION.

Above: A drawing of the original Macy's Underdog float from 1965. COURTESY OF TREAD COVINGTON. *Below:* The Underdog balloon was a perennial part of Macy's Thanksgiving Day Parade for almost 30 years.

A small book eponymously named *Underdog* came out in 1965 and mistakenly featured Riff Raff in the drawings while the text referred to him as "Cad Lackey." FROM THE AUTHOR'S COLLECTION.

Various Underdog products came out during *The Underdog Show*'s initial run. SOME ITEMS FROM THE AUTHOR'S COLLECTION.

176 CREATED AND PRODUCED BY TOTAL TELEVISION PRODUCTIONS

Above: A prototype drawing of Underdog by Joe Harris. *Below:* longtime *Hollywood Square* Wally Cox.

CREATED AND PRODUCED BY TOTAL TELEVISION PRODUCTIONS

CHAPTER 9

"GO GO GOPHERS WATCH 'EM GO GO GO!"

The first season of *The Underdog Show* featured reruns of *The Hunter* as its major supporting feature. The second segment featured a new segment called *Go Go Gophers*. *Go Go Gophers* featured two Native-American characters, Ruffled Feather and Running Board, who are constantly being pursued by Colonel Kit Coyote and Sergeant Okey Homa in a battle of territorial rights. The Colonel was an impersonation of President Teddy Roosevelt and voiced by Kenny Delmar. The Sergeant was an impersonation of John Wayne as performed by Sandy Becker, who also did Ruffled Feather.

As mentioned earlier, the partner who speaks gibberish idea that was originally planned for Chumley in *Tennessee Tuxedo* was revived here as part of Ruffled Feather character, with Chief Running Board interpreting his speech, as voiced by George S. Irving.

Gophers was originally planned as a segment for *Tennessee Tuxedo and his Tales*, which is why the copyright date states 1962, but it didn't appear until later on during *The Underdog Show*.

So popular was this segment that the Gophers received their own series, which debuted on CBS at 8 a.m., on September 14, 1968 and ran through September 6, 1969. This spin-off series consisted entirely of the 48 rerun segments.

The cast of the *Go Go Gophers* segment of The Underdog Show included Sergeant Okey Homa, Colonel Kit Coyote, Chief Running Board and Ruffled Feather.

"GO GO GOPHERS WATCH 'EM GO GO GO!"

Most *Go Go Gophers* merchandise appeared long after the series was out of production.

Original storyboard art and production background art from *Go Go Gophers*. ARTWORK COURTESY OF THE COLLECTION OF JOHN BRUSZEWSKI.

184   CREATED AND PRODUCED BY TOTAL TELEVISION PRODUCTIONS

CREATED AND PRODUCED BY TOTAL TELEVISION PRODUCTIONS

"GO GO GOPHERS WATCH 'EM GO GO GO!"

CREATED AND PRODUCED BY TOTAL TELEVISION PRODUCTIONS

CHAPTER 10

"DID I EVER TELL YOU ABOUT...?"

In early 1964, TTV was informed that the *Twinkles* advertising segments as well as the *Mr. Know-it-All* segments from *The Bullwinkle Show* were being discontinued. Twinkles, the cereal, was being phased out, and *Bullwinkle* was ending its run after five seasons (if one includes *Rocky and his Friends*). As a result, a new 1:30 length segment was required, one that would be used for *Tennessee Tuxedo* and the upcoming *Underdog Show*, but also Jay Ward's *Hoppity Hooper*!

The solution was to come up with a series of tall tales. The idea resulted in a segment ultimately titled *The World of Commander McBragg*.

The inspiration for Commander McBragg was British actor C. Aubrey Smith (1863-1948), who specialized in playing rotund military officers. McBragg can be traced more specifically to *The Four Feathers* from 1939. McBragg spun tall tales about his prior escapades to a usually disinterested friend.

Harris remembers in an interview by Nancy Basile, "One of my personal favorites was Commander McBragg. I always thought he was underrepresented and underutilized. He was the Baron Munchausen type of character. He did outrageous stories from his past. In a way I think he had the same…I know this may sound odd. I thought he had the same qualities as Mr. Magoo. Magoo couldn't see, and kept stumbling and fumbling. And McBragg can't help lying about everything. So I think he's funny, in that sense."

Most of the 48 *McBragg* segments followed the same pattern, but there was the occasional episode that broke from tradition, including at least two that proved that McBragg's tales weren't necessarily that tall after all.

According to Wikipedia, "Commander McBragg appeared in *The Simpsons* episode 'The Seemingly Never-Ending Story' voiced by Maurice LaMarche. He was acting as the judge for a scavenger hunt between Montgomery Burns and the Rich Texan, both eccentric millionaires in the same gentleman's club, known in the episode as 'The Excluder's Club' as it is known for being very exclusive."

While talking about Commander McBragg, Covington described the procedure of how episodes were created: "Each episode would run roughly five minutes. We had smaller segments like *The World of Commander McBragg*, which was more a three-minute thing. It was an in-between type filler [like three pages], and then the others would be about five or six pages. We usually did a bunch at a time, maybe three or four episodes at one time.

"There was no point in having the cast of one series and the cast of another series face off together just standing and waiting their turn. If it was a bunch of *Underdogs*, then Wally would be there, and so would Allen Swift.

"There's no question that the written conceptions of the first episodes and the cartoon ideas originated with Buck and Chet as the writers. I felt that my basic part on the creative side was the voice recording sessions, the soundtrack in other words. That was my area. The pictures or the visual characterizations were Joe's. Scripts were Buck and Chet.

"We knew the time that we had to have the storyboards ready to go to their next phase toward animation. From that we worked a production schedule. Buck and Chet would have to deliver their scripts to me, and then I in turn would have to get the voice tracks done, and then the storyboarding was done by Joe.

"The soundtrack had to go to him. I'd first get the script and I would time it; if it ran long, I could edit down. If a serious amount of editing had to be done, that would interfere with one of the jokes or the storyline, I would get in touch with Buck and Chet. Otherwise, I could just do it. After it had been timed down and we thought we had it right, then we would time it and if we ran long, we'd make a few cuts here and there. If we ran short, we'd expand on something, and then we would count in our effects time in our edits. We would count the seconds we thought we needed for action. For instance, if they were going to cut down a tree and you'd hear the tree fall and crash, we'd allow several seconds to get that across. The voice tracks that the artists got would be the voices, but with spaces left for sound effects."

Commander McBragg with a few of his usually disinterested friends.

Original storyboard art and production background art from *The World of Commander McBragg*. ARTWORK COURTESY OF THE COLLECTION OF JOHN BRUSZEWSKI.

CREATED AND PRODUCED BY TOTAL TELEVISION PRODUCTIONS

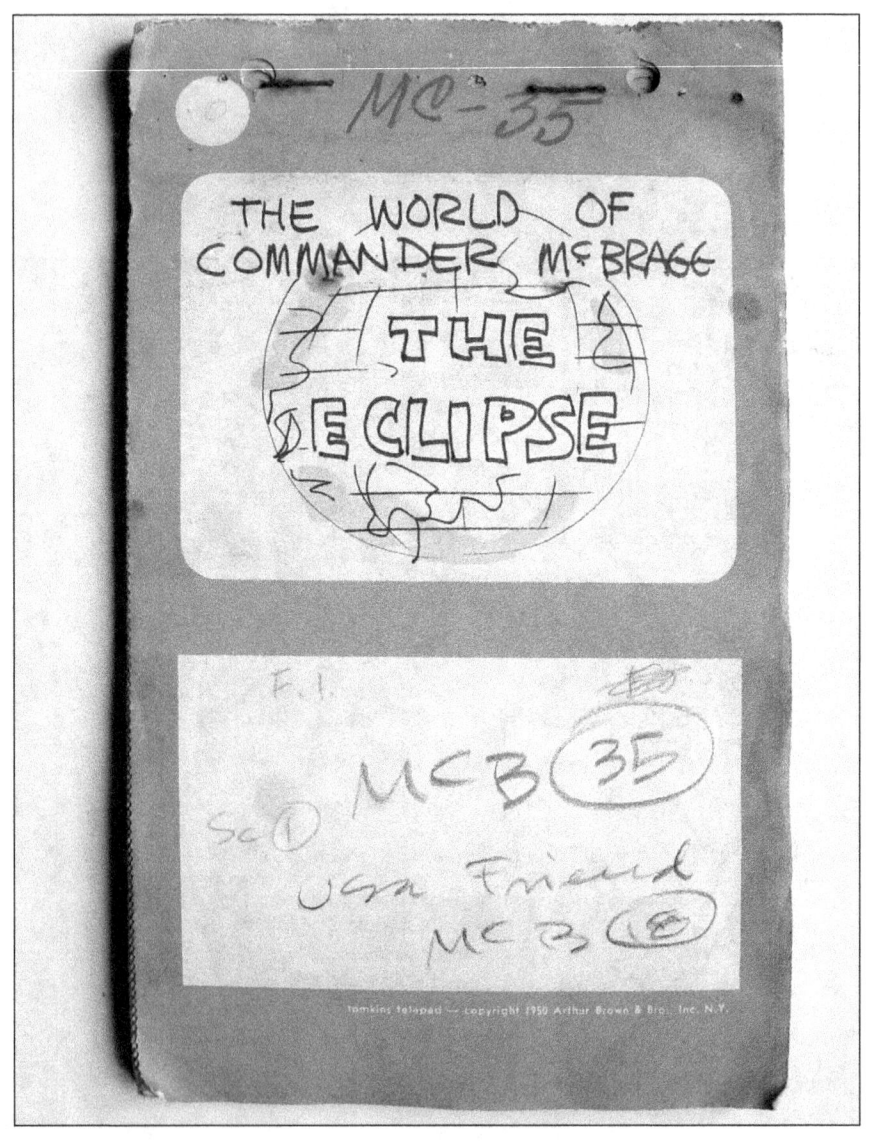

CREATED AND PRODUCED BY TOTAL TELEVISION PRODUCTIONS

CHAPTER 11

"KLONDIKE KAT ALWAYS GETS HIS MOUSE!"

During *Underdog's* original run, General Mills commissioned yet another new segment, so in *Underdog's* third season, a new segment appeared that debuted in 1966, and also appeared originally on *The Beagles*.

Klondike Kat featured a Canadian Mountie cat (not dissimilar to Jay Ward's Dudley Do-Right) that was always pursuing a mouse named Savoir Fare and his faithful dog companion Malamutt (who seldom spoke). Klondike worked for Major Minor at Fort Frazzle. 26 segments were made.

During this time, when *Klondike Kat* was in production in 1965, Harris paid a visit to Gamma in Mexico. "I went once and I stayed for, I think, a week. I watched the whole procedure all the way through. Have you ever heard anything about the Mexican operation? They didn't have any animators, so Sal Faillace and Harvey Siegel were the token amount allowed to go down there as representatives of the Yankee nation. The Mexicans were very strict on that. You had to have only 10% of the people down there could be Americans. We sent down two Americans and there were 20 people working there. Later on, there were three Americans and 30 people working there. In the beginning, the animation was quite crude. We had an arrangement with customs so that we could sneak things in and out. They paid them a lot of money to do that. I don't know if this should go in the book, but go ahead, what the hell.

"There was a key animator, who became so good that he wanted a raise equivalent to that of American animators. Now, I don't think that was he did. At any rate, he deserved it. He was really very good. He was a natural. They were hauling people out of art school and from what I heard from Harvey, they were picking them up off the street and teaching them. I remember some things, there was an earthquake down there that had preceded my visit, and there were huge cracks in the building, and as far as I know, that's the way they stayed. They had some people come in who had never seen the inside of a modern toilet and who were absolutely puzzled by what that white thing was."

When asked if Harris eyeballed what Jay Ward was doing with *Hoppity Hooper* during his visit, he commented, "I was really only concerned about Total TeleVision and also a trip to Mexico. I was getting pretty antsy at one point and had cabin fever and I said, 'I want to go down there,' and I did it legitimately, but I always felt guilty because my secondary motive was to go down to Mexico City. I did, but I spent all my time with Harvey and Sal. I did my job down there, but what I did come away with was a bunch of Xeroxes of Jay Ward's stuff — a lot of the storyboards. I used one of his animators to do one of the storyboards for me. I was hiring out stuff toward the end of the '60s, so I would establish characters and have other people doing the storyboards for me, so I hired one or two of the guys from Jay Ward who were freelancing."

Covington also paid a trip to Mexico once. "The main thing that took me to Mexico was the background music and occasional songs for our show. We started going to Mexico for recording our music because the situation in New York became exorbitant and expensive. *The Beagles* music was all done there."

The regular cast of the *Klondike Kat* segment of *The Underdog Show* and *The Beagles* includes Savoir Faro, Malamutt and Klondike himself.

No *Klondike Kat* merchandise was produced during the segment's original run, and this proposed Klondike Kat plush toy from 2006, pictured here with a similarly-proposed Tennessee Tuxedo plush toy, is the nearest they've come. FROM THE AUTHOR'S COLLECTION.

Original storyboard art from *Klondike Kat.* ARTWORK COURTESY OF THE COLLECTION OF JOHN BRUSZEWSKI.

CHAPTER 12

"LOOKING FOR THE BEAGLES"

After the success of *The Underdog Show*, things were rife for change from TTV. TTV hit a peak of sorts, as their next series, *The Beagles*, is barely remembered, if at all, despite its apparent ratings' success. Capitalizing on the success of The Beatles, "The Beagles" was actually a duo named Stringer and Tubby that more closely resembled The Smothers Brothers with a guitar and giant slap bass.

Their manager, Scotty, was always trying to get bookings for The Beagles in various exotic and unique locations. According to Harvey Siegel's great-nephew, Scotty was named after Harvey's son. No new voice talent was recruited for *The Beagles* as Kenny Delmar handled the narration.

Tread Covington recalls the voices for the show. "I know Mort Marshall was the voice of Tubby. Allen Swift did a sort of a laid-back Dean Martin kind of voice. Yes, Stringer. Of course, Allen could do any voice. I think he did a very laid back sort of a quiet voice. Mort Marshall was more frantic."

After a quick adventure lasting two to four episodes, the story culminated with The Beagles singing their latest hit song similar to how *The Archies* and *Fat Albert* would do in a few years, but The Beagles did it first, at least in animation. *The Beagles* probably drew upon *The Monkees* live-action show for the format.

The Beagles was somewhat of a departure for TTV as the program was the first not outright owned by General Mills. It was also the first show to mention the names of all four of its creators (Biggers, Stover, Harris and Covington) in the credits. Harris comments on the lack of "credits" on most TTV shows, "When you watch a scroll coming down after, say, any modern cartoon — there's a scroll of people and it goes on and on and it goes fast. Well, look at the scrolls that we had. It's a quick look and then TTV. Our names were never on it, but it wouldn't have made any difference. There were only three.

"Tread was named once [on *King Leonardo*] and I believe Buck said, 'Don't do that, Tread.' And I don't think he did it again. At any rate, the reason was that we all agreed that this was Total TeleVision and that's what we wanted to make it. We wanted to make a famous studio and individuals were subordinated to that desire, so we didn't give credits to each other. We decided that it was TTV that got the spotlight. Buck may have a different take on that."

Covington remembers, "I wasn't trying to develop my own personality as a public figure, that's right, but I delighted in being able to express my creative effort in the voice work, the voice tracks and the casting. So, that was the creative part, and then the rest was the business part, which I was glad to be involved in. I was in New York, living there on a full-time basis. All of the other partners lived out of town, and they were delighted to be able to live out of town.

"In the beginning, we had this sense of camaraderie and 'all for one and one for all' and I think that we agreed that that was a much more mature, much more profitable way to go to highlight the studio rather than the individuals. The thing was it wouldn't have meant anything to anyone anyway. It's an ego trip."

Biggers remembers, "Well, that was a huge ratings' success. I have somewhere a telegram from Fred Silverman congratulating us as the initial ratings came in for the show and how great it was doing. But, this was the first show that we had not sold to General Mills. It's the only show that we still own. The only show we EVER owned. We sold all the others outright to General Mills and this show we leased to Deluxe Toys, which was also a client of Dancer-Fitzgerald-Sample. They bought what amounts to nine half hours, but those nine half hours were combined with stuff from General Mills: *King Leonardo*, anything like that, to make a full 18 minutes. That's all the half-hour shows were. The rest was filled up with titles and bridges and stuff like that and six minutes of commercials. So, we only did the nine half hours in the first year and the CEO of Deluxe Toys absconded with all the company's money, nine or ten million dollars or something. And that was it; we had no sponsor.

"We had nothing and I don't know whether that spoiled *The Beagles* that association, but the point was unless someone was going to buy more, you can't do a hell of a lot with nine half hours. As much as kids like things repeated, nine half hours is just not enough. So, we had no real place to place them." It also sported the debut of the new TTV logo, a sort of a box with a fat letter T overlapping another T and a V, replacing the previous "arrow"-style TTV logo.

The show debuted on at 12:30 p.m., on September 10, 1966 on CBS, the network still airing *The Underdog Show*, and it ran through September 2, 1967. CBS also carried the similarly titled *The Beatles*, an animated series based on the real Fab Four and produced by Al Brodax Productions, who went on to animate the *Yellow Submarine* movie.

It was repeated the following season from September 9, 1967 through September 7, 1968 on ABC and then was quietly canceled, despite a record album being released of tunes from the show called *Here Come the Beagles*.

36 five-minute episodes were produced, totaling nine half hours. TTV set up Lancelot Productions (instead of Leonardo) to handle the merchandising, which only amounted to a single record album and even rarer single with picture sleeve. The original shows were padded out with repeat segments from previous TTV shows and some new ones of *Klondike Kat*.

It's long been rumored that the original negatives of *The Beagles* no longer exist, as the "Toontracker" website attests, "Joe Harris (the former Vice-President, Supervisor of Animation for Dancer, Fitzgerald, Sample Advertising, who left DFS in 1959 to found Total Television Productions with Treadwell Covington and writers Buck Biggers and Chet Stover) sent me the following regarding "The Beagles": '*The Beagles*. Now there's a sad story. The editor who worked on that series died while at work on them and apparently all the editing materials, including the master negatives, were tossed out by his widow. I've tried through John Gartenberg, the former archivist at Golden Books Publishing, to find out if the trail to those masters was still traceable but he came up with nothing. He was able to locate the masters on all but a very few of the rest of the TTV productions but drew a blank on the *Beagles*. I not only have the characters but the storyboards, although unfortunately on stats. I have no idea where the original boards are; possibly they went out with the rest of the materials. *The Beagles* were entirely TTV properties which makes it doubly painful to have lost them.'"

Biggers sets the record straight about how the episodes were supposedly destroyed. "I thought they were, but P.A.T. had them. They were the ones that handled all of the shows for General Mills. They had everything. When it came time for us to sell the shows, not *The Beagles* but all the others to Broadway [Video], we figured we go into the lab and give them *The Beagles*. Well, we couldn't find them; they were gone. But Joe Harris found them at Golden Books. Unfortunately, they are not in combination, they are all separate picture and track and it costs money just to put them together. A lot, so nobody's anxious to do that unless they're going to use them for something. We're still dickering around. I don't know if anything will come of it."

DVD reissue labels such as Shout Factory or Rhino would release them if demand dictates.

Harris recollects, not so fondly, "Oh, it was a terrible show. It was a terrible show. I have *The Beagles* sitting right here in my apartment. I have all of *The Beagles* episodes in interpositive. (An interpositive, IP or master positive is motion picture film with a positive image made from the edited camera negative.) I discovered them when I was working with Golden Books, who, as you know, owns the properties. There was an archivist there who said, 'Oh, I know where *The Beagles* are,' and she took me to a warehouse, and there were all the lost episodes. I had heard from Buck, that the editor of *The Beagles* had died, and his wife got rid of all the junk she had found lying around, but the interpositives —

all of the interpositives — I have, for all the shows. So I have the whole thing. In looking it over, it's like we did the other ones with our right hand, but now we are going to do this with our left hand, and it did not have any of the quality or the character development or the sparkle that any of the other shows had. It didn't and I know because I just looked at them again, trying to work a deal with some people I know who thought it would be a great idea to bring it back but in a different way, and so I looked at some of the episodes and I thought, 'Ooh boy! Not good.'

"I had to go through them, because I was trying to — I work with a writer, and we were trying to work on some shows, and he had the idea that the stories should be about two guys who are brought in by a studio head to do an animated show, and they are actually the show themselves, and they have *The Beagles* and they produced it, and they hated it, but the owner of the studio loved it. So, we were going to use clips of *The Beagles* to stitch this story together. Now it was really between the two guys, they were on opposite sides of the fence. They were the odd couple and they were told to produce a show. They thought that they were going to produce a worthwhile documentary and this guy said, 'No, I want you to do a cartoon show for kids,' and all they could come up with was *The Beagles*. So, they needed something to fill in and so in their eyes they thought, 'I got the perfect thing for you, the cartoon that everybody could love to hate.' Then he's a writer, and he started writing children's stories, and now he's on his sixth in the series called, *The Sisters Grimm*, and he's made a great success of it. So, he is no longer interested in following through. The world is full of these stories."

Original storyboard art and production background art from *The Beagles*. ARTWORK COURTESY OF THE COLLECTION OF JOHN BRUSZEWSKI.

Above: The Beagles' virtually impossible-to-find 1966 album on Harmony Records (HS 14561). It was, however, issued as a bootleg CD paired with *The Banana Splits* album and that's somewhat easier to find. FROM THE AUTHOR'S COLLECTION. *Below:* rarer still is the 45RPM single taken from the album on Columbia Records (4-43789). This is a photo of the promo copy, which is easier to find than stock copies.

The "Holy Grail" for *Beagles* collecting and TTV collecting would be this picture sleeve from the 45RPM single, boasting the single's B-side. FROM THE COLLECTION OF MICHAEL HAYDE.

CREATED AND PRODUCED BY TOTAL TELEVISION PRODUCTIONS

CHAPTER 13

"BUT FIRST, TIME FOR A LITTLE SONG."

The Sing-a-Long Family was a segment similar to the old bouncing ball cartoons that Fleischer and Famous/Paramount used to do. A story was told in song with the lyrics printed on the screen.

Biggers recalls: "Yeah, I wrote the music and the words. It's just that we had a need for some more 1:30s [cartoon segments of one minute, 30 seconds in length] and you remember from the book that we created *Commander McBragg* as a 1:30 element because all we had at that time was Bullwinkle as 'Mr. Know-it-All.' They needed more, so we did *Commander McBragg* and then at some point they wanted 13 more and I don't know if we did the whole order or not, but however many *Sing-a-Longs* were done, we did them."

Harris adds, "I remember them well. I ordered them. Three sounds about right. I remember the characters. I love the characters. They were little wooden figure like. They have a nice design to them, and I wanted to design them totally different from any of the other things in the show. So I gave this '30s-looking faces, and little stick figures, 'cause I knew we weren't going into full animation on any of them. *The Sing-a-Longs*. That was fun. I enjoyed that."

Gene Hattree and *Cauliflower Cabby* were two TTV cartoon ideas that were created and filmed circa 1964 as pilots for potential new segments or shows. Neither segment sold, though both eventually ended up in the syndicated *Underdog Show* package after 1973. When asked about these two segments, Joe Harris was amazed to discover that they had actually made it to air as they were only supposed to be pilots.

Hattree told the story of a singing cowboy horse; his name a play on singing cowboy star Gene Autry. The humorous element of this segment is that before he engaged in any gunplay, he would suddenly stop everything and say, "...but first, time for a little song." His deputy, Rabbit Foot, is earnestly trying to help bring in the bad guys, which always prompts Hattree to say, "Catching crooks is for sheriffs, sweeping is for deputies!" The bad guy, a fat Mexican bandit named Tortilla Fats, appears with his gang. In it, they rob the Parchesi Junction First National Bank.

Cabby tells the story of a dog cab driver that is secretly a superhero called The Champion. The bad guy here is a character named Boston Bully and another named Shifty. Cauliflower's girlfriend is named Pinky Knees. Though the character had some potential, the character designs weren't as strong as on other TTV shows, and they also didn't have as strong of characterizations. Also, the similarity to Underdog in concept is apparent.

How these segments made it to air at all had to do with General Mills' ownership of all things TTV. When the syndicated packages were created, every last morsel of TTV programming (save for *The Beagles*) was utilized for these packages. Unfortunately, in succeeding years, these packages have been rearranged so haphazardly that there are some segments of TTV shows that air numerous times, and some that do not air at all, and some even air in Hanna-Barbera's *Space Kidettes*, due to the fact that it is the one H-B show that is part of the DFS Program Exchange, a barter service in which TTV, Jay Ward and a few other TV series, including *Kidettes*, give TV stations the programs to air for free in exchange for a few spots taken by General Mills.

The rarely-seen Cauliflower Cabby and Pinky Knees.

CREATED AND PRODUCED BY TOTAL TELEVISION PRODUCTIONS

CHAPTER 14

"LOOKS LIKE THIS IS THE END!"

What happened next at TTV is the sketchiest part of the story. All Wikipedia says is, "Total Television folded when General Mills dropped out as the sponsor in 1969."

And what of Gamma, TTV's consistent animation house since the second season of *King Leonardo*? Adds Biggers, "As far as I know, I can't really speak for it, but that's my general thoughts, they tried to do commercial work and so forth and I think it just collapsed."

Apparently, TTV had trouble selling another series after *The Beagles*. The next known project that TTV tackled was called *The Colossal Show*. It is not known whether any animation still exists for *The Colossal Show*, although a single comic book issue did appear in October 1969 from Gold Key. As the General Mills sponsorship ended, so did any prospects of continuing on with this or any other series.

Recalls Biggers regarding *The Colossal Show*, "We had an agent named Jack Sobol, a very good agent, and he was the agent for some top comedians. He became our agent after the General Mills thing stopped and we were still trying to keep in the cartoon business. Now, you had to sell shows to the network. That's what changed. No longer could a company like General Mills buy a show and then put it on and now, thanks to Fred Silverman primarily, the networks were buying their own shows and we didn't have the contacts there. And we also didn't have a factory. They wanted their people to have a factory, like Filmation, instead of being people like us, hat in hand, where we had to go Mexico or Australia or someplace to get the animation done. They wanted someone primarily with their own animation house. We took Fred to '21' [a great New York restaurant] and he loved our presentation, loved our shows, but he never bought any. One of the pitches we made was to NBC, Bud Grant I think it was, and someone who was over him named Larry White. Anyway, we pitched *The Colossal Show*, which had a lead character that had the voice of Phil Silvers — an imitation of Phil Silvers as 'Bilko '— and each show there would be a different guest character doing a celebrity voice impersonation each week. On the pilot it was an imitation of Jack Benny."

When asked who voiced the characters, Covington couldn't quite remember. "It could be possible that Allen Swift was involved because he's such a pro, or Mort Marshall, or very possibly Kenny Delmar."

Biggers continues, "It was our typical stuff, a comedy, with Roman people, and we took it to them and they loved it. I remember he played golf with one of those spikey balls on a chain, you know, a mace. They laughed. And the plan was they wanted to buy it. We had another meeting and a handshake and they bought the series. With that handshake, Jack Sobol went to his friends at the comic book company and told him to quickly get a comic book out to take advantage of the debut. Then, when the comic book was already in the works, NBC backed out of the handshake. We never knew quite why that happened. It was nothing to do with the show, because nothing had changed."

Little exists of *The Colossal Show* besides the one-shot comic book. "There was a pilot, but I don't know where the hell it is. I think we did that at Terry-Toons. I'm not sure. I don't think it looked quite the same, but it was close. I would say that maybe our show had the same look, but it's hard to say," recalls Biggers.

Covington continues, "We gave the TV museum in New York City a collection of some of our 'one and only' copies of work along the way. When I moved to Southampton in 2004, I checked with Buck about some prints of various things I had that I was just holding for our company. I knew they would be better preserved if we gave them to the television museum. I have a complete list, but I didn't remember *The Colossal Show* ever appearing. We presented it as an idea and we just didn't sell it."

Harris remembers, "Oh yeah. I did the character designs. That's something else. I didn't know that was the name of it. Of course, it was now that I think back. I did all of the characters for that and again it was 'colossal' in the sense that there were dozens of characters. There didn't seem to be a central theme. There was the emperor, his wife, and all sorts of characters. Yeah, I did the characters for them, but I didn't remember what happened to them. It's odd that you bring that up because somewhere in a portfolio, somewhere in storage, I have all those characters. I will look, locally, but I don't know where that would be, but let's see. Too many things have happened. *The Colossal Show* I did not know about. I did a whole bunch of character drawings. Maybe those are the ones that went into a file, I don't know. But I never heard anything before."

Stover adds, "Actually, I've never heard of a comic book about it, but we did present a show to NBC. Mr. Colossal was Sgt. Bilko. It was a Phil Silvers-type voice. I don't remember doing that at all. We may have had a deal with Western while at DFS. DFS had a deal with Golden Books. I'm very vague about all that stuff at all. Terry-Toons — I don't know how they got involved with that. They operated somewhere out of Westchester County. I remember going out there to do a joint venture with somebody, and they were looking for a way to get back into television. No, but I do know that with *Tom Terrific* there was this guy named Jules Feiffer. He was involved with Terry-Toons also, I believe, and that was the only time I met him. I don't remember how that happened. We didn't go looking for Terry-Toons. It was a whole network sort of thing. Buck and I had an agent who somehow got involved with Terry-Toons. I think that's the way it worked. We had about five or six fully storyboarded presentations and we never sold anything more."

Harris adds, "That's funny now. It's too bad. Many years later, I started doing comic strips and I actually did one and it might have had an echo from *The Colossal Show*. I did one called *SVQR*. Whenever you look at a show with Richard Burton where he's dressed up as a gladiator and he's in one of the big marching scenes, you see them all carrying a banner, which has 'SVQR.' It means 'Senatis Publicus Romanus' or the Senate of the City of Rome. It goes all the way back to Goldwyn or whoever did the first of what they called sandal shows. Whenever they have one of those gaudy scenes, they're walking along with this big banner. It's a cartoon about a Roman emperor, who had a shrew for a wife. It's very simple, but that probably is an after-echo of that show. But, anyway, I couldn't do anything with it, either. I started doing comic strips and I did about five, and then I looked around for a buyer. I was out in Kansas City and I took one to the Kansas City syndicate and they turned it down because it was about a recently divorced man. The editors saw that and said, 'We can't do that!' So, later when I was living in Connecticut, I took it to Dik Browne, who did *Hagar the Horrible*, and he said, 'You don't want to get in comic strips.' I said, 'Why? Are they not good?' He said, 'No, no, no. They're fine. Come on over to my house.' So, I went to Dik Browne's house. This is a little house that you would never recognize belonging to somebody who had 1,000 comic strips. He worked like a dog, and I immediately sympathized with that, and I asked, 'Where do you work?' He took me down to the basement and he had one of those $42 kids' easels with one leg propped up with a brick, next to the side of the concrete wall was the furnace, and he worked there, and that's where he did *Hagar the Horrible*. And I said, 'I'm beginning to get the idea that this is not for me.' He said, 'Good, I'm glad you did. First of all, it will take you 8-10 years just to break into the '500' level. Then, there aren't many of us who do 1,000 in syndication. By that time, you're so exhausted; you'll wonder how you'll ever do the next 10 years.' I looked at him and he was wearing thick glasses, and he was dressed in a T-shirt and blue jeans and was worn out. I thought, 'No, not for me.' So, I still have them."

Besides *The Colossal Show*, a few other projects were attempted that didn't go anywhere. Biggers remembers, "*Parrot Playhouse* was the one that was mentioned; that was the one where we did a pilot called *Spoofs 'n' Saddles*, which was a takeoff on *Gunsmoke* and we did a fun pilot that was really a sales presentation where we introduced the characters and showed little bits of episodes. This was called *Noah's Lark*. It was a billionaire who built a spaceship and set out for planets and had all these people on board. It was animated. Different kind of animation totally from anything we'd done."

Another show attempted was alternately called *The Otters* or *The Otter Side*, featuring two otter characters that were to act as MC's and throw puns back and forth. Another show was to be called *The Clock*, featuring a hero with a clock for a face. Other ideas included shows called *Manley's Marauders* and *Tom the Water Baby*, but precious little is remembered about these concepts some 40 years on.

Yet another series was to feature some blue-skinned fish characters who lived underwater. For this series, Joe Harris drew some large drawings on some huge boards and a presentation was made once again to Fred Silverman, who asked his secretary what she thought while she was passing through the room. She couldn't comprehend the blue characters, and, ultimately, Silverman nixed the idea based on his secretary's opinion. Little did they all know that Hanna-Barbera would have a major hit animated series a little over a decade later with a cast of blue characters called *The Smurfs*!

Meanwhile, with no new TTV shows forthcoming, repeat TTV segments, such as *Commander McBragg*, were used on a new Peter Piech P.A.T.-Ward/TTV-Leonardo compilation show, *The Dudley Do-Right Show*, which debuted at 9:30 a.m. on April 27, 1969 on ABC and aired through September 6, 1970, forever cementing the TTV-Jay Ward mash-ups. Other Peter Piech mash-up shows include *Cartoon Cut-Ups*, *The King and Odie* and *Uncle Waldo*, all of which have sketchy airdates as they all originally appeared in syndication. *The Dudley Do-Right Show* became the final resting place for episodes #79-104 of *King and Odie* and episodes #40-65 of *The Hunter*, episodes that originally aired during the first season of *Tennessee Tuxedo and his Tales*.

"We were kind of in a vacuum. We hadn't been out there. We should have been out there doing something, developing contacts, but we had no reason really to expect things to change like they did and we weren't worried about anything and then all of sudden — Wham! — Then we tried to get out there and then when word gets around that you're not getting any sales, you really don't get any sales."

Stover agrees, "Gamma was put together by General Mills and DFS had a hand in it. We had nothing to do with it. I think basically the networks didn't want to have anything to do with DFS or an advertising agency and we had 'advertising agency' stamped all over us. That was the day when the agency and the client told the networks what they would draw. The networks didn't approach us with *King Leonardo* or *Underdog*. It worked the other way 'round. We gave the presentation to the agency and then General Mills went to the network. With the clout they had they could spend the money on Saturday morning TV and tell the networks what to put on and in what time slot. They worked out some kind of a deal. When Freddy [Silverman] came in, he didn't want to have anything to do with this, so we had a tough time after that. We wouldn't have minded being like Hanna-Barbera, however! No, we were sort of settled in the way that we did things."

Covington adds, "He may well have been because Fred felt he was very creative and wanted to definitely have a lot to say about what his network was trying to promote. We had some encouragement from Fred, but it may well be that Fred was not favoring us either. So Buck may have the correct assessment. Hanna-Barbera had become a big producing outfit and we had our successes, but production was farmed in different directions."

Arambula, mentioning his days after Gamma, says, "There was a lot of animation that was being done in Japan. You know in those days Japan was a burgeoning power in animation and they were cheaper than we were, and they have millions of people working in animation working there. I don't know if it was true, but that's what they told us, so they closed the studio and then I went to work in comic books. It was in 1970. So I came to Los Angeles and then went to Filmation, DePatie-Freleng, and Hanna-Barbera. They offered me a job at Filmation, but I liked the atmosphere at Hanna-Barbera."

Another obstacle was that there were now tighter rules governing "children's entertainment," with the advent of ACT (Action for Children's Television), formed in late 1968.

Harris had a different view on the events that led to the end of TTV. "Well, it was a shock for me, too. One day I was working and looking forward to the next job, and the next assignment, and then Buck, I think, called or Chet and said, 'Oh, by the way, we're out of business.' And it was like that. I don't know. If you've ever killed a chicken, which I have done, back in 10th and 11th grade. First you put their heads on a block and then you chop their heads off. That's the way I felt. It was just like a bang in 1969 after 10 years and it was that abrupt and that short. I didn't have any other job, so it was an absolute blow to me. I never spoke to Chet or Buck about what the real reason was. To this day I don't know how all of that worked out."

Covington provides his take on what happened during the waning days of TTV: "I don't believe that we had a fully-blown show or developed show that we were trying to sell before we stopped. We just agreed that instead of trying our damndest to sell new shows; our particular fortunes were probably better served by going in individual directions.

"My memory is that we carefully discussed the situation more than once. We were trying to resolve what to do. For instance, while Buck and Chet tried to develop new show ideas, Joe and I worked on presenting our adaptation of James Thurber's *The White Deer*, which TTV had purchased the film and TV rights from the Thurber Estate. We had greatly enthusiastic reception from our individual presentations to each of the three networks, and also Hallmark. Our adaptation was to be an hour-long special, but no sale. We had come to the end of our General Mills contract. I think they had decided that they had all the material that they needed for the present and didn't know when or if they would return to making more cartoons. At the time, there were three people that controlled the whole situation as far as cartoons were concerned — one from each of the three networks — the executives in charge of programming.

"General Mills did what we called a 'buy out,' so they owned the rights to the specific episodes that we wrote for them. General Mills was a wonderful sponsor, but eventually they simply had enough supply and, of course, they used the cartoons almost purely as a marketing tool and a way of bargaining for deals such as, 'We'll provide you with our cartoons if you give us so much commercial time.'

"It sort of just evolved. I'm sure we would have loved having *King Leonardo*, *Tennessee Tuxedo* and *Underdog* all in production at the same time, but one after the other seemed to be what General Mills preferred. They had a good library when we stopped.

"Of course, we were thrilled to become a creative entity with the sponsorship of General Mills. But we did not make enough effort to spread our wings and go truly independent with General Mills, maybe our primary sponsor, but not the only one. Whatever it was, we just didn't do it independently, or didn't have enough determination to strike out in a new direction.

"The four of us had a series of meetings to discuss what would make more sense, and we simply decided that we would go in separate directions and call it a day."

After the final curtain drop on TTV, Biggers and Stover still tried to continue. "Chet and I stayed together. We had a two-year contract with CBS Enterprises to develop shows for them and developed one at Terry-Toons and we developed a series called, *The Hatfields and the McCoys* and developed it for Fred with his blessing, but he never would commit at the last minute.

"We made some pitches to some other companies. They were all very nice but not a lot of them wanted to get into the business. They didn't want to get into the business of having somebody create shows. It's another business. General Mills got in there quite by accident at a time when there was nobody doing it, so they were willing to do it. Later, companies just weren't interested."

TTV became a licensing firm for their properties during the '70s as a number of items produced featuring *Underdog*, *Go Go Gophers* and some with *Tennessee*

Tuxedo, including comic books, coloring books, Pepsi drink glasses, and action figures.

Comments Biggers, "We didn't handle any of that. We got half the rights. Even now, somebody just put out a new set of glasses for Underdog and a new statue of Underdog, but you go to those companies and you sign with them and they just take off, you don't do anything. P.A.T. was handling it and they were called Leonardo at times, I don't know which ones, but the offices were called P.A.T. and Peter Piech and we got half the money."

Covington adds, "[Originally,] I didn't see a lot of our merchandising handled in a very good way. We tried to handle merchandising, but we hired the wrong person for it, and so that was a lot of wasted money." Merchandising improved in the 1970s after TTV was no longer a going concern. "It had something to do with some sales of rights in the development after the shows stopped, oddly enough. [Peter Piech] was involved with them a lot, and he tried to make similar deals for Jay Ward and for us. He was trying in his way.

"I think that any connection of merging of our characters in any way was definitely General Mills' marketing. It was my impression, although I'm not privy to all the business details, that they had a similar deal to ours. They were selling the rights of what they produced to General Mills, but then they were able to rise above it better than we did.

"Joe has had a lot to do with various things that tied in with our cartoons. He made it his point to merchandise what he had done and merchandise the characters that he drew visually. As an artist, he created their look. The looks of our characters were certainly not looks put together by committee and I don't take a bit of credit away from Joe, but he's become pretty impressive in his efforts to keep that material alive."

There was even a short-lived restaurant created by Ward vocalist Paul Frees, called "Bullwinkle's," that utilized a number of TTV's characters, including Underdog, Tennessee Tuxedo and Chumley, in their robotic stage shows that were similar to those appearing at Chuck E. Cheese's Pizza Time Theater. Tooter Turtle and Baldy Eagle also made appearances on menus and in the restaurant's decor. "I've heard about stuff like that, but it was all P.A.T. Somebody just sent me a menu from a small restaurant in New Jersey that has an 'Under Dog on Sweet Polly Pure Bread'! We didn't sanction any of that stuff," comments Biggers.

The *Underdog* comic book produced its last issue in 1979 for Gold Key/Whitman. During the '80s and '90s, further attempts were made to issue comic books, namely through Spotlight Comics and later Harvey Comics (who reprinted the early '70s Charlton Comics). Meanwhile, no new TTV shows were on the horizon, prompting many to think the company went bankrupt or closed.

Biggers clarifies, "Sure, we kept open. In fact, we had a bit of trouble with the IRS because they claimed that we couldn't file as 'Chapter S,' I think it was, and we had to file as a corporation and it was going to cost us an arm and a leg 'cause we hadn't done something. Well, anyway, we managed to get that all right. We sold the stuff and since selling the stuff about the only thing we've done is taken some option contracts of DVDs for *The Beagles*, something that we'd all sign."

"Peter [Piech] came to us and wanted to see if we could sell a new series of *Underdog*. In there is a write-up for that with new plots and stuff like that, so I don't know what year that was. It didn't sell, but we came close." The year was 1991, and Biggers and Stovers created a proposal for a new series of *Underdog* that was scheduled to debut on September 21, 1992. Unfortunately, nothing further happened.

Covington confirms, "I think it just never got to the point that some outfit or combination of interests was willing to say, 'Ok, let's draw up a contract and see what we can do with a series for next year.' It just never got that far."

But Underdog never completely went away. He was the poster boy for World Hunger Year in 1997 to help defeat world hunger in their hunger-thon drive.

Meanwhile, Biggers created a new episode of *Underdog* in 1999 as a half-hour radio show, narrated by Tom Ellis. In this story, Simon Bar Sinister develops a Switchpitch baseball to turn positive people negative, in order to become the king of Boston.

Harris mentions that there was an additional *Underdog* segment he did more recently for one of the DVD releases in 2001. "Did you see the little segment on *The Nug of Nog*? You know the story behind that? Well, I did that with a friend of mine, Vinnie Impala, and we didn't have anyone else to do the voice, so I did it. [As Underdog] There's no need to fear…Underdog is here."

Another latent Underdog appearance was at the tail end of a Visa Check Card commercial, which was really a showcase for the various Marvel superheroes, like Spider-Man, Captain America and Thor. In it, a lady cries for help because her card has been stolen, but the various heroes inform her that everything will be all right because she can dispute the incorrect charges. Underdog then flies in stating, "There's no need to fear…Underdog is…" But before he gets a chance to finish, the lady calmly says, "Never mind." The commercial originally aired during the 2005 Super Bowl. The spot was created by BBD&O in New York. It is unclear whether Wally Cox's voice was used.

For the 2008 Super Bowl, there was another Underdog sighting. The commercial was for Coca-Cola and features the Underdog and Stewie (from FOX's *Family Guy*) Macy's Thanksgiving Day balloons battling it out for the Coke bottle balloon. In the end, it's the Charlie Brown balloon that gets the Coke. It was all done with CGI.

Harris adds, "Well, they don't own the rights to the shows now, but they were the founding fathers. We made a contract with them that if they were to do new shows, then we would be the people who did it, and that was a little inclusion in the contract, and I think they might have signed it thinking to themselves, 'What's the difference? If that's what they want, because we're not going to do anymore anyway.' I believe that that's still floating somewhere in the contract. I was talking to Tread about this the day before yesterday, and he said, 'Joe, does that still exist? What rights do we still have?' We still have the music rights, thanks to Buck, who really created all the music, and did a terrific job of doing that, but I thought also that if there were to be new episodes for Underdog or any of those things, that they were contractually obligated to give us first crack. I don't know how the hell we'd ever do it.

"Alan Baldwin seems to be pretty savvy and I've never really sat down with him and talked, although I've sold him some of the original artwork that I did, because he wanted that, but we've never really sat down and had a talk. But I think that somewhere in the contract that he got from Golden Books, which they got from Lorne Michaels, somewhere there's a thing that says, 'If you're going to do more episodes, you have to clear it with the TTV people.' TTV is still current."

Wikipedia says, "In 1995, Biggers, Stover, Covington and Harris negotiated a sale of their creations to *Saturday Night Live* producer Lorne Michaels, who later sold the rights to Little Golden Books."

Comments Biggers of the sale, "When we sold all our properties, it was a co-deal with them [P.A.T.-Leonardo] when they sold all their properties to Broadway Video, and parts of them we were selling together because we were both producers. I don't know, but it's kind of like Total TeleVision productions, it's out there, but it doesn't do anything."

Adds Covington, "There were no more [cartoons] being produced and no one was making an effort to sell more episodes. I think it was Peter's desire to get as much money out of the product from both Jay Ward and us that he could manage. We were involved because we had been the creative side of the properties of ours that he worked with. Of course, we were involved in the contracts and the sales. Since we had stopped doing new things, we were happy to see some income from these sales. That would be the way I would say my impression is.

"We were very anxious to try to get something from what remained of our property and so we wanted to do something like that. I know Peter wanted to do something from his standpoint. He didn't pressure us. If anything, we pressured Peter."

In 2006, Entertainment Rights, owners of Classic Media, are the owners of all of the TTV properties, when they purchased Golden Books. Then, in 2009, Boomerang Media purchased Entertainment Rights, and is phasing out the Entertainment Rights name.

Above: This Gold Key comic book of *The Colossal Show*, issued in 1969, was the only public offering from this aborted series. Apparently, a pilot film was animated and filmed by Terry-Toons, and may still exist in the CBS vaults in New York. FROM THE AUTHOR'S COLLECTION. *Below: The Otter Side* was another aborted show that a few production sketches were produced. This one, as were all of the storyboard production drawings included in this book, was done by Joe Harris. ARTWORK COURTESY OF THE COLLECTION OF JOHN BRUSZEWSKI.

Though no Underdog comic books were produced during *The Underdog Show*'s initial run, many, many companies issued books from 1970-1994. FROM THE AUTHOR'S COLLECTION.

CREATED AND PRODUCED BY TOTAL TELEVISION PRODUCTIONS

CREATED AND PRODUCED BY TOTAL TELEVISION PRODUCTIONS

Original artwork from some of these comic books have also become highly collectible. *(Note: the comic book artwork was not done by Joe Harris.)*

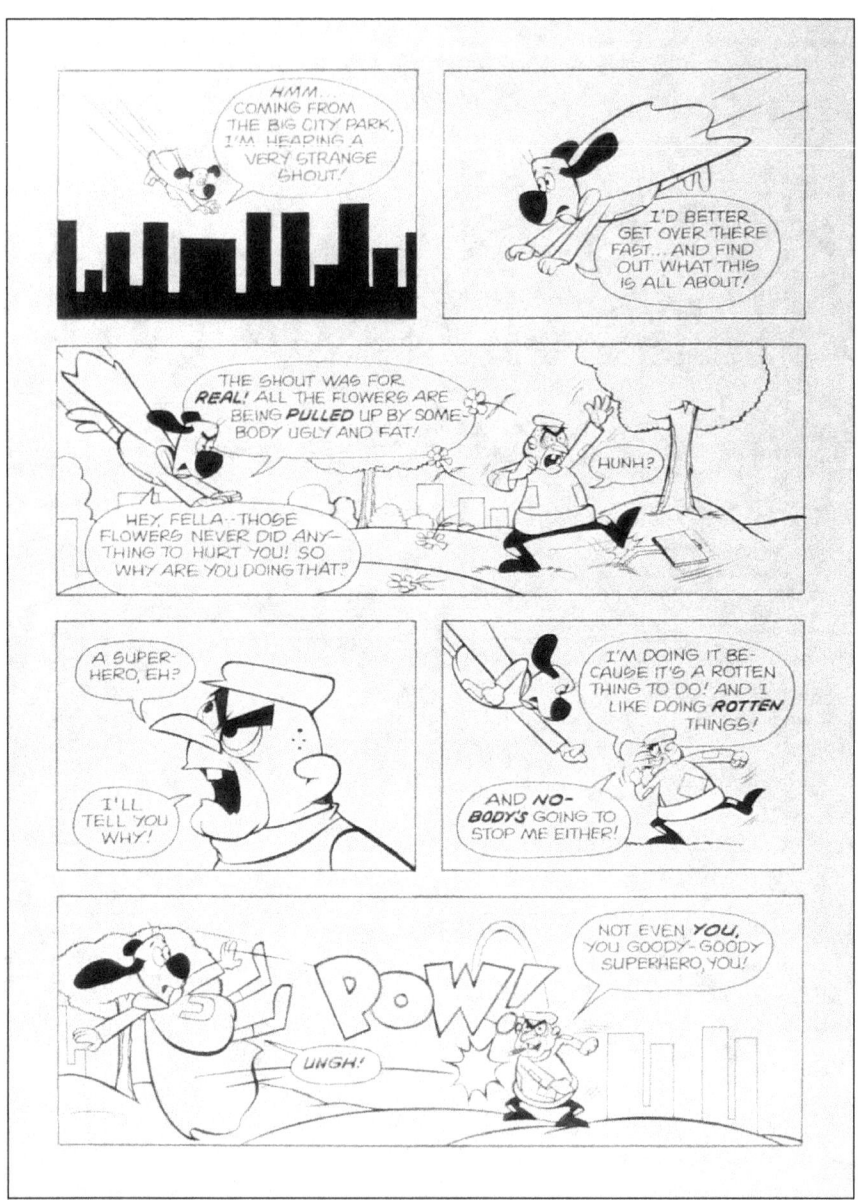

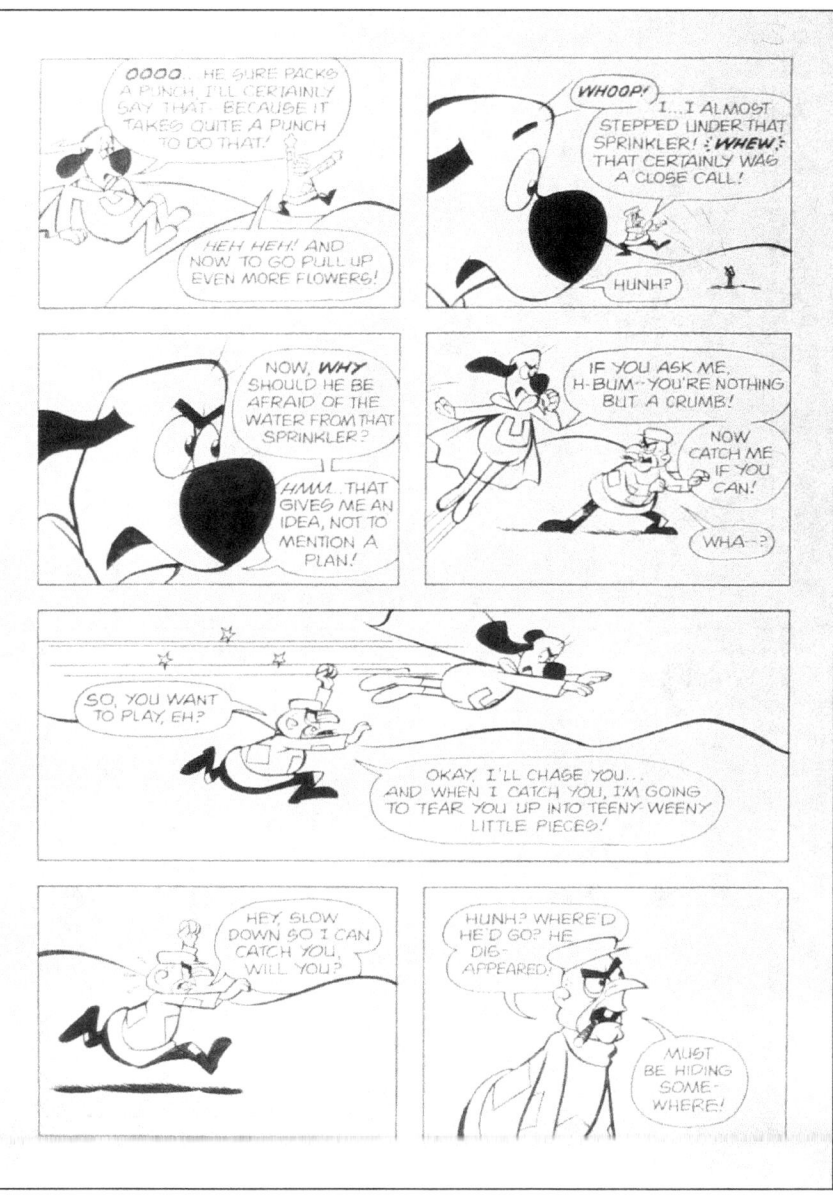

The original artwork for the cover of March of Comics #426 *from 1977.*

CREATED AND PRODUCED BY TOTAL TELEVISION PRODUCTIONS

Underdog became an even hotter commodity during the 1970s to the 2000s, long after the series and TTV ceased production. SOME ITEMS FROM THE AUTHOR'S COLLECTION.

CREATED AND PRODUCED BY TOTAL TELEVISION PRODUCTIONS

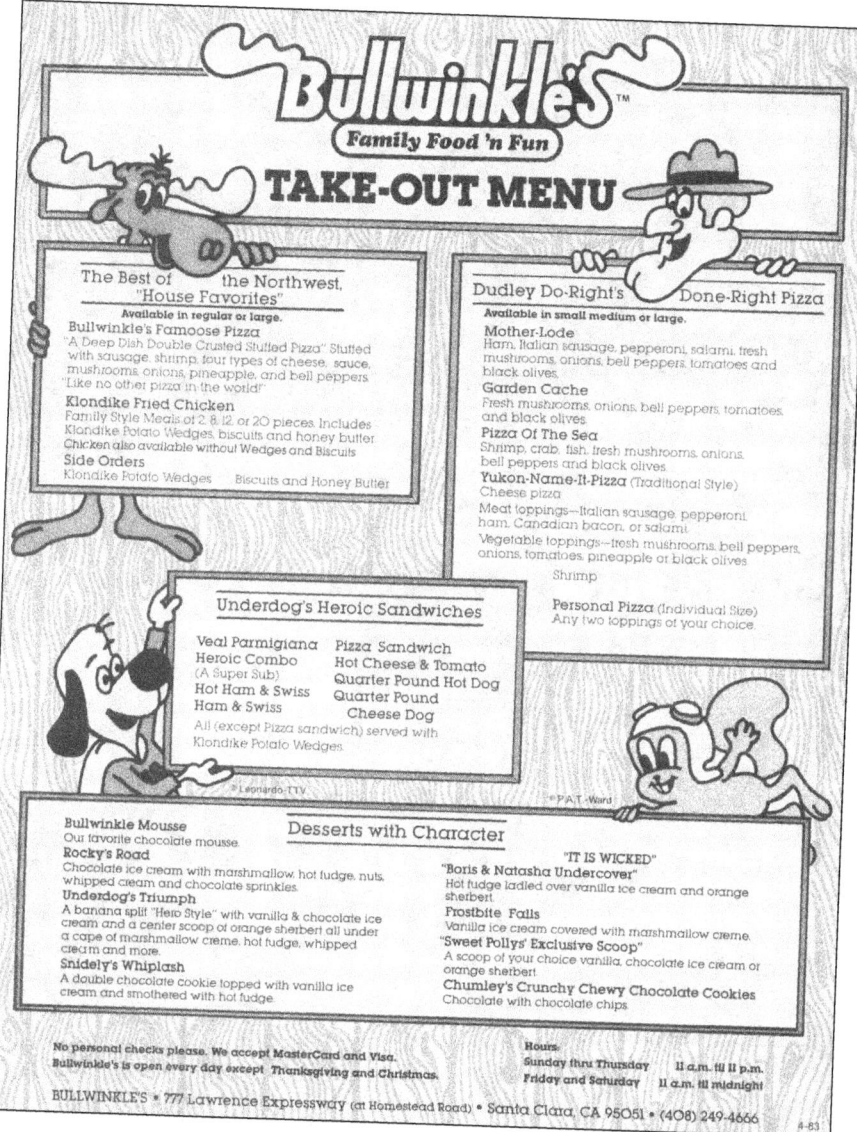

Bullwinkle's Restaurant was a short-lived restaurant chain from the 1980s and '90s that featured characters from the various shows produced by Jay Ward and TTV. Here are some photos, menu items and advertising from the author's collection.

CREATED AND PRODUCED BY TOTAL TELEVISION PRODUCTIONS

"LOOKS LIKE THIS IS THE END!"

DVDs have now become the preferred way to view old television shows. Here is a sampling of some various TTV releases from the past few years. FROM THE AUTHOR'S COLLECTION.

Joe Harris continues to keep the spirit alive with original drawings of Underdog offered for sale regularly through eBay and also with children's books such as 2008's *The Belly Book*. ARTWORK COURTESY OF JOE HARRIS.

Underdog, as he appeared in the 2005 Visa Check Card commercial.

CREATED AND PRODUCED BY TOTAL TELEVISION PRODUCTIONS

CHAPTER 15

WITHER UNDERDOG?

The future fame of the Total TeleVision characters is assured. The name "Total TeleVision" or "TTV" usually means nothing to the average person, but mention the name Underdog or Tennessee Tuxedo and a smile is sure to appear on the person's face. Biggers comments on Underdog's ongoing popularity, "Well, on Tuesday night, whoever was in charge of my appearance at the Writer's Conference here on the Cape, unbeknownst to me, printed up the 'Underdog Theme Song' and passed out the lyrics and we sang it and everyone was singing like fools!

"We [still] get the rights from music from ASCAP. I had an enjoyable time writing them. I [also] did some jingles for commercials, [but] they never got on! I had written a musical and all kinds of stuff, but nothing that had been performed or published, so one of the reasons I enjoyed doing the company is so that I could do the music. I had a lot of ulterior motives in forming the company!"

Covington agrees, "That's right. All four of us are members of ASCAP so our royalty is very small now compared to when everything was running all the time, but we still get checks from ASCAP. It was a strange situation because we owned the music rights, separately.

"That wasn't the case with our music. The case we made for the music was that they owned the music only in the sense that it was their right to have it in the episodes that had been bought out without them paying us continuing fees. So, in other words, it was not considered part of the actual buyout to the degree that they could take the music and run with it in other ways, but only as an integral part of the physical cartoons that they had bought.

"Originally, in our soundtracks, the music and the sound effects were done by music and sound effects people. They were bits of themes of music that were put into the cartoons, as could be done from a library, but then we started doing our own music, instead. Our later work is all our music. I worked a lot in Mexico on collecting a music library of our own. The themes, the sound effects and the melodies. We had a certain stock library. The music we did was written by the four of us, except our early episodes, which used canned music provided by a musical production house." This music was mainly composed by Winston Sharples, who worked for Paramount's Famous Studios, which is why you can hear the same stock music in *King Leonardo* and *Tennessee Tuxedo* as well as in 1940s and '50s *Popeye* and *Casper* cartoons.

Stover states that, in the years following TTV, "I went on to do a number of things. I worked for a couple of years over at Milton-Bradley and did a couple of their commercials. I did all of their advertising. They had a house agency. I also flew out to Australia and did a series called *Around the World in 80 Days*. It was a cartoon. I did that for General Mills directly, and it was animated down there."

Harris explains that, post-TTV, "I did [go back to DFS] briefly, but I ran into a problem in advertising in that I met people who did not want me to succeed, so I did not continue. I was back for one year with Dancer-Fitzgerald-Sample, and I ran into such enmity. I never did the first time, but coming back, I had certain laurels to wear with Trix and all that and there was a lot of enmity and a lot of backstabbing, and after a year I quit. I opened my own company, and did commercials." Biggers also went back to DFS for a time and worked with Gordon Johnson again, who was with the agency until 1974.

Harris comments on the rarity of TTV animation cels and drawings, "This kills me. When I was living in Connecticut, I had a big house, and a big garage, and part of the garage is where I kept all of the storyboards, cels. I had stacks of cels. I had all of the stuff that we worked on — preliminary stuff — the stuff that I had done since 1959. I remarried and my wife said, 'You know, I would be very comfortable if I could move out of this house, which has all these memories where your two children feel at home. As a new wife, I would like to have my own home.' And I said, 'You're on. Fine.' I sold that house and one of the things that I did was at the last minute was to go in the garage, go up on the loft, take out all of the cels, all of the storyboards, and anything else relating to the first 10 years, and put them in the back of a huge dump truck, and my wife said later on when I told her, she said, 'You saved your old Marine Corp. uniform, but you threw out all of your cels?!' And I said, 'You know, they're not worth anything.' Sure enough, she was smarter than me, 'cause a few years later, those cels were selling for a premium. On the storyboards, I went online once and I found an organization gallery that was selling my storyboards, done in pencil for $100 a panel. I had several packs of them, but who knew? Who knew? Go back to the 1980s when nothing was happening with Underdog."

Covington adds, "It's a shame. These things would be nice to have. We had some marvelous animation cels of the very first episodes that were done, and we were sent them from Mexico. We thought we would be able to make something of them, but then we got sidetracked and didn't look into it carefully enough. By the time we could do something with them, they'd all been stored and stuck together. I have a few left."

Harris offers a glimmer of hope for those wanting a TTV original. "If you're really interested, I do original drawings in color of Underdog. I do them in mixed media and I recreate sheets from the episodes and so I have one now on eBay. If you're interested, go to eBay and look up "animation>characters>art." It's up there. I keep putting them on, so take a look. I just put it on four days ago, and it's Underdog breaking through a wall to get to Simon and Cad. They've got Polly strapped to a surgical table. It looks really nasty, but we know that he's going to prevent that."

In 2007, a live-action feature film was made by Disney. Biggers comments, "Right. It's in Providence, Rhode Island. I think they're wrapping. Nancy and my daughter visited the set. I was invited but I didn't go with them. They went to the set a couple of times and I don't have any idea what kind of movie it'll be or whether it will be a success, but I hope it is a success."

Harris was less than thrilled with the results of the *Underdog* feature film. He explains the film's genesis: "Well, I was working with Bob Griffin over at Classic Media, and I said to him, 'You're going to do *what* with Underdog?' And he said, 'Don't get your ax hackled. This is thoroughly thought out and thoroughly planned.' And I said, 'Why are you doing it with live dogs? Why are you not doing it CGI like *Roger Rabbit*?' And he said, 'No, that wouldn't work.' And I said, 'Of course, it works. It worked fine. It's a titillation to see the animated characters dealing with real people.' If you look carefully at the show, you'll realize that there are real people in all of the episodes. All the people in the background are real.

"The main characters are animals so I said, 'Please, let's do it *Roger Rabbit* style. It'll be great,' and they said, 'No, no, no.' I even presented them with a scenario. Talk about being ahead of the game. I sent them a scenario and gave it to him in his office. He said, 'I like it. I'll take it out to the West Coast.' I guess he was talking to Disney at that point. This was a couple of years ago, and it was all about Simon Bar Sinister, who had now come out of prison, and was totally rehabilitated, and he decided he was going to be a businessman, and he started buying the tops of all the mountains he could, and he started buying all sorts of places way up high, and the reason he was doing that, was because he had discovered a machine that would melt the ice caps, and he was going to plant communities up on all of these mountains. Then he was going to turn the machine on, melt the ice, and everyone would have to go up there and live, and he would be a multi-millionaire, and he'd own the yachts. And then, Bob said, 'You know, you've got to get out of the 1960s, because this sounds an episode from one of the shows, rather than a movie.' I said, 'Wait a minute. You've just heard the skeleton of it. There's a lot more to it. There are subplots and so on.' He said, 'No, no, no. I'll take it out there, but I don't think anything will happen.' By that time, they already had a writer, and then they went through I don't know how many writers. I had a mole at Classic Media, a nice gal that I knew fairly well, and she kept sending me all the scripts and I couldn't believe how bad they were.

"It just stunned me. I think I ended up with seven or eight scripts. The latter two began to shape up, and the last one that I got was the one that they used. I sent Bob a lot of cartoons about Underdog: one where he and Polly were in their dressing room, and this rather important looking man in a suit walked in and said, 'Hi there, kiddies, I hope that I'm not interrupting anything, but we're just want to try on some costumes for the upcoming movie.' Outside the casting door are these two trainers with leashes. And he said, 'Ok, I get the idea. I get the idea.' Then I sent him one, which showed everyone getting an Academy Award, and Underdog came up and they gave him a silver bowl that said 'Dog' on it. Bob didn't like that one either. So that's where we're at."

The four owners are still friends, but don't talk with each other as frequently as they had in the past. "Yes. I don't talk to him much anymore since he moved to Long Island. He's in real estate and I think he wanted to get out of the hubbub. I've talked to him, I guess, once in the last year and I've talked to Joe a couple of times."

The 2007 *Underdog* feature film spawned a whole new line of merchandise.

CREATED AND PRODUCED BY TOTAL TELEVISION PRODUCTIONS

I. KING LEONARDO AND HIS SHORT SUBJECTS

    NBC Network: 1960-61
                      1961-62
                      1962-63

    Now in various syndication:

    1. "King & Odie"
    2. "The Hunter"
    3. "Tooter Turtle"
    4. "Twinkles"

II. TENNESSEE TUXEDO AND HIS TALES

    CBS Network: 1963-64
                      1964-65
                      1965-66

    Now in syndication:

    1. "Tennessee Tuxedo" Cartoons
    2. "Klondike Kat"

III. THE UNDERDOG SHOW

    NBC Network: 1964-65
                      1965-66

    1. "Underdog" Cartoons
    2. "Go Go Gophers"

    Beginning 1966-67 - CBS Network

IV. THE BEAGLES

    Beginning 1966-67 CBS Network

    1. "Beagle" Cartoons
    2. New cartoons from some of our previous series

A full schedule of TTV shows courtesy of Tread Covington from the final active days of TTV.

APPENDIX

TOTAL TELEVISION EPISODE GUIDE

Please note: special thanks to The Big Cartoon Database at *http://www.bcdb.com* for their airdate information, but even their site has errors, and I have made adjustments to their information as I saw fit and used it only as a guide. Please take everything in this listing with a huge grain of salt in regards to run dates. I tried to use logic and common sense to what aired when, originally. Except for the season opening date and time, all dates mentioned here are to *not* be taken for gospel because I assumed that all shows ran with new episodes each week until the season allotment was aired. I did not account for holiday breaks or any other repeats. I can confirm that a new episode of *The Underdog Show* did air on Thanksgiving Day 1965, but cannot confirm any other such "new" holiday airings.

Original airdates and episode compilations have proved to be impossible to find as General Mills had a habit of mixing and matching segments more and more as time went on. As Buck Biggers confirms on the existence of an original episode airdate listing, "It doesn't exist as far as I know. If it does, it would have to be General Mills that would have it. They scheduled any way that they wanted to and they did it station by station any way they wanted to. *Underdog* was the one on the network longest. Nine years on the network. That set a record for kids' shows on Saturday morning. Most of it was syndicated. So, I doubt you'd find schedules. If you found them, you wouldn't be able to read 'em." I contacted General Mills and Saatchi & Saatchi many times to no response.

Tread Covington offers a slim possibility. "I used to do the blurbs that would appear in *TV Guide*, the brief description of the show that week. I did those for them and then I turned them over to Dancer-Fitzgerald, and then they in turn submitted them, so I might even find those." Should such schedules turn up; this section will be corrected in any future editions of this book.

I have also tried to be as accurate as possible with episode titles. Many titles have been incorrectly listed over the years, a good example being "Underdog vs.

Overcoat," which was, is and always should be "Underdog vs. Overcat." And, if the title card used quotation marks or other punctuation, I have tried to replicate that, as well. Episodes marked with an asterisk (*) have been personally viewed by the author in order to confirm the actual title card that appears on screen.

Episodes not viewed personally by me were due to their availability only being on *The Dudley Do-Right Show* (which has never aired in my area), or completely out of circulation, due to the haphazard way that these cartoons have been aired or issued on home video. Hopefully, such omissions will also be corrected in future editions.

Special notice should be taken that the following Columbia Pictures theatrical cartoons were part of early NBC airings of *King Leonardo and his Short Subjects*. They are in no way, shape or form part of anything to do with TTV other than this inclusion and are listed here for completeness sake, and their titles are sometimes mistakenly cited as *King and Odie* episode titles. They are "Midnight Frolics" (1938), "Tito's Guitar" (1942), "Fiesta Time" (1945), "The Carpenters" (1941), "Cat-Nipped" (1946) and "Dog, Cat and Canary" (1945). The inclusion of these had to do with *King Leonardo* replacing *Ruff and Reddy* in its timeslot and something to do with Screen Gems, which distributed early Hanna-Barbera material, as well as the Columbia cartoons, and were included due to contractual obligations.

KING LEONARDO AND HIS SHORT SUBJECTS
(39 SHOWS)

THE KING & ODIE
(104 EPISODES)

FIRST SEASON: 10/15/60-4/8/61
NBC (52 EPISODES, 2 PER SHOW)

King & Odie #1: *Riches to Rags* *............................10/15/60
Part 1: Biggy Rat and Itchy Brother plot to take over the kingdom. Odie Colognie, who is listening in, is soon discovered by Biggy and Itchy, who proceed to tie him up. Then, Biggy and Itchy tell King Leonardo that he has lost touch with his people. Itchy says he'll sit on the throne while Leonardo goes to talk with the people. Note: This episode is available on DVD on *The Underdog Chronicles*.

King & Odie #2: *Nose for the Noose* *..........................10/15/60
Part 2: Itchy's on the throne; Odie's tied up; and Leonardo's trying to get back in the castle, but it is difficult as Leonardo is now on Wanted posters. Meanwhile, Odie gets himself free and then helps Leonardo get back in the castle by pole-vaulting him. Biggy and Itchy parade around as Leonardo and Odie until they get hosed down and are revealed. Then the real King and Odie take over and throw Biggy and Itchy in jail. Note: This episode is available on DVD on *The Underdog Chronicles*.

King & Odie #3 *Drumming Up the Bongos* *....................10/22/60
Part 1: There is a surplus of bongo drums in Bongo Congo. It turns out that Biggy and Itchy have been circumventing the drum shipments causing chaos with the economy and making it easier to overthrow the government. Odie decides to check into the shipment, which is approved by Leonardo, because apparently America is still ordering a lot of bongo drums. Biggy and Itchy (in disguise) take the King and Odie for a ride and dump them off a cliff.

King & Odie #4 *How High is Up?* *............................10/22/60
Part 2: The King and Odie are falling, but are saved by a branch sticking out of a cliffside. The fall has had traumatic effects as Leonardo's hair has fallen out and he looks more like Itchy. A passing taxi picks up Leonardo and Odie and takes them to the palace, but the driver reveals that Itchy is now on the throne. Leonardo comes in to take back the throne, but he is unrecognizable, so for the

moment it looks like Biggy and Itchy have won. Odie shows further proof that it is Leonardo and everything gets back to normal.

King & Odie #5 *Royal Amnesia* *.............................10/29/60

Part 1: Bongo Congo have entered the space race and soon it will be time for the countdown. Biggy and Itchy are planning to sabotage the effort by protesting the astronauts being sent, and want Leonardo to fly his own ship. Leonardo boots them out, so Biggy and Itchy take it to the public, who agree to have Leonardo fly. Leonardo goes up and crash-lands. Is he alive?

King & Odie #6 *Loon from the Moon* *..........................10/29/60

Part 2: Itchy Brother is certain that King Leonardo is dead and assumes the throne. King Leonardo has returned from the crash, unharmed except that he had lost his memory. Leonardo believes that he's from the moon. Odie tries to prove otherwise, but fails, and they are thrown in jail. The old cliché of another blow to the head returns Leonardo's memory and Leonardo and Odie take back the throne.

King & Odie #7 *Royal Bongo War Chant* *.......................11/5/60

Part 1: The story opens at Koko Loco, the kingdom south of Bongo Congo. Biggy and Itchy convince King Loco III of Koko Loco to declare war on Bongo Congo. If Bongo Congo gets defeated, Biggy and Itchy can take over. They go to Leonardo to tell him about the war and Leonardo agrees to fight. Leonardo wants to fly a plane and attack, but all they have is a balloon, a ship and six soldiers.

King & Odie #8 *Showdown at Dhyber Pass* *.....................11/5/60

Part 2: King Leonardo goes up in his hot air balloon and is shot down by the Koko Loco Air Force, but the pressure of the gas from the balloon blows the Air Force out of the sky. Next, Leonardo defeats Koko Loco's Navy. Finally, Leonardo battles the Koko Loco Army at Dhyber Pass. Leonardo fools the Koko Loco Army by placing fake cannons and they surrender by thinking they were outnumbered.

King & Odie #9 *Duel to the Dearth* *..........................11/12/60

Part 1: Biggy and Itchy have attempted to overthrow King Leonardo time after time, and they still haven't given up. This time they plan to overthrow him by spreading rumors that Leonardo is a coward, and Itchy challenges Leonardo to a fight, which Leonardo agrees to defend his honor.

King & Odie #10 *Ringside Riot* *..............................11/12/60

Part 2: Leonardo thinks he's going to fight Itchy Brother, but instead they put him up against Terrible Tim, a huge opponent. Sure to lose, Odie helps Leonardo by tunneling underneath the ring and creates a trap door, which drops Tim out of the ring, and Leonardo is declared the winner. Biggy and Itchy are arrested again.

King & Odie #11 *Bringing in Biggy* * 11/19/60
 Part 1: Leonardo reminisces about how Biggy and Itchy first plotted against him in boyhood days, when Leonardo and Odie built a tree house. As a child, Leonardo's mother also made him pay a bongo buck every time he said, "Confound it!" Itchy Brother says he can help Leonardo stop saying it for one day, if he can have the right to the throne.

King & Odie #12 *Confound it! Confusion* * 11/19/60
 Part 2: Leonardo and Odie finish the tree house while Itchy and Biggy try to get him to say "Confound it!" to get the throne, but Leonardo ends up saying, "Constantinople" and other things. He does last the day and saves the throne, but never truly stops saying, "Confound it!"

King & Odie #13 *Paris Pursuit* * 11/26/60
 Part 1: Things are running smoothly in Bongo Congo, so Leonardo and Odie decide to go on a vacation in Paris. Biggy and Itchy find out about it in the papers and discover that Leonardo and Odie will be traveling with the royal yacht, so Biggy and Itchy get hired as the new crew on the yacht, in order to off the King, and it appears that they do so, by blowing up the yacht.

King & Odie #14 *The Awful Tower* * 11/26/60
 Part 2: Leonardo and Odie escape from their plight on a speedboat and end up in Paris. They check into a hotel and want to be shown the tourist attractions. Meanwhile, Itchy and Biggy try to kill the King with an arrow. King and Odie chase after Itch and Big with taxis and end up on the Eiffel Tower and later the Bastille. Leonardo is happy as the Bastille is one of the most famous jails in the world and Itchy and Biggy are trapped. King and Odie go on their way.

King & Odie #15 *Beatnik Boom* * 12/3/60
 Part 1: Everyone in the kingdom is happy, except Biggy and Itchy, who aren't because they may have to go to work. They decide to get everyone in Bongo Congo to stop working and become beatniks. This leaves all of the factory work to be done by the King and Odie. What's worse is that the workers want Itchy Brother to become king!

King & Odie #16 *Call Out the Kids* *. 12/3/60
 Part 2: With the kingdom a land of beatniks, the kids realize that no work by the parents, means no money for any toys. This cannot happen, so the kids emu-

late their beatnik parents and the parents turn their allegiance back to Leonardo. The people go back to work and Leonardo wins the vote by a landslide.

King & Odie #17 *Trial of the Traitors* *........................12/10/60
   Part 1: Leonardo and Odie are sick of Biggy and Itchy's tricks so they decide to put them on trial for being traitors. At the trial, they use footage from the first 10 *King and Odie* episodes to prove their point.

King & Odie #18 *Battle-Slip* *............................12/10/60
   Part 2: The jury declares Biggy and Itchy guilty and banish them from the kingdom. Biggy swears revenge. Soon, the soldiers of Bongo Congo site a battleship captained by Biggy and Itchy. They declare war on the kingdom and a battle with cannons begins. Leonardo takes the Army (because they don't have a Navy or Marines) and they overwhelm the traitors.

King & Odie #19 *Heroes are Made…With Salami* *...............12/17/60
   Part 1: King Leonardo is in his country house counting out his bongos. Odie is making bread and honey. Biggy and Itchy call on Professor Messer to get a new gadget to take over the kingdom. He comes up with an exploding hero sandwich for the King. Afterwards, Biggy, Itchy and Messer also eat hero sandwiches, but one of them is ticking, as Itchy gave the wrong sandwich to Leonardo, and the three explode.

King & Odie #20 *The Big Freeze* *..........................12/17/60
   Part 2: After the explosion, Messer comes up with an ice cube ray. This ray will freeze solid anything it touches. Biggy and Itchy make a skating rink and then they zap the King and Odie and proceed to dump the frozen duo into the river and they floated downstream like ice cubes, but the ice melts as the river has warm water. In the end, they capture Biggy and Itchy after capturing the ray gun.

King & Odie #21 *The Legend of Leonardo the Neat* * 12/24/60
   Part 1: Odie conducts tours of the kingdom. Meanwhile, Itchy tells Biggy that there is a royal treasure buried under the palace. They make a few attempts to scale the castle wall and then to dig underneath. Finally, they cover the palace with garbage and destroy the castle, so King Leonardo claims that the palace is a ghastly mess and puts it up for sale.

King & Odie #22 *Home Neat Home* *.........................12/24/60
   Part 2: As soon as King Leonardo leaves, Biggy and Itchy move in. Leonardo then discovers that he left his storybook in the palace and goes back to retrieve it. Biggy and Itchy make fun of Leonardo when he sees them, and then throw

him in the dungeon. Odie comes back to rescue Leonardo and falls in the moat and gets covered with mud so he is virtually invisible. Biggy and Itchy are in the dungeon digging up the treasure and think Odie's a ghost. Biggy and Itchy are knocked unconscious, and Leonardo is freed. The treasure turns out to be a broom and dustpan to help clean up.

King & Odie #23 *Sticky Stuff* * 12/31/60
Part 1: Chinese detective Charlie Chin is visiting Bongo Congo and says that Itchy Brother is rotting the family tree and something should be done. Leonardo commands that Odie and Chin must find him and do something about it. Meanwhile, Biggy and Itchy consult with Professor Messer and want a foolproof way to steal the King and they decide on sticky glue to do the job. Note: This episode is available on DVD on *The Ultimate Underdog Collection Volume 1*.

King & Odie #24 *Am I Glue* * 12/31/60
Part 2: Biggy wants to glue King Leonardo to the palace wall and pretend that he is missing. Meanwhile, Odie and Charlie Chin are searching for Professor Messer while they dine at a restaurant which Messer is portraying their waiter. Then a secret message comes through that needs to be decoded by the Odie Decoder and Odie and Chin now know the glue plan. Leonardo is missing and Itchy assumes the position of king. It's only temporary as Odie and Chin use a Leonardo cutout to prove that he was still the leader. Note: This episode is available on DVD on *The Ultimate Underdog Collection Volume 1*.

King & Odie #25 *Double Trouble* * 1/7/61
Part 1: Leonardo wants to become friends with Itchy and Biggy and they are shocked when he offers not only his crown but his entire head! It turns out to be a robot of Professor Messer's and together the three plot another takeover using the Professor's Leonardo double. Note: This episode is available on DVD on *Underdog Nemesis* and on *The Ultimate Underdog Collection Volume 2*.

King & Odie #26 *Switcheroo Ruler* * 1/7/61
Part 2: The robot doubles of Leonardo and Odie confuse the guards and the real Leonardo and Odie are thrown in the dungeon. Meanwhile, the three villains take over Bongo Congo. King and Odie escape and replace the robots, fooling the three villains and they take back their kingdom and lock up the villains. Note: This episode is available on DVD on *Underdog Nemesis* and on *The Ultimate Underdog Collection Volume 2*.

King & Odie #27 *Perfume Panic* * 1/14/61
Part 1: Odie is in charge of the royal perfume. One day the public protests

the smell of the perfume, as they feel it smells bad. It turns out to be a scam by Itchy and Biggy in order to corner the perfume market.

King & Odie #28 *Style Awhile* *............................... 1/14/61
Part 2: Biggy and Itchy have taken over the perfume business in Bongo-land. Biggy plans to use the money from the perfume to buy out the bongo business. Odie suggests his sister Carlotta Colognie to help, but can she do it?

King & Odie #29 *No Bong Bongos* *............................ 1/21/61
Part 1: It has been discovered that there is no bong in the bongos manufactured in Bongo Congo. It turns out that Itchy and Biggy have been tampering with the drums at the manufacturing plant. The drumheads were soaked in water and the drumheads aren't tight enough. With the problem solved, a new problem arises as no one wants bongo drums from Bongo Congo anymore, so they have to figure that problem out next.

King & Odie #30 *The Ad Game* *............................... 1/21/61
Part 2: Odie feels that advertising would help the bongo drum industry be revitalized in Bongo Congo. He calls the help of an ad agency. Meanwhile, Biggy is selling his bongos and has taken control of the industry. The agency comes up with the slogan "Stand up for Bongo Congo Bongos" and "The bong is back in the bongos." Biggy's industry takeover is easily defeated.

King & Odie #31 *De-Based Ball* *............................. 1/28/61
Part 1: The Bongo Bruins are playing against the Koko Cards in a baseball game. All of Bongo Congo is watching as they haven't won a game in 432 years. King Leonardo is pitching and Odie is catching so they feel confident that they will win.

King & Odie #32 *Bats in the Ballpark* *...................... 1/28/61
Part 2: Biggy and Itchy do not want the Bruins to win, so they obtain a jumping ball from Professor Messer, and with Itchy as umpire, it doesn't look like they will win. All seems hopeless until Odie gets a jumping bat from his Uncle Sintilatin Skunk.

King & Odie #33 *Long Lost Lennie* *.......................... 2/4/61
Part 1: Lawyers from the United States stop by to show Leonardo a will of his late Uncle Lennie. Leonardo is left an entire town called Gravestone, supposedly stocked with silver. Leonardo and Odie go out to see his land, but no one will take them the entire way, because Gravestone is haunted with ghosts.

King & Odie #34 *Ghosts Guests* *. 2/4/61
Part 2: Itchy and Biggy also go to Gravestone to try to take away Leonardo's new inheritance. Leonardo and Odie make it to the Hotel Prairie Queen, which does have some ghosts. Then they go to a bar and their drinks are stolen by ghosts. The ghosts, of course, are really Itchy and Biggy, and Leonardo and Odie soon figure this out and turn the tables on them. Odie finds a safe and when they open it, they find a silver spoon, the sole sum of silver stored in the town.

King & Odie #35 *Fatal Fever* *. 2/11/61
Part 1: Odie is going on vacation and Leonardo is in a panic about who's going to do things. Odie has already made arrangements. Meanwhile, Biggy and Itchy take advantage of Odie's absence and convince Leonardo that he's sick. Then, they switch Leonardo's and Itchy's manes to fool the kingdom and take over.

King & Odie #36 *Pulling the Mane Switch* *. 2/11/61
Part 2: Itchy, in disguise, takes Leonardo to Dr. Bugosi to get his mane cut. They put Leonardo on the rack. Meanwhile, the Bongo Congo guards are aware of Leonardo's disappearance and a call goes out for Odie's return. Odie arrives just in time to save the day and Itchy gets shaved instead of Leonardo.

King & Odie #37 *Dim Gem* *. 2/18/61
Part 1: Leonardo and Odie go to London to get the royal jewels polished, as London is the best place in the world for polishing. Biggy and Itchy travel to London as well and Itchy disguises himself as Scratchy Jewel, a jeweler, and steals the royal jewels.

King & Odie #38 *The Clanking Castle Caper* *. 2/18/61
Part 2: Odie gets the jewels back by opening a beatnik coffee shop and fooling Itchy (wearing some of the jewels) who falls into a trap and leads him to Biggy, who has the rest of the jewels.

King & Odie #39 *The King and Me* *. 2/25/61
Part 1: King Leonardo leaves Bongo Congo for Hollywood to make a movie. Of course, Biggy and Itchy catch wind of this and begin making their own plans.

King & Odie #40 *The Loves of Lynetta Lion* *. 2/25/61
Part 2: While in Hollywood, Leonardo and Odie meet up with the beautiful lion starlet, Lynetta Lion. In the end, Leonardo concludes that Hollywood is not for him, and returns to Bongo Congo.

King & Odie #41 *The Sport of Kings* * 3/4/61
   Part 1: King Leonardo is the best Steeplechase rider in the kingdom due to the fact that he has the best horse, called White Star. In fact, White Star is so good that no one wants to race him anymore. Leonardo decides to put the entire kingdom as the prize for anyone who can beat White Star in a race. Biggy and Itchy decide to enter and know that the only way they can win is to switch horses.

King & Odie #42 *Black is White* * 3/4/61
   Part 2: Itchy is now racing a horse called Old Paint, which is really White Star in disguise. Of course, Leonardo can't get his horse, the fake White Star, to do anything. Meanwhile, the milkman confesses that his horse has been stolen to Odie and he sees that there has been a switch. Odie sends a balloon up to make it rain and all the paint washes off and White Star wins with Itchy on his back and Leonardo keeps his kingdom.

King & Odie #43 *True Blue Blues* * 3/11/61
   Part 1: Leonardo and Odie go ice-skating, but Leonardo falls in the ice, so instead they go sledding, skiing and play ice hockey. Leonardo is still unhappy as these sports don't cheer him up, so Odie buys him a dog. Biggy Rat has a new plan that Itchy disguises himself as a dog, while they steal the king's dog, so they get into the palace.

King & Odie #44 *My Dog has Fleas* * 3/11/61
   Part 2: Biggy tricks Odie and does the dog switcheroo. Unfortunately for Biggy, Leonardo's dog attacks him after the switch. In the meantime, Itchy, as the dog, is waiting for his chance to take the palace gold until fleas are noticed on Itchy, so a bath is in order. The ensuing chase reveals Itchy and then the real palace dog brings Biggy in and they are both arrested.

King & Odie #45 *Lead Foot Leonardo* * 3/18/61
   Part 1: Leonardo is sent a go-cart from the US and soon he declares go-carting a national pastime and starts a go-cart race. Of course, Itchy and Biggy enter the race.

King & Odie #46 *The Rat Race* * 3/18/61
   Part 2: It's the day of the big race and Biggy continues to sabotage Leonardo's car. Later, Itchy throws tacks on the road and Leonardo gets four flats. The King gets 40 laps behind. Biggy, disguised as a police officer, pulls Leonardo over for speeding, but he is discovered and Leonardo speeds up to actually pass up Itchy Brother and wins.

King & Odie #47 *The Obey Ball* *................................3/25/61

Part 1: Biggy and Itchy are hard at work plotting another takeover. Professor Messer stops by with his latest invention, the Obey Ball, a ball that follows all of your commands. Meanwhile, Leonardo and Odie are playing catch. Leonardo overthrows the ball and Biggy and Itchy throw back the Obey Ball, controlled by Messer. Leonardo gets clobbered by the ball so many times, he fires Odie. Leonardo hires a replacement, which is really Itchy Brother.

King & Odie #48 *Out of the Depths* *..........................3/25/61

Part 2: Itchy, taking Odie's place, puts Leonardo's feet into a washtub and pours quick-drying cement on Leonardo's feet and throws him in the river. Back at Biggy and Itchy's hideout, Biggy gets mad when he discovers that Itchy had put the Obey Ball in Leonardo's mouth. Messer says not to worry and uses the remote control to retrieve the Ball and Leonardo, too. Odie witnesses all this and rescues Leonardo, who realizes his mistake in firing Odie. Biggy and Itchy take over Bongo Congo until Leonardo and Odie shows up. Odie takes the control box and controls the Obey Ball.

King & Odie #49 *The Loco Play* *................................4/1/61

Part 1: King Loco wants to see a stage play of *Romeo and Juliet*. King Leonardo decides to appease his wishes and asks for popular movie actress Lynetta Lion to star. Biggy and Itchy plot to capture Lynetta to ruin the play.

King & Odie #50 *Romeo and Juliet* * 4/1/61

Part 2: Biggy and Itchy hold Lynetta Lion hostage for a hefty ransom. Some lipstick on a suit of armor foils the plot, Lynetta is rescued, the play goes on without a hitch and Itchy and Biggy are thrown in jail. Note: For those who don't know, Joliet is the name of a city in Illinois.

King & Odie #51 *If at First you Don't Succeed* *...................4/8/61

Part 1: Leonardo feels that the world should hear more about Bongo Congo. He decides to fly an airplane higher than any airplane has flown before. He fails in his attempt. Then he decides to set foot on the bottom of the Pacific Ocean. He fails here as well. Finally, he discovers a newspaper article that says that he'll win $100,000 for climbing Big Rock Candy Mountain. Of course, Biggy and Itchy have the same idea.

King & Odie #52 *Try, Try Again* *...............................4/8/61

Part 2: Leonardo and Odie prepare to climb the peak. Biggy and Itchy climb as well. Leonardo and Odie accidentally climb the incorrect peak, but use a mountain goat's butt to sail to the correct peak. The force of Leonardo's crash into the proper peak causes Itchy and Biggy to lose their footing and the $100,000.

SECOND SEASON: 9/30/61-12/23/61
NBC (26 EPISODES, 2 PER SHOW)

King & Odie #53 *Long Laugh Leonardo* * 9/30/61

Part 1: Odie pours too much of a certain chemical, called Papa Colognie's Smile, into the annual batch of the royal perfume, creating a laughing gas. Leonardo sniffs it and starts to laugh uncontrollably. Odie closes the lid in time and searches for an antidote. Biggy Rat and Itchy Brother take advantage of the situation by stealing the "laughing gas" perfume.

King & Odie #54 *He Who Laughs Last* * 9/30/61

Part 2: Leonardo is growing weaker with all his laughing and while Odie goes for help, he gets trapped in a vat. With Odie out of the way, Biggy and Itchy bottle the perfume and pass it out to take control of the kingdom with laughing. Odie finally escapes and discovers that onions are the antidotes as it makes Leonardo cry. They soon spray it on the kingdom and capture the crooks.

King & Odie #55 *East Side West Side* * 10/7/61

Part 1: Things were running smoothly in Bongo Congo, so King Leonardo turns his attentions to other countries and decides to come to America. This trip to New York is considered an ideal way to do away with the King, according to Biggy and Itchy. They disrupt the ticker-tape parade by dropping stuff on Leonardo. This fails, but Biggy and Itchy try again when they find out the King and Odie are going to Coney Island.

King & Odie #56 *Coney Island Calamity* * 10/7/61

Part 2: Biggy and Itchy disguise themselves as cabbies, but still fail. Now at Coney Island, Leonardo and Odie decide on what rides to ride. They ended up riding on Biggy and Itchy's Shooting Gallery, but they miraculous did not get shot. Next, they go on a Ferris wheel that goes at a dizzying speed and are thrown and land on the roller-coaster tracks. Next, Leonardo decides to go through the funhouse while Odie sits it out and discovers Biggy and Itchy's sabotage, and knocks them out with a pop bottle. The King is safe.

King & Odie #57 *An Ode in Code* * 10/14/61

Part 1: In 1752, the last battle raged between Bongo Congo and Koko Loco. At the end of the war, there was some hidden treasure and, 200+ years later, Biggy and Itchy try to find the treasure, but they need a decoder from Odie to help find it. They drop a big rock on Odie and tie him up and get the decoder. Will the two villains get the hidden treasure?

King & Odie #58 *Two Beneath the Mast* * 10/14/61
Part 2: After deciphering the map, Biggy and Itchy arrive at the island where the long-lost treasure of Bongo Congo is supposedly hidden. Leonardo and Odie are not far behind and order Biggy and Itchy to surrender the royal treasure, and they are soon captured.

King & Odie #59 *Hip Hip Hypnosis* * 10/21/61
Part 1: Biggy takes up hypnotism and after practicing on Itchy (making him act like a dog and such), he decides to hypnotize Leonardo while Leonardo is in bed reading a *King Leonardo* comic book.

King & Odie #60 *Odie Hit the Roadie* * 10/21/61
Part 2: Biggy begins hypnotizing the King to takeover his kingdom. The hypnotism works and he makes Itchy Prime Minister and Biggy Royal Treasurer and dumps Odie. After Odie leaves, he investigates and finds out about the hypnotism and breaks the trance. Leonardo then plays like he's hypnotized and they capture Biggy and Itchy and put them in the dungeon.

King & Odie #61 *Hunting a Hobby* * 10/28/61
Part 1: Odie suggests that Leonardo takes up a sport for a hobby. At first, he tries bowling. He doesn't like it and wants something with a little more action. Then, he tries tennis, but Leonardo isn't very good at this, either. Then, the King and Odie try kite flying and croquet and diving. Finally, they try the golf course and Leonardo isn't any good at it, either, until he was hit by a golf ball and becomes a star player.

King & Odie #62 *Teeing Off* * 10/28/61
Part 2: So, Leonardo sets up the Blue Blood golf tournament and, of course, Biggy encourages Itchy to play, so they can win the big cash prize. While playing, Biggy plays tricks and helps Itchy to tie with Leonardo on the last hole. Leonardo needs a hole-in-one to win and he gets it.

King & Odie #63 *Smarty Gras* * 11/4/61
Part 1: In New Orleans, plans for the Mardi Gras are being made and they are trying to find out who would be best to be King for the Mardi Gras, and King Leonardo is chosen. Biggy and Itchy, of course, read about it and make their plans. Leonardo and Odie take a riverboat there, captained by Captain Stonewheel Jackson. Biggy and Itchy are aboard and stick Leonardo's cape into the

giant paddlewheel. Odie soon sets him free, but Biggy and Itchy are trying to keep Leonardo from getting to New Orleans and plan to shoot him next.

King & Odie #64 *Bayou Blues* *............................11/4/61
Part 2: Before shooting him, Biggy and Itchy gamble against Leonardo and Leonardo accuses Itchy of cheating and so Itchy challenges Leonardo to a duel. Biggy provides the pistols until Odie intervenes, and Biggy and Itchy's costumes come off and King and Odie jump overboard and hold on to a log. King and Odie get rescued by a small boat. Meanwhile, Itchy disguises himself as Leonardo and gets to New Orleans first and becomes King. Leonardo and Odie finally get to New Orleans themselves and disguise themselves as waiters and take their rightful places back.

King & Odie #65 *Stage Struck*...............................11/11/61
Part 1: Synopsis unavailable.

King & Odie #66 *One Way Ticket to Venus*....................11/11/61
Part 2: Synopsis unavailable.

King & Odie #67 *Back to Nature* *...........................11/18/61
Part 1: It is time for the Olympics and for the first time Bongo Congo is entered a team. While enthusiastic, the team has a fighting heart, but weak physiques, causing the citizens of Bongo Congo to be in an uproar. Leonardo sends for a Health Minister to figure out what to do. The Health Minister says that modern conveniences have made the team weak, so Leonardo proposes a "Back to Nature" program to set a good health example.

King & Odie #68 *My Vine is your Vine* *......................11/18/61
Part 2: Leonardo really wants everyone to go back to nature and live in a tree house without any modern conveniences to make the Bongo Congo Olympic Team stronger. King and Odie also hunt for their own food by fishing. Meanwhile, Biggy and Itchy are scheming and pull the King and Odie into the water and over a waterfall. Soon Biggy and Itchy are taking over, explaining that the King and Odie are no more, but the King and Odie are not hurt as they are rescued by an ape man.

King & Odie #69 *The Tourist Trade* *.........................11/25/61
Part 1: King Leonardo and Odie are making their annual inspection of the Bongo Congo Airport. While there, they discover an American tourist, who's unhappy. He feels that he's stuck in a crummy dump of a place called Bongo Congo. Leonardo blows his top and asks Odie to tell the man of the tourist attractions.

When they can't think of anything, Leonardo decides to test new things like skin-diving, surfboarding and other things to offer as tourist attractions, but none are good. They begin to despair. Then, they think of a bicycle race to attract tourists.

King & Odie #70 *Bye Bye Bicycle* *................................11/25/61
    Part 2: The day of the big race is at hand for bicycles built for two and Biggy and Itchy enter the race. They don't want the villains to win because it will ruin the tourist trace, so Leonardo and Odie decide to race themselves to ensure that the bad guys won't win. Biggy and Itchy almost win, but the King and Odie stop that and ultimately, two Americans win, Wilbur and Orville Wrong.

King & Odie #71 *Chicago Shenanigans* *........................12/2/61
    Part 1: Leonardo is angry because he is not getting a decent steak dinner, so he and Odie race off to Chicago when he finds out that he can get a good steak there. Of course, Biggy and Itchy hear about it. Biggy calls his friends, the Natty Brothers Gang (Notty, Nitty and Nutty), to help get Leonardo. Meanwhile, Leonardo is very happy with his steaks and is now playing Bongo Bongo with Odie.

King & Odie #72 *Loop the Loop* *...............................12/2/61
    Part 2: Finally, the Natty Brothers succeed in kidnapping the King and knocking Odie out. Odie follows them and discovers Leonardo bound and gagged and having his feet bound in cement to "off" him. Odie tells the police and the Natty Brothers are sent to jail and Leonardo enjoys yet another steak.

King & Odie #73 *Uranium Cranium* *...........................12/9/61
    Part 1: An old prospector who discovered uranium into Bongo Valley comes into town, causing a uranium rush. The old prospector turns out to be Itchy Brother. The reason for this is because Biggy Rat owns all the land in Bongo Valley, land that is useless. Everyone bought, even King Leonardo. It is supposedly barren land, but Leonardo does find uranium. Now, Biggy and Itchy want the land back.

King & Odie #74 *Mistaked Claim* *.............................12/9/61
    Part 2: Leonardo and Odie start digging for the uranium while Biggy and Itchy plan to hurl a giant rock on them, but the rock lands directly on Biggy. Then, they decide to offer all the money they've earned for Leonardo's lot. Odie says yes, much to Leonardo's disagreement. After the sale, it turns that the only uranium was in Itchy's missing watch, left on Leonardo's plot of land.

King & Odie #75 *The Trail of the Lonesome Mine* *..............12/16/61
    Part 1: Odie is worried that the Bongo Congo treasury is almost empty, so Leonardo and Odie go mining to dig up some buried gems. An old prospector

named Death Valley O'Days helps them stake their claim. Meanwhile, Odie discovers a tunnel.

King & Odie #76 *The Treasure of Sierra Bongo* *................12/16/61
Paul 2: In Death Valley, Leonardo and Odie find diamonds in the tunnel and haul them out. Unfortunately, they meet up with some bandits who take the diamonds. The chase is on and the bandits are defeated by a large boulder.

King & Odie #77 *Fortune Feller* *........................12/23/61
Part 1: Biggy and Itchy open up a fortuneteller business with Itchy portraying the gypsy. Biggy made sure that the fortunes come true and pick pocket the customer's wallets. Itchy wants to go back to overthrowing kingdoms. Biggy says that they should read Leonardo's fortune to make him go away. Leonardo is looking for a place to vacation when they see Biggy and Itchy in disguise as fortunetellers and Leonardo brings them into the palace to tell his fortune. Itchy predicts that Leonardo will go traveling.

King & Odie #78 *Wild and Wobbly* *........................12/23/61
Part 2: Itchy predicts that the King and Odie will be going to the far west and they soon are on a plane to America and soon encounter Indians, which are really Biggy and Itchy in disguise. Next, Leonardo and Odie take a wild stagecoach ride in which they are out of control for a time. After that, Leonardo goes into a bar and orders lemonade. Biggy and Itchy dress up as cowboy bandits and start shooting at Leonardo. Odie, meanwhile, dresses up as El Squaro and stops them. Leonardo, unaware that he was in danger, laughs it off. Note: Biggy and Itchy strongly resemble Ruffled Feather and Running Board in their Indian costumes.

THIRD SEASON: 9/28/63-3/21/64
CBS (AS PART OF *TENNESSEE TUXEDO AND HIS TALES*)
(26 EPISODES)

King & Odie #79 *Introducing Mr. Mad*.....................9/28/63
Part 1: Synopsis unavailable.

King & Odie #80 *Falling Asleep* 10/5/63
Part 2: Synopsis unavailable.

King & Odie #81 *Hup-2-3-Hike*...........................10/12/63
Part 1: Synopsis unavailable.

King & Odie #82 *Spring Along with Itch* 10/19/63
Part 2: Synposis unavailable.

King & Odie #83 *Left Alone Leonardo* 10/26/63
Part 1: Synposis unavailable.

King & Odie #84 *A Tour de Farce* 11/2/63
Part 2: Synposis unavailable.

King & Odie #85 *Get 'Em Up Scout* 11/9/63
Part 1: Synposis unavailable.

King & Odie #86 *The King Camps Out* 11/16/63
Part 2: Synposis unavailable.

King & Odie #87 *Offensive Defensive* 11/23/63
Part 1: Synposis unavailable.

King & Odie #88 *A Long Long Trail A-Binding* 11/30/63
Part 2: : Synposis unavailable.

King & Odie #89 *Treasure Train* 12/7/63
Part 1: Synposis unavailable.

King & Odie #90 Handcar Heroes 12/14/63
Part 2: Synposis unavailable.

King & Odie #91 Honey Business 12/21/63
Part 1: Synposis unavailable.

King & Odie #92 Bye Bye Bees 12/28/63
Part 2: Synposis unavailable.

King & Odie #93 *The Royal Race* * 1/4/64
Part 1: Yachts are practicing for the Royal Yacht Race, even though the King and Odie always win. Biggy and Itchy also enter and see Professor Messer for help in winning the race.

King & Odie #94 *The Shifty Sail* 1/11/64
Part 2: Synposis unavailable.

King & Odie #95 *Asleep on the Deep* 1/18/64
   Part 1: Synopsis unavailable.

King & Odie #96 *An Ace for a King*. 1/25/64
   Part 2: Synopsis unavailable.

King & Odie #97 *Odie Takes a Dive* * 2/1/64
   Part 1: The King and Odie take up a new sport...skydiving. They jump together many times, but one day Leonardo is busy with royal duties (working on his stamp collection!), and tells Odie to go it alone. Odie parachutes into a crater and is lost. Meanwhile, Biggy and Itchy are with Mr. Mad, who orders them to kidnap Odie.

King & Odie #98 *Go and Catch a Falling King* .2/8/64
   Part 2: Synopsis unavailable.

King & Odie #99 *Royal Rodeo* *. 2/15/64
   Part 1: Leonardo wants the people of Bongo Congo to be even happier, so Odie suggests having a rodeo. Nobody is entering the cowboy contest so Biggy and Itchy do, and use Professor Messer to help them win. It turns out that Itchy will win because no one has entered, so Leonardo decides to enter as well. Note: This episode is available on DVD on *The Ultimate Underdog Collection Volume 3*.

King & Odie #100 *Ride 'em Cowboy* * 2/22/64
   Part 2: At last it is time for the great spectacle in Buffalo Bill's Wild West Wingding. They do a bucking bronco contest, roping and steer throwing. Itchy wins everything until he is caught cheating. Leonardo wins. Note: This episode is available on DVD on *The Ultimate Underdog Collection Volume 3*.

King & Odie #101 *S. O. Essex Calling* 2/29/64
   Part 1: Synopsis unavailable.

King & Odie #102 *The Big Falling Out* 3/7/64
   Part 2: Synopsis unavailable.

King & Odie #103 *Long Days Journey Into Fright* 3/14/64
   Part 3: Synopsis unavailable.

King & Odie #104 Making A Monkey Shine. .3/21/64
   Part 4: Synopsis unavailable.

OPENING AND CLOSING

The cast sings the theme song describing themselves and their show. There are two versions of this, one with the General Mills mentions from the original network airings and the syndicated versions *sans* any sponsor mention. The closing has more of the same and the lengthiest credit role of any TTV show.

There is also a version of this when it went into syndication as *The King and Odie Show* with a different version of the theme song and everyone in a conga line.

Opening: A quick history of Bongo Congo mentioning the chief industry being the manufacture of bongo drums, the principle product of the kingdom.

Bumpers: "Confound it, it's a TV set."

Here comes Leonardo,
Leonardo Lion,
King of Bongo Congo,
A hero lion or iron.

Where Leonardo travels
His subjects all go, too
There's Odie O. Colognie,
The Fox and Hunter, too.

Toonerville and Wizard,
They're ready set to go,
So, everyone come join the fun
On King Leonardo's show!

TOOTER TURTLE
(39 EPISODES)

FIRST SEASON: 10/15/60-4/8/61
NBC (AS PART OF *KING LEONARDO AND HIS SHORT SUBJECTS*)
(52 EPISODES, 2 PER SHOW)

Tooter Turtle #1 *Two Gun Turtle* *............................10/15/60
   Tooter wants to be a cowboy as Mr. Wizard the Lizard typically protests against. As sheriff, Tooter battles Black Bark. Note: A recurring gag is a man walking through the scene yelling, "Mr. Melon, oh Mr. Melon," a parody of the character Chester from *Gunsmoke* yelling, "Mr. Dillon." Tooter calls for Mr. Wizard when he ends up at the wrong side of a gun.

Tooter Turtle #2 *Tailspin Tooter* or *Plane Failure* *...............10/22/60
   Tooter wants to be a fighter pilot in WWI. His assignment is to bring down the German Messerschmitts and the Black Baron, but when his plane gets in trouble, Tooter calls for Mr. Wizard. Note: This episode available on DVD on *The Underdog Chronicles*.

Tooter Turtle #3 *Sea Haunt* *...............................10/29/60
   Tooter is hankering for adventure in the briny deep. A woman calls Tooter the "Sea Haunter" to rescue her brother at the bottom of the ocean. Tooter makes many attempts trying to rescue the brother, but encounters torpedoes, dynamite and giant sea creatures. The brother is rescued, but is a troublemaker, so more explosions occur after he's rescued causing Tooter to cry for help. Note: This episode is a sort of take-off on *Sea Hunt*, a popular show on at the time starring Lloyd Bridges.

Tooter Turtle #4 *Highway Petrol* or *Road Blockhead* *..............11/5/60
   "I want to be a highway petrol man," claims Tooter, so Mr. Wizard complies. He patrols the highway in his car #44444 with a lot of "Roger" jokes. Tooter is on the hunt for a Roger Schmodger. He finds the hideout, but the only thing inside is a bundle of dynamite, which explodes. Afterwards, Tooter calls all of the other squad cars to the intersection that he's at and they all crash into him, prompting Tooter to call for Mr. Wizard.

Tooter Turtle #5 *Knight of the Square Table* or *the Joust and the Unjoust* *
....11/12/60
   Tooter wants to be Sir Laffalot de Puddle, a Knight of the Square Table, and Mr. Wizard complies. Tooter goes through various chivalrous events, such as

jousting. Tooter keeps getting thrown from his horse and is almost disqualified. Finally, Tooter engages in swordplay, but calls for Mr. Wizard just as he's going to be sliced in two.

Tooter Turtle #6 *Mish-Mash-Mush* or *Panting For Gold* *..........11/19/60

Tooter wants to be a prospector. He goes to the bar to order lemonade and is told that there is no gold. Turns out not to be true, so Tooter takes out a dogsled to the mountains. On the way, Tooter causes an avalanche, but survives. He also survives claim jumpers but calls Mr. Wizard when he runs his dog team off the cliff.

Tooter Turtle #7 *The Unteachables* or *The Lawless Years* *...........11/26/60

Tooter wants to be an FBI Unteachable (Untouchable). At one point Tooter gets trapped, causing him to cry for help.

Tooter Turtle #8 *Kink Of Swat* or *Babe Rube* *....................12/3/60

Tooter wants to be a big baseball player. He thinks he's good enough for the team, but Mr. Wizard warns about the Manager. The Manager puts Tooter through all the paces during training practice. Now, it was time for the big game. During his time at bat, Tooter swings too hard and hurls himself into space, calling for Mr. Wizard.

Tooter Turtle #9 *One Trillion B.C.* or *Dinosaur Dope* *.............12/10/60

Tooter comes in carrying a big stone and wants to be a caveman. Wizard narrates about the Stone Age man swinging through the trees and caring for his kid and his nagging wife, and capturing a dinosaur for dinner. Catching a dinosaur is not as easy as it looks. Finally, caveman Tooter succeeds, but not before he's almost eaten by a T. Rex.

Tooter Turtle #10 *Olimping Champion* or *Weak-Greek* *............12/17/60

Tooter asks Mr. Wizard to send him back through time to the days of ancient Greece to perform in the original Olympics.

Tooter Turtle #11 *Stuper Man* or *Muscle Bounder* *...............12/24/60

Tooter practices to be a bodybuilder and feels that he can be a superhero. As Stuperman, Tooter can fly. He also appears disguised as mild-mannered Cluck Kent. Lois Loon tries to help him out by tipping him off about crime, but Stuperman keeps bringing in the wrong people and messing up. Shades of Underdog! Finally, Tooter gets in so much trouble with sneezing powder that he calls for Mr. Wizard.

Tooter Turtle #12 *Buffaloed Bill* or *Custard's Last Stand* * 12/31/60

Tooter wants to be a scout like Buffalo Bill, leading a cavalry unit. Wizard warns to watch out for the Indians. General Custard sends Tooter to scout the territory, but, of course, the Injuns cause Tooter to cry for help.

Tooter Turtle #13 *Moon Goon* or *Space Head* * 1/7/61

Tooter wants to fly to the moon and be a "Space Head." Tooter successfully lands on the moon and starts exploring. When he discovers a moon monster, Tooter cries out for Mr. Wizard.

Tooter Turtle #14 *Robin Hoodwink* or *Thimple Thief* * 1/14/61

Tooter desires to be Robin Hoodwink (Robin Hood) but promptly gets stuck with an arrow. He wants to rob from the rich and give to the poor. Of course, he gets trapped with a shower of arrows and asks to be sent home.

Tooter Turtle #15 *Steamboat Stupe* or *Captains Outrageous* * 1/21/61

Tooter wants to be a riverboat captain. Mr. Wizard recommends that Tooter be a turtle boy. It takes strength and practice to become a good riverboat captain. Tooter does a race against Big Blackie Bart. Tooter's miscalculations cause him to come home.

Tooter Turtle #16 *Souse Painter* or *Brush-Boob* * 1/28/61

Tooter wants to do painting and decorating. Finally, Mr. Wizard agrees that this may be a safe job, but warns Tooter to do a good job. Tooter has a helper and somehow gets more paint on himself than on the house. His helper is no help at all and Tooter gets in trouble with the person whose house they're redecorating.

Tooter Turtle #17 *Railroad Engineer* or *Stupefied Jones* * 2/4/61

Tooter wants to be a railroad engineer. Amazingly, Mr. Wizard approves of the idea and lets Tooter become one. Everything is fine until a mishap with the engine, that causes it to fly through the air, causes Tooter to want to come back home.

Tooter Turtle #18 *Quarterback Hack* or *Pigskinned* *. 2/11/61

Tooter is a major football fan and desires to play football. He does fine until a big kickoff causes him to ask Mr. Wizard to bring him home. Note: This episode is available on DVD on *Underdog Nemesis*.

Tooter Turtle #19 *Drafthead* or *Overwhere?* * .2/18/61

Tooter wants to join the Army and Mr. Wizard helps him out. Tooter goes through boot camp training, but once he engages in real battle, he calls for help. Note: This episode is available on DVD on *The Ultimate Underdog Collection Volume 2*.

Tooter Turtle #20 *Lumber-Quack* or *Topped* * 2/25/61
    Lumberquacks (lumberjacks) have a hard job, but Tooter wants to be one. Tooter keeps up with arm wrestling with Pierre Le Barque and also chopping down mighty trees. After his training, Tooter is on his own, but he has no strength for any of this. Then, Pierre and Tooter do logrolling and also send chopped logs down the chute. The logs sometimes get jammed and dynamite has to be used to free it up, but a call goes out for Mr. Wizard when the explosion goes awry.

Tooter Turtle #21 *Jerky Jockey* or *Kenducky Derby* * 3/4/61
    Mr. Wizard is trying to talk Tooter out of being a jockey, but it doesn't work. Tooter races on the horses until he sinks into some quicksand and calls for help.

Tooter Turtle #22 *Fired Fireman* or *Hook and Batter* * 3/11/61
    Tooter wants to be a fireman this time. Tooter is assigned to steer the back end of the fire truck, but isn't very good at it. They finally get to the fire and Tooter is told to run up many flights of stairs to save a small boy. He tries but fails, then uses the extension ladder to try again. The kid goes down with another fireman and Tooter is trapped in the burning building, calling for Mr. Wizard.

Tooter Turtle #23 *Sky Diver* or *Jump, Jerk, Jump…!* * 3/18/61
    Tooter wants to be a skydiver. Mr. Wizard advises Tooter to be a stamp collector, but Tooter persists. As a skydiver, Tooter practices landing before going up in a plane. Then he practices with his parachute. After continually falling and crashing, Tooter gets fed up and cries for Mr. Wizard.

Tooter Turtle #24 *Tuesday Turtle* or *Private Pie* * 3/25/61
    Tooter wants to be one of those real detective fellers. As Tuesday Turtle, Tooter is sent on the hunt to find a pie thief. The pie thief is also a pie thrower. Finally, a few are caught for a police line-up. The guilty party hurls a pie with a bomb in it, prompting Tooter to call for help. Note: This almost seems like a *Hunter* episode.

Tooter Turtle #25 *Snafu Safari* or *Trackdown Tooter* * 4/1/61
    Tooter wants to be a big game hunter. Tooter puts on the proper equipment and heads out to the jungle. After some snakes and crocodiles, Tooter has had enough.

Tooter Turtle #26 *Anti-Arctic* or *North Pole Nuisance* *..............4/8/61
Tooter wants to be an Arctic explorer despite Lizard's protests. Tooter goes to the North Pole via ship and then hiking. On the way Tooter builds an igloo and paddles a kayak. An angry polar bear brings Tooter home.

SECOND SEASON: 9/30/61-12/23/61
NBC (AS PART OF *KING LEONARDO AND HIS SHORT SUBJECTS*) (13 EPISODES)

Tooter Turtle #27 *The Master Builder* or *Rivet Riot* *...............9/30/61
Tooter claims he will no longer try to be something he is not, and says he's going to get a real job…as a construction worker! He works on building a high skyscraper with rivets and jackhammers. After getting in a fight with the foreman, he falls off the skyscraper and calls Mr. Wizard just in time.

Tooter Turtle #28 *Taxi Turtle* or *My Flag is Down* *...............10/7/61
Tooter wants to be a taxi driver, but Wizard warns against this, too. After a series of misadventures, Tooter finally gets a fare in his "Tooter Taxi," but gets into an accident. Later, Tooter proves he can maneuver through heavy traffic. Tooter calls for help when he stops paying attention to the traffic rules and goes the wrong way on a one-way street.

Tooter Turtle #29 *Canned Camera* or *Peek a Boob* *...............10/14/61
Tooter wants to make movies of people like on *Candid Camera*. At first, Tooter smashes a watch and pretends that it's the antique watch of a customer. The customer beats up Tooter until Tooter reveals that he's on hidden camera. Next, Tooter hides in a cannon and says he's a talking cannon, but the plan backfires. Finally, Tooter flies in a plane and pretends to hijack the plane while filming, but the angry crowd tosses Tooter out of the plane and a call goes out for Mr. Wizard.

Tooter Turtle #30 *Muddled Mountie* or *One, Two, Buckle My Snowshoe* *
....10/21/61
Tooter rides a horse on a stick as he wants to be a Canadian Royal Mountie. There is a test to see if Tooter is ready and after getting whacked by a number of paddles, he is ready to get his man, Black Bark. There is so much snow; it is hard to chase Bark, who rolls a giant snowball down on Tooter. Tooter still doesn't give up. He grabs what he thinks is Bark, but is really a snowman in disguise and while falling, calls for Mr. Wizard.

Tooter Turtle #31 *Duck Haunter* or *Decoy Drip* *.................10/28/61
   Tooter desires to be a duck hunter. Lizard tries as usual to talk him out of it. Of course, Tooter finds himself in a mess and asks to be brought back home.

Tooter Turtle #32 *Bull Fright* or *Olay Down* *.....................11/4/61
   Tooter wants to be a bullfighter until he realizes how mean and nasty bulls really are.

Tooter Turtle #33 *News Nuisance* or *Sub Scribe* *.................11/11/61
   Tooter comes into Mr. Wizard's home flashing pictures and blinding Mr. Wizard. Wizard changes him into a newspaper photographer, and his editor sends him out on the beat to get some pictures. Tooter gets caught up with volleying flagpoles and doesn't get the photo. Ultimately, his paparazzi ways gets him thrown in jail. Note: This episode is available on DVD on *The Ultimate Underdog Collection Volume 1*.

Tooter Turtle #34 *The Sheep of Araby* or *Beau Geste Goes West* *.......11/18/61
   Tooter wants to join the foreign legion. As a legionnaire, Tooter gets lost in the desert and sees a mirage. Soon, Tooter is captured by Arabs, but when Tooter is told he is to be beheaded, he calls for Mr. Wizard.

Tooter Turtle #35 *Waggin' Train* or *California Bust* *..............11/25/61
   Tooter sings "California, Here I Come" in Mr. Wizard's house and wants to be a wagon master in the days of the Wild West. Tooter engages in a Wild West fight with Big John and then leads the wagons on the best trail — off a cliff! Later, with an Indian attack, the wagons are formed into a circle. Finally, they end up in California…or do they? When they find out they're in Chicago, a call goes out for Mr. Wizard.

Tooter Turtle #36 *Anchors Awry* or *Nautical Nut* *.................12/2/61
   Tooter sings "Sailing, Sailing" and wants to be a sailor in the days of the old sailing ships. Tooter is referred to as Mr. Blister in this story. The ship rocks so much that Mr. Blister keeps spilling food and garbage everywhere. Finally, he gets to weigh anchor and raise the main sail. After causing more trouble, the captain orders Mr. Blister overboard, prompting Tooter's usual call for help. Note: This episode is available on DVD on *The Ultimate Underdog Collection Volume 2*.

Tooter Turtle #37 *Vaudevillain* or *Song and Dunce Man* *...........12/9/61
   Mr. Wizard is setting down to watch *You Want to be a Star*. Tooter wants to be a song-and-dance man. He tries to get a good agent. The agent is trying to

determine Tooter's talent and Tooter claims that he's a dancer, but he's no good at that either. The agent makes him "Moon Shot, the Singing Banjo Player." That doesn't work, so they try making Tooter a rodeo singer, but he's soon bucked from his horse. Tooter attempts, one more try as Daryl Devil, singing and hanging upside down from an airplane, but someone shoots at Tooter, and that's the end of his show-business career. Note: This episode is available on DVD on *The Ultimate Underdog Collection Volume 3*.

Tooter Turtle #38 *Rod and Reeling* or *Field & Scream* * 12/16/61

Tooter shows Mr. Wizard that he's good at casting and wants to become a fisherman. He does all of the typical fishing stuff like fishing from a boat and everything, but when Tooter catches a huge fish and heads over a waterfall, he calls for Mr. Wizard. Note: This episode is available on DVD on *The Ultimate Underdog Collection Volume 1*.

Tooter Turtle #39 *The Man in the Blue Denim Suit* or *Hay! Hay!* * 12/23/61

Tooter goes to Mr. Wizard to become a farmer thinking that life will be easy. Wizard warns him that it is hard work and he is right and soon Tooter is calling for help.

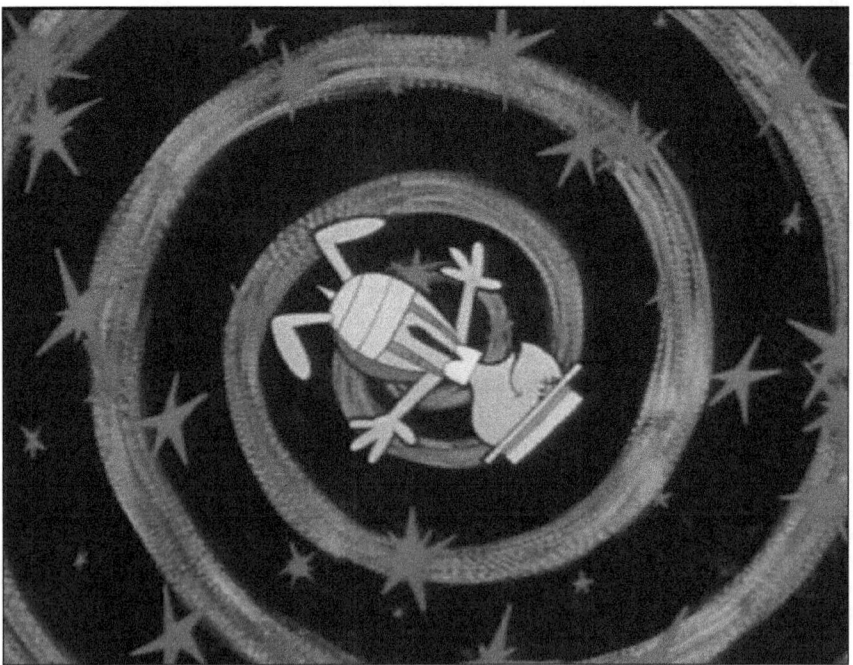

"...Drizzle druzzle drazzle drone. Time for this one to come home."

OPENING AND CLOSING

Bumper: King Leonard and Odie are trying to guess what Tooter will be in his next episode. ("Believe me, Tooter, I am certain you wouldn't be happy as king.")

Opening:
Tooter: Deep in the forest grows a tall tall tree,
Of course it was a short tree, but it, uh, grew.
And down at the bottom of that tree is a little old box
That's really the home of Mr. Wizard the Lizard.
(*knocks*)
Lizard: (wakes up) Yes, who is that?
Tooter: It's Tooter the Turtle, Mr. Wizard.
I've got another favor to ask.
Lizard: Come in, come in, my boy.

Closing:
Tooter: Gee, Mr. Wizard, I guess I made a mess out of things again.
Wizard: (laughs) Always, always I tell you, Tooter:
Be just what you is,
Not what you is not,
Folks who do this,
Is the happiest lot.

(The theme song has no lyrics.)

CREATED AND PRODUCED BY TOTAL TELEVISION PRODUCTIONS

THE HUNTER
(65 EPISODES)

FIRST SEASON: 10/15/60-4/8/61
NBC (AS PART OF *KING LEONARDO AND HIS SHORT SUBJECTS*)
(26 EPISODES)

The Hunter #1 *Brookloined Bridge* *...........................10/15/60
In New York City, the Brooklyn Bridge has been stolen. It is concluded that The Fox has stolen it and a call goes out for The Hunter. The Hunter starts making calls, little knowing that The Fox is hiding in his own Wanted poster, and knocks The Hunter on the head. The Hunter searches around for more clues to the whereabouts of the bridge, and drives across the water when there's no bridge. The Fox, meanwhile, reconstructs the missing bridge and literally bumps into The Hunter, who takes him off to jail. Note: This episode is available on DVD on *The Underdog Chronicles* and *The Ultimate Underdog Collection Volume 1*.

The Hunter #2 *Counterfeit Wants* *...........................10/22/60
The Hunter is on the prowl for a desperate criminal, but stops for a cup of tea. He takes in a kindly old grandmother, but is soon set free. It turns out The Fox is making fake Wanted posters and innocent people are being caught. The Fox impersonates a cop putting up the posters, and Flim Flanagan arrests him for impersonation.

The Hunter #3 *Haunted Hunter* *...........................10/29/60
The Fox stumbles on a Civil War treasure map stating that there is a treasure hidden in City Hall. On top of that, the employees of City Hall feel that it is haunted. Meanwhile, The Hunter is upset with a new driving law and so goes to City Hall to complain. He gets in the way of The Fox who has been haunting the place and looking for the treasure. Police go to City Hall to investigate the ghostly explosions and Flim Flanagan sees that The Hunter has once again inadvertently caught The Fox. Note: This episode is available on *The Ultimate Underdog Collection Volume 2*.

The Hunter #4 *Fort Knox Fox* *...........................11/5/60
The Fox disguises himself as a 10-star General and steals all of the gold in Fort Knox. A call goes out to Officer Flim Flanagan, who says that The Fox has stolen the gold and only The Hunter can capture The Fox, which he does. At the end of the episode, President Dwight D. Eisenhower makes a cameo appearance

asking Flim Flanagan who the hero is. Note: This episode is available on DVD on *Underdog Nemesis* and on *The Ultimate Underdog Collection Volume 2*.

The Hunter #5 *Stealing a March* * 11/12/60
The Hunter and Flim Flanagan are looking forward to the annual St. Patrick's Day Parade, but there isn't any. The Hunter goes on a search for the missing parade and its music. The Fox is selling the stolen music, but is captured by a pile of sheet music.

The Hunter #6 *Horn-a-Plenty* * 11/19/60
The Fox plots to steal the Hunter's horn and succeeds. Officer Flim Flanigan helps him get it back.

The Hunter #7 *Concrete Crook* * 11/26/60
Cement trucks are disappearing everywhere. No cement means roads and sidewalks go unfinished and so a call goes out for The Hunter. Of course, it is The Fox who's using the cement trucks to mix ice cream. The unsuspecting Hunter can't figure out at first that the ice-cream trucks are really the missing cement trucks, but eventually he figures it out and catches The Fox.

The Hunter #8 *Subtracted Submarine* * 12/3/60
The giant atomic submarine Hautilus has been stolen, so they call in Officer Flim Flanagan, who calls in The Hunter to get The Fox. Meanwhile, The Hunter needs a vacation and goes into Oxfay Travel Agency to book a trip somewhere. The Fox suggests a cruise, which just happens to be on the stolen submarine. While The Fox steers, The Hunter happens to get caught on the outside, making it hard to see, and he must surface. He is now seen by Flim Flanagan, who takes The Fox away.

The Hunter #9 *Risky Ransom* * 12/10/60
The Hunter picks up his mail in his office, which informs him that his nephew Horrors Hunter will be staying with him. Hunter tries to hide before Horrors shows up, but is unable to get away. Horrors is truly a pain in the neck, but The Fox kidnaps him anyway. The Fox ends up mailing Horrors back and gets caught at the post Office. Note: This is the first appearance of Horrors Hunter.

The Hunter #10 *Unfaithful Old Faithful* * 12/17/60
All the world's reservoirs are stolen and Flim Flanagan sends The Hunter on the case. He finds The Fox selling hot water at inflated prices.

The Hunter #11 *The Armored Car Coup* * 12/24/60
The Hunter goes on a fishing trip when armored cars start disappearing. Flim

Flanagan goes to California to find Hunter. The Hunter insists on staying on vacation, but Flanagan doesn't give up and finally Hunter agrees to search for the Fox. Finally, he discovers the Fox selling the armored cars as well-constructed homes. His duty done, Hunter wants to go back to California.

The Hunter #12 *Telephone Poltergeist* * 12/31/60

The Hunter is desperately trying to call San Francisco. He can't get through, so he calls LA to check up on SF. It turns out that nothing's wrong with SF or LA; there's something wrong with the telephone system. Every telephone pole in the country has been stolen by The Fox. The Hunter is searching for clues at a Pole Vaulting Contest and a May Pole Dance, but these are all dead ends. The Fox is found selling cut-rate log cabins using the poles that he has stolen. After a scuffle and explosion, The Fox is caught.

The Hunter #13 *Sheepish Shamus* * 1/7/61

The Fox has stolen a great many things and now has stolen all the sheep in the US. He shrinks the sheep and sells them to people who need to count sheep to sleep. The Hunter is set on the trail and puts on a sheepskin in order to get caught by the Fox and succeeds in getting back all the stolen sheep.

The Hunter #14 *Rustler Hustler* * 1/14/61

This time buffalo are being stolen by the Fox. Officer Flim Flanagan is called to contact the Hunter. Hunter rides to the desert on a horse and meets the Fox disguised as an Indian. As per usual, the Hunter inadvertently catches the Fox just as Flim Flanagan arrives.

The Hunter #15 *The Case of the Missing Muenster* * 1/21/61

The Hunter wants cheese on his sandwich, but there's no cheese to be found. Cheese had been stolen all over the country, so Flim Flanagan calls in the Hunter to solve the case. Hunter feels that a mouse stole the cheese so he builds a trap. It turns out that the Fox has stolen the cheese and is selling it as part of the moon. The mousetrap becomes a Fox trap.

The Hunter #16 *The Great Train Robbery* * 1/28/61

The Fox steals a train and it's the Hunter on the trail. He goes to the roundhouse and gets run over, but finally catches up with him. The Hunter inadvertently brings in the Fox by rowing the train back home across the ocean.

The Hunter #17 *Florida Fraud* * 2/4/61

The Hunter takes a vacation in Florida. The Fox sabotages this by claiming that Martians are invading to get everyone to leave the state. The Hunter goes to investigate and finds a Martian, who is actually The Fox in disguise. After that, The Fox steals the entire state of Florida and makes it his own island resort. Flim Flanagan orders The Hunter to go to Atlanta, Georgia, to investigate. The Hunter finds The Fox and everything is put back in order.

The Hunter #18 *The Great Plane Robbery* * 2/11/61

Somebody has stolen an airplane, and, of course, Flim Flanagan accuses The Fox. The Hunter, meanwhile, is on a duck-hunting vacation. The Fox convinces The Hunter to take the plane up where the ducks are. The Hunter shoots a machine gun at the ducks and soon there is a shower of Mallard ducks on the ground. The Hunter keeps shooting and wrecks the plane. They crash-land just in time of Flanagan's arrival and they capture The Fox.

The Hunter #19 *Girl Friday* * 2/18/61

The Hunter's paperwork has been piling up, so he places an ad for a secretary in the paper. The Fox, in disguise, answers the ad to help, and throws The Hunter's paperwork out of the window. The Fox also takes dictation and now knows all of The Hunter's personal business. They send a letter to Flim Flanagan who arrives just in time to see The Fox's costume fall off. Note: This episode is available on DVD on *The Ultimate Underdog Collection Volume 3*.

The Hunter #20 *Stamp Stickup* * 2/25/61

A boy named Bill comes home to work on his stamp collection, but he is not alone. Stamps are stolen across the country. Mr. Phil Attely issues a statement and Flim Flanagan assigns The Hunter to the case. He starts looking at the post office, but keeps getting referred to the next window and doesn't get anywhere. As usual, it is The Fox who stole the stamps for his used-stamp lot, a cut-rate post office. The Hunter meets up with him and firmly shakes his hand and shakes off The Fox's costume. He is then captured.

The Hunter #21 *Statue of Liberty Play* * 3/4/61

The wily Fox has pulled a caper long before David Copperfield did. He has stolen the Statue of Liberty and the President of the United States puts out a call for The Hunter. Hunter reasons that The Fox can't hide a statue that big very well. Hunter accuses Honest Sam the Souvenir Man and Flim Flanagan says that he's not the thief. The Hunter takes the case to cold Crussia and there he finds The Fox selling Liberty to the Crussians and arrests him.

The Hunter #22 *Frankfurter Fix* * 3/11/61

At the baseball stadium, there is a rash of frankfurter thefts. Flim Flanagan sends the Hunter to Hankie Stadium as a hot dog vendor to capture the culprit whom he suspects to be the Fox. Hunter goes to Frankfort, Germany, to find the villain, but is sent home. He finally discovers the Fox selling hot dogs, and captures him. The Fox has the last laugh by giving Hunter an exploding dog (dynamite).

The Hunter #23 *The Case of the Missing Mowers* * 3/18/61
    The Hunter is weary from the recent ice-cream caper and is coming back from his vacation to see tall grass out in front of his house. There are no lawnmowers to be found and Flim Flanagan sends The Hunter to find The Fox. Hunter questions Flanagan about what a mower sounds like to help him find the mowers. Hunter confuses other motors for that of mowers. Hunter finally meets up with The Fox who has taken the mowers for his go-carts.

The Hunter #24 *Fancy Fencing* * 3/25/61
    Officer Flim Flanagan is overworked as a wave of disappearances hits the town. He calls the Hunter for help and he knows that the Fox has been behind it. The Fox is selling fencing made from old jail cells. Meanwhile, the Hunter is tied up learning how to fence. As usual, he inadvertently catches the Fox with one of his fences.

The Hunter #25 *Raquet Racket* * 4/1/61
    All tennis racquets in the country have been stolen by the Fox. A call is made for the Hunter. The Hunter goes to the tennis court for some clues. In the end the Hunter succeeds as usual.

The Hunter #26 *Seeing Stars* * 4/8/61
    The giant telescope at the observatory has been stolen and a call goes out for The Hunter by Flim Flanagan. The Fox sets up the stolen telescope on a hill in New Jersey to charge people to take peaks at New York. The Hunter takes a peak into the telescope and sees Flanagan in a helicopter. As he comes into town, The Fox is captured and Flanagan thinks The Hunter did it.

SECOND SEASON: 9/30/61-12/23/61
NBC (AS PART OF *KING LEONARDO AND HIS SHORT SUBJECTS*)
(13 EPISODES)

The Hunter #27 *Elevator Escapade* * 9/30/61
    The Fox has stolen every elevator in the city and The Hunter is put on the trail. He finds The Fox selling homes that rise up and down and, of course, puts the clamp on him when Flim Flanagan arrives.

The Hunter #28 *Hula Hoop Havoc* *.............................10/7/61
Hula-hoops are really popular, then no longer, but the remaining hula-hoops in storage have been stolen by The Fox, so it's The Hunter to the rescue. After making some mistaken accusations, like looking at hula dancers and a tiger tamer using hoops, The Hunter gets taken by The Fox to his ring toss game and, of course, gets caught.

The Hunter #29 *The Counterfeit Newspaper Caper* *................10/14/61
R.E. Hearse reads a copy of his own newspaper and realizes that it is a counterfeit newspaper. Newspapers have been stolen across country and counterfeit papers replaced. Flim Flanagan calls out for The Hunter. Hunter is sniffing out the case and finds a fish salesman who wraps their fish in newspapers. Meanwhile, The Fox buys worthless stock and prints in his counterfeit newspaper that the stocks are booming. The Hunter sees the moving news headlines on the building and finds they are faked and soon catches The Fox in the stock exchange.

The Hunter #30 *Diamond Dither* *............................10/21/61
Jewelry stores and wealthy people with jewels are having their diamonds stolen, so a call goes out to Officer Flim Flanagan who calls The Hunter to get The Fox. Meanwhile, The Fox is selling diamond glasscutters. The Fox demonstrates on The Hunter's glasses (who is in disguise) and he catches The Fox.

The Hunter #31 *Grand Canyon Caper* *........................10/28/61
The Grand Canyon is missing and there is nothing left but water. The Hunter is on the trail only to discover that the US Army has taken over his case. It turns out that it was The Fox who filled up the Grand Canyon and renamed it Lost Canyon Lake. This time The Hunter actually catches The Fox and locks him away.

The Hunter #32 *Borrowed Beachland* *.........................11/4/61
Sam is proud of his beach and The Hunter goes out to sun bathe, but finds it missing when he gets there. The Hunter says not to cry, he will return the beach. He and Sam go on the hunt and The Hunter gets caught in the machinery of a sandpaper factory (among other things). They still are on the trail for the beach sand, when they come across The Fox selling sand for a sandlot baseball game. The Fox is soon caught by The Hunter.

The Hunter #33 *Peek-a-Boo Pyramids* *........................11/11/61
The Hunter flies to Egypt as soon as he hears the theft of the great pyramids. He lands at an "X" that turns out to be a railroad crossing. He escapes just in

time. He then gets a camel to look for The Fox. He finally arrives at a sphinx and gives it a kick. The Fox, in disguise, tries to sell The Hunter some bricks when his disguise comes off when Flim Flanagan arrives.

The Hunter #34 *Lincoln Tunnel Caper* *. 11/18/61

Everyday tons of traffic goes through the Lincoln Tunnel until one day the tunnel is missing. A call goes out for The Hunter. The Hunter looks for the tunnel underwater. Meanwhile, it turns out that The Fox has moved the tunnel to the Pennsylvania Turnpike and is starting to make money as most people wouldn't know there is another toll road. There are so many of them already. The Hunter drives on the Turnpike and he searches frantically for a quarter for the toll and in the scuffle discovers that it is The Fox running the tollbooth and arrests him.

The Hunter #35 *TV Terror* *. 11/25/61

In every home, television sets are disappearing everywhere, causing chaos. Flim Flanagan is sure that it is the work of The Fox, so a call goes out to The Hunter. On the hunt, The Hunter takes an antenna as evidence, causing a small child to wonder what is going on on the roof. The Hunter then arrests everyone at the movie theater. Finally, The Hunter finds wall-to-wall TVs for sale at a new housing development, which just happens to be sold by The Fox. The Hunter inadvertently catches The Fox again.

The Hunter #36 *Bye Bye Bell* *. 12/2/61

The Fox perpetrates a crime in Philadelphia when he steals the Liberty Bell. Everyone is searching and The Hunter is put on the case. He searches for bells in various locations. He gets caught up in a clock tower. Meanwhile, counterfeit Liberty Bells are being created by The Fox, so they would think they are returning the actual bell. Everything is working fine until The Hunter is sold a bell and he captures The Fox.

The Hunter #37 *Time Marches Out* *. 12/9/61

Clocks and watches are being stolen by (guess who?) the Fox. Flim Flanagan calls in the Hunter, who gets on the trail and captures the Fox in record time.

The Hunter #38 *Fox's Foul Play*. 12/16/61

Synopsis unavailable.

The Hunter #39 *Bow Wow Blues* *. 12/23/61

Snow is falling in the city and then crimes start happening. People's dogs are being stolen and so The Hunter is put on the case. The Hunter's nephew Horrors drops by and wants to help find the dognapper. Horrors has brought a trained flea. Flim Flanagan warns that the snow is really deep. Meanwhile, The Fox is renting dog sleds, but soon the flea causes all the dogs to escape. The Fox is then caught, and The Hunter catches the flea.

THIRD SEASON: 9/28/63-3/21/64
CBS (AS PART OF *TENNESSEE TUXEDO AND HIS TALES*)
(26 EPISODES)

The Hunter #40 *Breaking in Big* * 9/28/63

The Hunter is locked out of the office by his nephew Horrors. As it is April Fool's Day, Horrors decides to play with The Hunter and not allow him back into the office. Meanwhile, the phone is ringing and The Hunter desperately tries to get in. When he finally does, he realizes that the ringing phone was also an April Fool's Day prank.

The Hunter #41 *The Bank Dicks* * 10/5/63

The Hunter and Horrors are told to guard a bank on the day The Fox is supposed to plan a robbery there. The Hunter shows Horrors how to guard, but he messes everything up. Meanwhile, The Fox arrives in costume and The Hunter shows The Fox the vault. Horrors sees through the costume and an arrest is made.

The Hunter #42 *Eye on the Ball* 10/12/63
Synopsis unavailable.

The Hunter #43 *Breakout at Breakrock* * 10/19/63

The Fox escapes Breakrock Prison and vows revenge on The Hunter. He follows The Hunter and Horrors to their summer cabin and emulates Goldilocks and the Three Bears. The Hunter and Horrors start looking for Goldilocks, thinking she is messing up their house. The Fox then dresses up as a ghost and chases the duo until they bump into Flim Flanagan who makes an arrest.

The Hunter #44 *Getting the Business* 10/26/63
Synopsis unavailable.

The Hunter #45 *An Uncommon Cold* * 11/2/63

Horrors is told to take cookies to his sick Uncle Hunter. The Fox tries in vain to stop Horrors. They go through the whole Red Riding Hood bit, but eventually the Fox is captured.

The Hunter #46 *The Pickpocket Pickle* * 11/9/63

The Fox picks pockets at an amusement park and then sets up his own carnival game with the stolen wallets as prizes. The Hunter arrives and gets his wallet stolen, which is on the end of a long line so that he can follow The Fox. The Fox realizes what The Hunter has done and winds the string through a number of places in the park, including the shooting gallery and the fun house. Finally, the string leads to a hole, which The Hunter puts his head through. People start throwing baseballs at his head. The Hunter sees The Fox and gets so angry he crashes through the wall and arrests him.

The Hunter #47 *Goofy Guarding* * 11/16/63

Horrors Hunter is back in town and causing havoc once again. The Hunter is called to find The Fox in a department store, and Horrors insists on coming. The Hunter hides in a washing machine in the store and Horrors innocently starts it. Meanwhile, The Fox arrives and steals diamonds dressed as a little old lady. He is defeated when Horrors runs him over. Note: This episode is available on DVD on *The Ultimate Underdog Collection Volume 3*.

The Hunter #48 *The Big Birthday Blast* * 11/23/63

The Fox steals all the dynamite in the city and then sells the dynamite as party favors. Horrors wanders into the store and buys the party favors for his Uncle Hunter's party. After The Hunter blows up, he drags Horrors back to the shop to complain. The Fox gives The Hunter a cigar and before he can light it, The Hunter discovers that he is The Fox and turns him in to Flim Flanagan.

The Hunter #49 *Under the Spreading Treasure Tree* * 11/30/63

The Hunter and Horrors camp under The Fox's Treasure Tree, a hollowed-out tree that contains all of The Fox's stolen goods, which are discovered after Horrors saws the tree down. The Hunter and Horrors also have a run-in with a bear.

The Hunter #50 *School Days, Fool Days* 12/7/63

Synopsis unavailable.

The Hunter #51 *Fall of the House of the Hunter* * 12/14/63

The Fox is stealing birdbaths. The Hunter and Horrors don't want theirs stolen, so they build a house around it. Like The Three Little Pigs, they go through hay, sticks and then bricks. The Fox plays along like the wolf in the story and blows down everything but the bricks. The Hunter then blows his horn and the bricks rain down on The Fox.

The Hunter #52 *Oyster Stew* 12/21/63

Synopsis unavailable.

The Hunter #53 *The Stolen Spoon Saga* 12/28/63
   Synopsis unavailable.

The Hunter #54 *Under Par* 1/4/64
   Synopsis unavailable.

The Hunter #55 *Chew Gum Charlie*. 1/11/64
   Synopsis unavailable.

The Hunter #56 *Using the Ole Bean* *. 1/18/64
   The Fox has been stealing beans and sets up a stand where he claims that they are "magic beans" just like in Jack and the Beanstalk. Meanwhile, The Hunter has been kicked out of his office because he hasn't been paying his rent and sends Horrors to spend their last dollar on food for them. Horrors buys some of the beans and The Hunter angrily goes back to The Fox who convinces him that they are "magic beans." The next morning, The Fox has painted a telephone pole green and claims that it is a beanstalk. The Hunter climbs up but the pole soon falls, smashing The Fox's bean stand in the process.

The Hunter #57 *The Case of the Hunted Hunter* * 1/25/64
   The Fox dons a "Hunter" suit and commits crimes while he's dressed as him. Flim Flanagan and everyone else think The Hunter has gone crooked and he's thrown in jail. Horrors believe his uncle is innocent and sets about to clear his name and get him released.

The Hunter #58 *The Purloined Piano Puzzle* * 2/1/64
   The Hunter insists that Horrors needs to practice the piano every day. One day all the pianos are stolen and Horrors is happy. The Hunter and Horrors travel around to find the missing pianos and come across "musical trampolines," which are really the missing pianos. The Hunter tries one out and jumps too high and comes crashing down on The Fox, removing his disguise in the process. After a fight inside a piano, Flim Flanagan arrives to arrest The Fox.

The Hunter #59 *Record Rocket* * 2/8/64
   Parties all over have come to a standstill as The Fox has stolen all of the records. There is no music to be found save for an old Rudy Vallee record that The Hunter has kept in his safe. The Hunter and Horrors decide to use it to lure The Fox out of hiding. They eventually find The Fox selling the discs at a stand for use like clay pigeons. The Hunter decides to take a shot, but ends up blowing up The Fox's stand in the process.

The Hunter #60 *The Hunter's Magic Lamp* *......................2/15/64
While cleaning out his storeroom, The Hunter stumbles across an old lamp. The Hunter rubs the lamp and a genie appears and grants him wishes. The Hunter wishes for a million dollars, when suddenly, a briefcase full of money appears. Flim Flannigan shows up and tells the Hunter that there has just been a million-dollar robbery at the bank. Then he sees the Hunter's case of money and takes it back, assuming the Hunter had already solved the case. The Hunter is angry, realizing that the genie had stolen the money. Horrors suggests that The Hunter wish for something that would benefit society instead. The Hunter agrees and wishes for the genie to get rid of The Fox. However, with no Fox around, there are no more crimes for the Hunter to solve, and soon the Hunter begins to regret his wish. Horrors wishes for the genie to bring back the Fox, and everything returns to normal.

The Hunter #61 *Hunter Goes Hollywood*........................2/22/64
Synopsis unavailable.

The Hunter #62 *Two for the Turkey Trot* 2/29/64
Synopsis unavailable.

The Hunter #63 *Captain Horatio Hunter* *......................3/7/64
The Hunter decides to tell Horace the story of his ancestor, Horatio Hunter. Horatio and his men are out in search of the Pirate Redbeard (who is actually the Fox). Soon, they meet up with Redbeard's ship and a fight breaks out. Redbeard captures Horatio and makes him walk the plank. At the last second, Horatio does a back flip on the plank, lands on Redbeard and knocks him out. The Admiral of the Queen's Navy (who resembles Flim Flannigan) arrests Redbeard and his men.

The Hunter #64 *The Horn of the Lone Hunter* *...................3/14/64
Horace reads that his uncle, The Hunter, is the world's greatest detective. The Hunter claims this should not seem surprising, and tells Horace the story of one of his ancestors, the Lone Hunter. Billy the Fox is on the loose and has single-handedly robbed a stagecoach, rustled the cattle, and held up a train. Lone Hunter rides into town to assist Sheriff Flannigan in apprehending the criminal. He chases The Fox into a gulch, and when his horse stops short, he flies off, knocks over The Fox and pins him down. The Lone Hunter is credited with the Fox's capture.

The Hunter #65 *Little Boy Blues* * 3/21/64
The Fox has stolen Little Boy Blues' magic horn. Unable to get the cattle to come home, Papa Blues calls The Hunter to find it. The Hunter drives out to the Blues' farm and tries blowing his own horn to call the cattle home. Unfortunately,

the Hunter's awful playing sends the cattle stampeding in the opposite direction. The Hunter bumps into the Fox, disguised as a shepherd. The Fox offers to let the Hunter use the magic horn to call the cattle for five bucks. The Hunter agrees, but as he plays the horn, the Fox is knocked down and his disguise falls off. Papa Blues recognizes his son's horn and the Fox is caught.

OPENING AND CLOSING

Opening 1: Have nose, will hunt: "Here a blow for your cartoon show."

Opening 2: "We're calling, we're calling the Hunter" song.

TENNESSEE TUXEDO AND HIS TALES
(70 SHOWS)

TENNESSEE TUXEDO
(70 EPISODES)

FIRST SEASON: 9/28/63-3/21/64
CBS (26 EPISODES)

Tennessee Tuxedo #1 *Mixed-Up Mechanics* *..................... 9/28/63

This episode tells of how Tennessee and Chumley are rescued from the freezing South Pole by Stanley Livingstone and his assistant Flunky, but discover that they are to live in the zoo. After seeing a newspaper ad for Mr. Whoopee and one for being car mechanics, they decide to leave the zoo to work as mechanics. T&C's first customer is Rocky Monanoff, who wants his car repaired right away. They can't do it so go to see Mr. Whoopee to learn about car engines. They repair the car; take it for a test drive, run down Rocky in the street, who's then taken to jail. T&C are also captured by Stanley and Flunky.

Tennessee Tuxedo #2 *The Rain Makers* *....................... 10/5/63

Tennessee and Chumley decide to become weathermen. Everything is fine until a farmer barges in with a shotgun claiming that it hasn't rained and his cauliflower crop is wilting. Chumley finds a book on Indians doing rain dances. Tennessee finds that ridiculous but can't offer an alternative, so they go see Mr. Whoopee about how to make it rain. The duo follows Whoopee's advice and do make it rain, but they piss off everyone who didn't want it to rain. Note: This episode is available on DVD on *The Underdog Chronicles* and *The Best of Tennessee Tuxedo and his Tales*.

Tennessee Tuxedo #3 *The Lamplighters* *...................... 10/12/63

The light is too dim in Tennessee and Chumley's cage so they stack boxes to get up closer to the light, which proves to be precarious. Soon, there is a fire in the zoo. It turns out that T&C have set it to read by. This doesn't work either when the fire department arrives. Next, Tennessee tries to build a light bulb, but fails, so they go see Mr. Whoopee to learn about light bulbs. In the end, Tennessee goes out and buys a lamp. Note: In one brief scene right after Mr. Whoopee opens the 3DBB, you can hear Chumley's original voice, as it is obvious that it isn't Bradley Bolke. This episode is available on DVD on *The Underdog Chronicles* and *The Best of Tennessee Tuxedo and his Tales*.

Tennessee Tuxedo #4 *Telephone Terrors or Dial "M" For Mayhem* * . . . 10/19/63

Stanley wants Tennessee to spread the news about his piano concert that evening. By noon, Tennessee is exhausted. He decides that an extension phone would be a better way to spread the news, but Stanley says that the only way they will get phones is if they build them themselves. Eventually, Tennessee and Chumley go see Mr. Whoopee to learn about telephones. Ultimately, they create a series of tin-can telephones made with simple wires. Unfortunately, the wires they use come from Stanley's piano, which means he plays a silent concert. Note: This episode is available on DVD on *The Best of Tennessee Tuxedo and his Tales*.

Tennessee Tuxedo #5 *Giant Clam* * 10/26/63

Stanley wants deep-sea divers to find the giant clam and Tennessee answers the ad. Stanley says no and hires two men for the job. Tennessee clobbers the men and he and Chumley take over. Once they take over, they realize they don't know everything so they go see Mr. Whoopee to learn about undersea diving. Now experts, they go to sea to get the clam. Chumley is sent down and is immediately eaten by the clam. Tennessee hoists him and the clam up and they return to the zoo. Stanley is impressed and he claims he will not punish T&C. Rather, they must share residence with the clam in the zoo. Note: This episode is available on DVD on *The Best of Tennessee Tuxedo and his Tales*.

Tennessee Tuxedo #6 *Tick Tock* * 11/2/63

The mayor of Megapolis dedicates a new clock tower to the zoo. Later, Chumley is shooting arrows and shoots one right at the face of the clock. Stanley sees this and demands the arrow be removed. While climbing up the clock, Chumley slips and hangs on for dear life on the long hand. Tennessee rescues him, but soon they damage all the gears in the clock. They try to repair it but can't, so it's off to Mr. Whoopee to learn about clocks. They repair the clock and still forget about the arrow. When they go get it again, they naturally break the clock again! Note: This episode is available on DVD on *The Best of Tennessee Tuxedo and his Tales*.

Tennessee Tuxedo #7 *Scuttled Sculptor* * 11/9/63

Stanley tells Tennessee to spread the news about a new statue that will be unveiled at 3 p.m. Tennessee and Chumley ride around on a scooter to spread the news, but they soon speed up, lose control and crash into the statue. After a number of escape attempts, they make it to Mr. Whoopee's to learn about statues. Back at the zoo, Tennessee and Chumley create a replacement statue, but this statue is much inferior to the original, so that the unveiling is greeted with laughter, and Tennessee and Chumley are thrown into jail where they smash rocks. Note: This is the first episode in which Stanley Livingston has a fringe of hair instead of a few strands. This episode is available on DVD on *The Best of Tennessee Tuxedo and his Tales*.

Tennessee Tuxedo #8 *Snap That Picture!* * 11/16/63

Chumley receives a package and Tennessee (not paying attention) tells him to toss it in the trash. It turns out to be Tennessee's new camera and soon they opened a camera business (T&C Photography). T&C get an assignment to take a new portrait of the mayor. Chumley suggests practicing taking pictures, but when Tennessee is done, there are no pictures inside the camera. They go see Mr. Whoopee who teaches them about film and cameras. T&C leave before Whoopee tells them about film developing and soon they are back. After learning more, they finally take the mayor's pictures, but it turns out that T&C's photography skills leave a lot to be desired in regards to framing and composition. Note: Mr. Whoopee states that Chumley is six feet tall!

Tennessee Tuxedo #9 *Zoo's News* * 11/23/63

Stanley has gotten some new wallpaper to prepare for the mayor's visit next week. He tells Tennessee to spread the news. Tennessee is annoyed and then is tired from his work and wonders if there could be an easier way to spread the news. Yak, Baldy and Chumley suggest a radio broadcast. Tennessee says that is silly and instead suggests that they do a newspaper and go to Mr. Whoopee to learn about newspapers and spreading news. Whoopee gives them a small printer and says that all they need is the paper. Chumley discovers "rolls and rolls" of paper, which turns out to be Stanley's wallpaper, which hasn't been used yet. Stanley discovers the thievery and has a new "scoop" for their next edition. Note: The various names suggested for the paper include *The Yakkety Yak, The Morning Eagle, The Walrus Street Journal* and *The Tennessee Tablet*.

Tennessee Tuxedo #10 *Aztec Antics* * 11/30/63

People are no longer watching Tennessee Tuxedo at the zoo; they are coming to see the newest attraction, Jerboa Jump. Very soon, the mayor comes to visit and says that he wants Stanley to go to Mexico to look for evidence of zoos from the days of the Aztecs. Tennessee needs help, so he and Chumley go see Mr. Whoopee. Tennessee and Chumley use various ways in every episode to sneak out to see Whoopee, but this one is the best, where they go riding in the interior of a tire. Whoopee pulls out a big book to show proof of the Aztec zoos. They would be in Mexico City. Meanwhile, Stanley is sending two archeologists. They do find proof and bring it back in crates. Unfortunately for Stanley, proof is Tennessee and Chumley. In the end, Tennessee and Chumley get the attention they want when Stanley installs a ball game in which T&C's heads are in the centers of the targets.

Tennessee Tuxedo #11 *Coal Minors* *..........................12/7/63

Tennessee and Chumley are freezing in the zoo. They obtain a heating stove, but have no coal to burn in it. They ask Stanley for coal, but he refuses to give them any as they are a penguin and a walrus and they are supposed to be able to withstand the cold. So, T&C go to Mr. Whoopee's for advice and he tells them about coalmining. Back at the zoo, Tennessee and Chumley dig for coal and succeed in tapping into Stanley's coal bin, leaving Stanley out in the cold.

Tennessee Tuxedo #12 *Hot Air Heroes* *........................12/14/63

Stanley once again wants Tennessee and Chumley to spread the news about some event, this time a picnic with the mayor to be a guest of honor. They go see Mr. Whoopee for help and he teaches them about hot air balloons, but T&C use all of the picnic supplies, such as the basket and tablecloths, and get in typical hot water with Stanley Livingstone.

Tennessee Tuxedo #13 *Irrigation Irritation* *....................12/21/63

Tennessee's watermelon patch dries up. In the meantime, there's a draught and anyone using too much water will be thrown in jail, according to the Mayor and Sergeant Badge. Stanley stops Tennessee's watering, prompting Tennessee and Chumley to go see Mr. Whoopee, and he tells them about irrigation. Back at the zoo, T&C take the rain gutters off of Stanley's office. Stanley soon gets a second warning about using too much water and he puts locks on the water faucets. A second trip to Mr. Whoopee teaches about dams and wells. So, T&C go back to dig for water. They do hit water right away… the zoo's water main! The police come to take Stanley away, but Stanley leads Sergeant Badge to take Tennessee and Chumley away.

Tennessee Tuxedo #14 *T.V. Testers* *..........................12/28/63

Tennessee and Chumley want jobs as TV repairmen. Rocky Monanoff needs a repair and so T&C are hired. They try, but eventually see Mr. Whoopee to learn about television. Mr. Whoopee says that TVs should only be repaired by experts and offers to repair the set. Tennessee brings over the set and asks Whoopee to hurry. As Tennessee and Chumley bring back the repaired set, they get caught up in the crossfire of Rocky's bank robbery and he's hauled off to jail and T&C go back to the zoo.

Tennessee Tuxedo #15 *By the Plight of the Moon* *.................1/4/64

Jerboa Jump is breaking in a sensational new act, and Tennessee gets jealous, so he decides to top him by going to the moon. They rush off to Cape Canaveral to take a flight, but the Cape says no. Then they go to Stanley for help and Stanley throws Tennessee and Chumley out with such force that it knocks Tennessee out, and he proceeds to dream about flying to the moon in a fantasy sequence. In his dream, Tennessee consults Mr. Whoopee with his "Teletopper" about how to fly to the moon. Tennessee and Chumley watch on their viewer as they hurtle through space. After learning, they land on the moon, but Tennessee wakes up before they crash. While he was dreaming, Tennessee was jumping and had attracted all of Jerboa's audience away.

Tennessee Tuxedo #16 *Lever Levity* * 1/11/64

This is a sequel to the episode #11 where Tennessee and Chumley were digging for a coal mine, as now Stanley's building is now sinking into the ground as the foundation is damaged. Stanley says he'll get someone to fix the foundation, but Tennessee says that he'll do it. Soon, Tennessee and Chumley escape to Mr. Whoopee's to learn about "simple" machines, including the lever, the wedge, the pulley, the screw, the inclined plane and the wheel and axle. Ultimately, they use the lever to lift the building, but to level it out they raise the building 40 feet in the air! After the building falls, Stanley chases them to fade out.

Tennessee Tuxedo #17 *The Bridge Builders* *. .1/18/64

Tennessee wants him and Chumley to become bridge builders. Meanwhile, Rocky Monanoff and his gang are planning a bank robbery that requires a bridge for their getaway. They catch T&C at the office and make demands that they need the bridge right away. Under pressure, T&C decide to go to Mr. Whoopee to learn about bridges. Tennessee and Chumley build the bridge out of a log, and not very well, so Rocky and his gang end up in the river and are caught by the police. Note: This episode is available on DVD on *The Best of Tennessee Tuxedo and his Tales.*

Tennessee Tuxedo #18 *Howl, Howl the Gang's All Here!* * 1/25/64

It's Tennessee's birthday and he receives a gift of a large white sheepdog named Howler. It's a gift from his Uncle Admiration. Stanley hears the dog and says that no dogs are allowed in the zoo. Tennessee and Chumley hide Howler and temporarily convince Stanley that there are no dogs. Tennessee and Chumley ask Mr. Whoopee to meet them in the woods to learn about building a doghouse for Howler. Soon after Whoopee leaves, Stanley spies on our heroes and falls into the lake. Howler rescues Stanley and changes his mind about Howler, making T&C live in the doghouse, and Howler in T&C's cage. Note: This is the first episode in which Chumley's look is slightly modified. His nose is now completely black instead of white with two nostrils as in previous episodes. Stanley Livingstone is also modified to have a little more hair. This is also the first appearance of Howler, the dog. Episode #24 is a sequel to this episode. This episode is available on DVD on *The Best of Tennessee Tuxedo and his Tales.*

Tennessee Tuxedo #19 *Sail-Ho!* * 2/1/64

Tennessee wants to start a yacht club since everyone seems to own a boat. Tennessee assumes the role of Commodore, until Jerboa challenges him to a race for the title. T&C decides that this is a good time to talk to Mr. Whoopee about boats. On the day of the big race, Jerboa's tricks prevent T&C from making initial progress, but soon they take over and eventually win as Jerboa is spending more time trying to come up with more ways to cheat than trying to win. Note: This one features Chumley and Stanley's original design. This episode was adapted into a book called *Tennessee Tuxedo and the Sailboat Race*. This episode is available on DVD on *The Best of Tennessee Tuxedo and his Tales*.

Tennessee Tuxedo #20 *Tell-Tale Telegraph* * 2/8/64

A dream episode where Tennessee is in the Union Army during post-Civil War times and is told by General Livingstone to guard the fort from Indians. Tennessee and Chumley go see Mr. Whoopee in Dodge City to learn about the telegraph. Everything they try doesn't work, and so Stanley kicks Tennessee out of the Army, to get massacred by the Indians, prompting Tennessee to wake up, relieved to discover it was all a dream. Note: This episode is available on DVD on *The Best of Tennessee Tuxedo and his Tales*.

Tennessee Tuxedo #21 *Rocket Ruckus* * 2/15/64

Jerboa is exaggerating about tales of space travel to the annoyance of Tennessee. Tennessee shows him - he and Chumley decide to build their own rocket into space. Failing this, they go to Mr. Whoopee to learn about rockets. They tell Whoopee about Jerboa's bragging and Whoopee has a solution. They borrow a rocket ride from a carnival and ask Jerboa to ride it, but he's too afraid and his claims are found to be fraudulent. Tennessee then offers everyone else rides on the carnival rocket ride. Note: This episode is available on DVD on *The Best of Tennessee Tuxedo and his Tales*.

Tennessee Tuxedo #22 *All Steamed Up* * 2/22/64

Stanley has an old locomotive called the Old '97 that takes zoo guests around the park on Saturdays. One Saturday, Stanley is going to be out of town, so he posts a sign saying that there will be no train rides that week. Tennessee and Chumley don't want to disappoint the kids, so they decide to run the train themselves, which leads to a horrible accident because they forgot to throw the switch. They quickly go to Mr. Whoopee to learn about trains and come back and repair the train. Before they let the public ride the train, they test drive the train and forget to throw the switch a second time and crash the train again, just as Stanley is returning to the zoo. Note: This episode is adapted into a book called *Tennessee Tuxedo and Old '97*.

Tennessee Tuxedo #23 *Tale of a Tiger* * 2/29/64

    Stanley's new zoo acquisition is a tiger named Tiger Tornado who's passive until he hears the ring of a bell. Jerboa teams up with Tiger to take over the zoo by bullying all the animals. Soon, Tennessee and Chumley challenge Tiger and are defeated, so they go see Mr. Whoopee. Whoopee teaches them about armor. Now, suited up in armor, Chumley easily defeats Tiger. Note: This episode features the first appearance of Tiger Tornado. A major error has Baldy's voice coming out of Yak's mouth. This episode is available on DVD on *The Best of Tennessee Tuxedo and his Tales*.

Tennessee Tuxedo #24 *Dog Daze* * 3/7/64

    Howler, Tennessee and Chumley's dog, is overly protective over Stanley and when the Mayor plans to pin a medal onto Stanley, Howler chases the Mayor up a tree. Stanley then orders Tennessee to chain Howler in his doghouse. Howler escapes and chases the Mayor into the lake. Stanley himself takes care of everything this time and ties Howler to a stump. Chumley comes by and lets him go, not knowing that he's supposed to be tied up. The Mayor says that no dogs are allowed in the zoo, but Tennessee promises to train Howler, as he's become unbearable. T&C go see Mr. Whoopee for advice. Mr. Whoopee teaches T&C how to train their dog. For some reason, they train Howler to sit when he says "Gesundheit!" Of course, when the medal award ceremony is underway, Tennessee forgets the word but he sneezes and unknowingly Stanley says "Gesundheit!" just in time, right before tackling the Mayor. Note: This episode is a sequel to episode #18.

Tennessee Tuxedo #25 *Brushing Off a Toothache* * 3/14/64

    Chumley has a painful toothache and is tearing up the house because he's in so much pain. Tennessee tries to help Chumley remove his tooth, but nothing works. They try to use Stanley's scooter to pull it, but destroy it in the process. They beat a hasty retreat to Mr. Whoopee to learn about dentists. After the visit, Tennessee takes Chumley to Drs. Drillum and Fillum. Chumley turns the table and sends in Tennessee in his place, but ultimately they both get their teeth fixed. They get back to the zoo just in time to fix Stanley's motor scooter.

Tennessee Tuxedo #26 *Funny Honey* * 3/21/64

    Tennessee wakes Chumley up to go into the honey-making business to sell to the bears in Bearville at the zoo. The bears think it is great. Big Bill Bear warns them if they don't get their honey, they get nasty. Next, Tennessee captures a bee and sticks him in a box. The next day he reaches in the box to get the honey, but gets stung. T&C go to see Mr. Whoopee to learn about bees and honey. They come back to the zoo and follow a bee back to its hive. Tennessee wants Chumley to dance with a giant flower to attract the bees so Tennessee can remove the honey, but the bees attack. Covered with bee stings, they go back to Mr. Whoopee's for more lessons about hives. Big Bill Bear comes by after Tennessee gets set up to say that the bears are going to buy direct from the manufacturer.

SECOND SEASON: 9/12/64-2/20/65
CBS (24 EPISODES)

Tennessee Tuxedo #27 *The Treasure of Jack the Joker* *.............9/12/64
Tennessee and Chumley like going through the Megapolis Museum. They discover a room that they've never been in before, and find a bottle that has a map in it that has pirate treasure hidden by a pirate named Jack the Joker. They try to read the map, but don't know how, so just they just dig randomly. Yak stops by and finds out what T&C are doing and soon everyone is digging for treasure, until Stanley stops it. Next, they go to Mr. Whoopee to ask him how to read the map. After they follow the map, they find that the treasure is right in front of Stanley's office. Stanley locks them up, but not before they hide the final box. In jail, they open the box, and it is all a joke from Jack the Joker.

Tennessee Tuxedo #28 *Wreck of a Record* *......................9/19/64
Tennessee and Chumley want Baldy to don a wig so they can perform in Stanley's talent show. Stanley has no such intentions of having them in his show and only wants Tennessee to post signs about the show. Stanley also says that he only wants singers who have had hit recordings. So, Tennessee and Chumley see Mr. Whoopee about recording, while Baldy puts up the posters. After Whoopee, T&C try to get their song recorded. No one is interested. Back at Whoopee's, he suggests that they perform their song around the zoo to stir up interest. Finally, at the big night of Stanley's show, he's forced to let "Tennessee Tuxedo and his Folk Singers" perform due to their newfound popularity. Note: While it was obvious in 1964, the purpose of Baldy wearing the wig was so they could look like folk singers Peter, Paul & Mary. The song "Abracadabra, Change-o Range-o Ree" was good enough that it should have been released as a single. This episode is available on DVD on *Underdog Nemesis* and *The Best of Tennessee Tuxedo and his Tales*.

Tennessee Tuxedo #29 *Miner Forty-Niner* *.....................9/26/64
Gold is discovered in California and in Muddy Flats. Stanley is having Tennessee and Chumley sweep the floor and uncrate the crackers. Jerboa Jump and Tiger Tornado meet a man who has a map that leads to his gold mine. In the scuffle, the map ends up in the hands of Tennessee and Chumley, who make a paper airplane out of it. Tennessee figures out that it is a treasure map, so they consult Mr. Whoopee for advice on how to read maps and how to pan for gold. Tennessee and

Chumley quit Stanley's store to strike it rich. Jerboa and Tiger plan to take the gold away, but fall asleep, so they have to chase after T&C. They escape and go to Stanley to gloat about their treasure, until the man whose map had been stolen, lays claim to his own gold. In the end, T&C are working again for Stanley.

Tennessee Tuxedo #30 *Helicopter Hi-Jinx* * 10/3/64

It's a very hot day at the Megapolis Zoo and Tennessee and Chumley are hoping to sneak out in order to get some fans. Stanley and Flunky stop all of their attempts to escape. They realize that the only way they can get out is to go straight up and Tennessee recalls a time they went to Mr. Whoopee and he told them about helicopters. They fabricate a makeshift helicopter that doesn't get them off the ground, but the spinning of the blades ultimately ends up cooling them and all of the other zoo animals off.

Tennessee Tuxedo #31 *Oil's Well* 10/10/64

Synposis unavailable.

Tennessee Tuxedo #32 *Parachuting Pickle* * 10/17/64

Rocky Monanoff and Pretzel rob a bank and fly off in a plane. While they are over "Lost Valley," Pretzel makes a wrong turn and the money falls out of the airplane. They place an ad in the paper and Tennessee and Chumley answer thinking it is about diving into a swimming pool, but it's actually skydiving. So they go see Mr. Whoopee about skydiving. Whoopee warns them that skydiving is dangerous, but T&C do the dive anyway and retrieve the money and climb into a large basket. Rocky and Pretzel pick up T&C but they refuse to climb out of the basket to the plane so Rocky climbs down and, due to the added weight, the three of them and the money crash through police headquarters. Note: This episode is available on DVD on *The Best of Tennessee Tuxedo and his Tales* and *The Ultimate Underdog Collection Volume 1*.

Tennessee Tuxedo #33 *Wish Wash* * 10/24/64

Stanley has purchased a prefabricated tool shed. Meanwhile, Tennessee and Chumley are washing clothes and then decide to wash clothes for others as a business called Tennessee Tuxedo's Laundry. Soon, they have too much business and a mountain of clothes. They build a bigger invention to wash many loads of clothes, but they need power, so they go see Mr. Whoopee for ideas. They make a windmill out of Stanley's tool shed. Stanley makes them take it down, so it's back to Mr. Whoopee who says to make a water wheel. This time they use Stanley's shovels. Stanley takes those back and so it's back to washing by hand. Note: This episode is available on DVD on *The Best of Tennessee Tuxedo and his Tales* and *The Ultimate Underdog Collection Volume 1*.

Tennessee Tuxedo #34 *Telescope Detectives* *.....................10/31/64
Tennessee tells Chumley they are to become detectives. They are hired to be hotel detectives by Mr. Hothead, and to capture Slippery Hood, the hotel robber. As they try to capture Slippery, he uses a little old lady disguise to get by our heroes more than once. In desperation, they go see Mr. Whoopee, who tells them about telescopes to spy on Slippery. Chumley discovers Slippery's disguise and the chase is on. Slippery is caught, but, in the process, frustrate Mr. Hothead so much, they are fired. In the end, they use the telescope and charge money for people to look at the stars.

Tennessee Tuxedo #35 *The Eyes Have It* *.......................11/7/64
Tennessee, Chumley, Yak and Baldy want to be bowling champions and Jerboa takes steps to make sure this doesn't happen. Jerboa and Tiger Tornado offer free eye examinations before the big bowling championship and prescribe dark glasses for Tennessee. At the bowling tournament, Tennessee bowls horribly due to his dark glasses, but happens to bump into Mr. Whoopee, literally, who tells Tennessee about glasses. T&C come back to the bowling alley and Tennessee bowls a lopsided ball, but still happens to make a strike, winning the tournament. Note: There is an error when the corrective lens is placed on the near-sighted eyeball.

Tennessee Tuxedo #36 *Mad Movie Makers* *....................11/14/64
Tennessee and Chumley decide that they want to make movies, but don't have a clue about how to do it, so they consult Mr. Whoopee to learn about moviemaking.

Tennessee Tuxedo #37 *Snow Go* * 11/21/64
Tennessee decides to develop a ski area in the Megapolis Zoo, which is an idea Stanley promptly rejects. Soon, refrigerators are missing all over the zoo, which causes Stanley and Flunky to accuse "Tennessee Tuxedo!!" and they are right. Meanwhile, Tennessee and Chumley are skiing down their makeshift ice cube mountain. After everything is taken away, T&C try again, this time with ice cream. Stanley and Flunky take the ice cream away after catching them in the act. Third time's the charm, as they try with grease. Defeated again, Tennessee and Chumley see Mr. Whoopee to learn about snow and where it comes from. Tennessee tries out Whoopee's solution and it works! Meanwhile, Stanley is showing the Mayor around and they slip down the mountain of snow.

Tennessee Tuxedo #38 *The Big Question* * 11/28/64
Stanley and Flunky are listening to a radio show called *The Big Question*, and feel they are going to get a call and win on the next show. Meanwhile, Tennessee

and Chumley have the same idea and "borrow" Stanley's radio for the next show. They try to get it by "fishing" for it, but end up "fishing" all of Stanley's furniture as well. Stanley and Flunky get everything back, so Tennessee disguises himself as Santa Claus to take back the radio because Stanley's been a bad boy all year. Tennessee is discovered, so the next way they try to get the radio is by sucking it up into their vacuum. Stanley stops everything, so T&C go to Mr. Whoopee to learn about radios. T&C make their own radio, but need an antenna. Chumley gets an antenna wire, which so happens to be the antenna for Stanley's radio. The radio show is on and Stanley gets the winning call, but as he has no reception, he has no idea what song is playing, and loses the contest, which has the prize of a free luxury cruise. As a result, he puts Tennessee and Chumley to work rowing a boat with Stanley in it, thus giving him his much deserved "cruise."

Tennessee Tuxedo #39 *Brain Strain* *. 12/5/64

Chumley resembles a local millionaire, so Tennessee convinces Chumley to impersonate the millionaire. Soon, Chumley loses his memory and truly believes that he is the millionaire. Tennessee tries to convince Chumley of who he really is, but is continually caught by the butler. In the end, Tennessee succeeds and Chumley's memory returns.

Tennessee Tuxedo #40 *Rocky Road to Diamonds* * 12/12/64

Tennessee and Chumley are hired by Mr. Stonecutter to work at a jewelry store. Soon, Rocky Monanoff stops by and robs the store. Afterwards, T&C try to get the diamonds back by sailing on a ship that Rocky has escaped on. After a couple of failed attempts, they go see Mr. Whoopee to learn about where to find diamonds, especially since they are now accused of stealing the diamonds. Whoopee just happens to be a passenger on the ship and together they go to his stateroom to learn. In the end, T&C are let go, and Rocky is captured on the ship as Mr. Whoopee saves the day, by telling the whole story to the ship's captain.

Tennessee Tuxedo #41 *X-Ray X-Perts* * 12/19/64

Stanley Livingstone has a rare coin from 1796 that Tennessee and Chumley use to pay Stanley's newspaper bill. Soon they are on the chase to find the coin. The coin goes to an ice cream truck. They rent a car and chase the ice cream truck onto a ferryboat. The ice cream truck man says he paid the coin to a baker. They go back to the bakery and while Tennessee is talking with the baker, Chumley eats a fresh batch of cookies, which apparently has the coin baked inside. It's time for Mr. Whoopee, who explains x-rays to the boys. After x-raying Chumley, it is revealed that Chumley has not eaten the coin after all. Relegated to the rock pile, Chumley removes his hat and finds an uneaten cookie hidden there. He proceeds to bite into the remaining cookie and bites into Stanley's rare coin, prompting Tennessee to chase him for his forgetfulness. Note: The ferryboat is named *Nancy* (after Biggers' wife).

Tennessee Tuxedo #42 *Food Feud*. 12/26/64
Synopsis unavailable.

Tennessee Tuxedo #43 *How Does Your Garden Grow* *. 1/2/65
Tennessee is tired of eating fish, so he decides to grow a garden for the vegetables. Stanley is totally against it until the Mayor's wife sides with Tennessee. Tennessee and Chumley go to Mr. Whoopee for advice about gardening and when they come back, get Stanley to do all of their gardening for them. Stanley complies until he discovers that the Mayor's wife is on a trip around the world and cannot supervise so closely.

Tennessee Tuxedo #44 *Perils of a Platypus* *. 1/9/65
Stanley raves to Flunky about his new acquisition, a platypus. As there is no place for him to stay, Stanley puts him in Tennessee and Chumley's swimming pool. T&C chase out the platypus, raising Stanley's ire, so they go see Mr. Whoopee to learn about platypuses, which are like fish, snakes, beavers and ducks. T&C leave for Australia to help recapture the platypus. Recapturing the platypus proves harder than they thought, but Tennessee strikes up a bargain and gives the platypus his tuxedo in order for him to come back to the Megapolis Zoo. Note: This is the character created to appease the wishes of Sy Plattes.

Tennessee Tuxedo #45 *Hail to the Chief**. 1/16/65
Jerboa feels that he should have been Zoo Police Chief instead of Tennessee and causes trouble to get everyone mad at Tennessee. Tennessee recruits Chumley, Yak and Baldy to help capture the crooks. In their first attempt, Tennessee is captured by his own trap. Soon, Tennessee and Chumley go to Mr. Whoopee to learn about how a real police force operates. The only thing they get out of it is they need uniforms, but there is more to it than that. Jerboa laughs it up with Tiger Tornado about it, because he knows his plan is working and he will be Police Chief soon. Tennessee soon accidentally discovers that Jerboa was behind all the robberies and arrests him.

Tennessee Tuxedo #46 *Physical Fitness* *. 1/23/65
Tennessee is annoyed about Tiger Tornado being a famous boxer (loosely based on Cassius Clay, later Muhammad Ali) and decides to train Chumley to be a boxer. Jerboa laughs, but agrees to a fight. Chumley does a practice fight, but loses, so Tennessee takes Chumley to Sillyman's Gym to train. Soon, they are thrown out, so T&C go to see Mr. Whoopee about exercise. On the day of

the fight, it is shown that Tiger has not bothered to train and, in fact, is sitting eating a box of candy, thinking he will knock out Chumley easily. Chumley's training has paid off and he wins the fight.

Tennessee Tuxedo #47 *Playing it Safe* * 1/30/65
Rocky Monanoff and Pretzel are in the middle of a bank robbery. They escape with a safe and try to blow it up with dynamite. The safe doesn't bust so they put in a want ad for someone who knows how to open a safe. Tennessee and Chumley answer the ad and get the job. They go to Mr. Whoopee because they need to know about locks. After they get back, Rocky begins to lose patience as T&C don't have the combination and still are not able to open the safe. Rocky is going to "play a tune on his violin" just in time for the cops to arrive.

Tennessee Tuxedo #48 *House Painters* 2/6/65
Synopsis unavailable.

Tennessee Tuxedo #49 *Admiral Tennessee* * 2/13/65
Tennessee falls asleep and dreams that he's an Admiral in search of pirates. He thinks the battle will be easy, but he is incorrect. He goes to Mr. Whoopee's to learn about ships and pirates, and, armed with this new information, it is still a struggle for Tennessee.

Tennessee Tuxedo #50 *Three Ring Circus* * 2/20/65
Tennessee and Chumley decide to join the circus. Initially, they try to get jobs as trapeze artists. Failing that, they try to become lion tamers. Ultimately, they get offered a job playing the calliope, but they don't know what one is. They find out from Mr. Whoopee. The calliope runs on steam, but Whoopee warns them of using too much steam. This advice is not heard and Tennessee keeps playing faster and faster in order to not burn his fingers. Chumley, meanwhile, tries to replace the broken valve. Stanley and Flunky finally arrive at the circus to retrieve our heroes.

THIRD SEASON: 10/2/65-2/12/66
CBS (20 EPISODES)

Tennessee Tuxedo #51 *The Big Drip* * 10/2/65
Tennessee feels that he and Chumley should become plumbers. Meanwhile, Rocky Monanoff and his henchman have a leaky faucet in their hideout, and call a plumber. It turns out to be Tennessee and Chumley, who have just purchased a plumbing business. They try to fix Rocky's faucet, but can't, and actually break the pipes. They decide to go to Mr. Whoopee to learn about faucets and plumbing. Armed with new knowledge, they replace the broken pipe and washer.

Unfortunately, they create a maze of pipes that leaks horribly, and close the door behind the flooding room. Rocky and his henchman come back to the hideout, open the door and the four are washed to the police station.

Tennessee Tuxedo #52 *Boning Up on Dinosaurs* *................. 10/9/65
Stanley introduces a dinosaur exhibit at the zoo. Tennessee and Chumley are told to stand guard, but their dog, Howler, keeps stealing bones from the exhibit and burying them. T&C recover all of the bones, but have no idea how to reconstruct the skeleton, so they go to Mr. Whoopee to learn about dinosaurs and skeletons. Armed with this new knowledge, T&C quickly reconstruct the structure before Stanley returns.

Tennessee Tuxedo #53 *Smilin' Yak's Sky Service* *................. 10/16/65
Yak inherits an airplane and doesn't know what to do with it. Tennessee does, and opens an airplane business. They take a flight that is less than successful and conclude that before any further flying, they should learn how to fly a plane. Rocky Monanoff tells Tennessee that he wants him to fly him out of there after he does his "bank business." Tennessee, Chumley and Yak all learn about airplanes and come back in time for Rocky's flight. Tennessee is not any better than he was earlier, so the flight is shaky at best and soon they are grounded and Officer Badge hauls Rocky to jail.

Tennessee Tuxedo #54 *Teddy Bear Trouble* * 10/23/65
Stanley brings a koala bear from Australia as the newest addition to the zoo, but the koala quickly disappears. It turns out he's in Tennessee and Chumley's house, and Stanley threatens to kick Tennessee out of the zoo if he messes with the koala again. The next morning, the koala is back in Tennessee cage, and Stanley is ready to throw Tennessee out. Tennessee and Chumley go to Mr. Whoopee to learn about fingerprinting to prove Tennessee's innocence. After fingerprinting everyone at the zoo, it turns out that Chumley was the guilty party as he let the koala into the cage in his sleep as he missed his toy teddy bear, which was lost in the closet.

Tennessee Tuxedo #55 *Sword Play* * 10/30/65
Stanley gives Tennessee a job of cleaning up the museum, which Tennessee hates doing. While cleaning, he notices a suit of armor and starts pretending he's a knight and hits the suit, causing the headpiece to fall on his head and knock him out. Tennessee then dreams that he's Sir Tennessee commanded by King Stanley to fight a fire-eating dragon. Sir Tennessee and Chumley keep losing battles until they go see Mr. Whoopee, who tells them about steel and swords. With a steel sword, Sir Tennessee goes back into battle, but is tricked by the dragon and comes to, in time to be chewed out by Stanley.

Tennessee Tuxedo #56 *Phunnie Munnie* *...................... 11/6/65

Rocky Monanoff tells Pretzel about his counterfeit money scheme. He takes his printing plate to Tennessee Tuxedo Printer and wants 10,000 images of George Washington printed in green ink by 2 p.m. As Chumley, Tennessee and Baldy try to run the printing presses, it is obvious they don't know what they are doing as they get stuck repeatedly in the presses, so they soon go see Mr. Whoopee for help. After the lesson in printing, they tell Whoopee what they are printing and Whoopee calls the police after they leave. So as not to get shot, they comply with Rocky's request and when they are about to deliver, Chumley sneezes the money and Rocky and Pretzel get caught up in the machinery just like Tennessee and Baldy, and are stalled long enough for the police to arrive.

Tennessee Tuxedo #57 *Romance of Plymouth Rock* *................ 11/13/65

Tennessee is auditioning actors for his play about pilgrims. Chumley, Yak and Baldy all audition. Baldy wins the part of Priscilla, Chumley is Miles Standish, Tennessee is John Alden and Yak is an extra. Tiger Tornado and Jerboa Jump observe Tennessee's auditions and decide to sabotage the play so Tennessee doesn't win the award for best play. They get the parts of Indians and insist on playing them as fierce. Tennessee brings Tiger and Jerboa to Mr. Whoopee to learn about Thanksgiving. The play goes on without a hitch and Tennessee wins the award. Note: This episode is available on DVD on *The Ultimate Underdog Collection Volume 3*.

Tennessee Tuxedo #58 *The Zoolympics* *....................... 11/20/65

Stanley decides to start the first annual Zoolympics. Jerboa Jump's team competes against Tennessee's. So far Jerboa's does much, much better. Eventually, Yak, Baldy, Chumley and Tennessee go to Mr. Whoopee to discover why they don't have enough energy to compete. Whoopee teaches them about food for energy and proper nutrition. So, Tennessee's team improves their performance. Jerboa's team feels that they have the competition in the bag, so they party, and eat poorly and don't get any rest. As a result, they fall behind. They decide to sabotage the Zoolympics, but it doesn't work as the conditioning of Tennessee's team has made them better athletes and they still win.

Tennessee Tuxedo #59 *The Tree Trimmers* 11/27/65

Synopsis unavailable.

Tennessee Tuxedo #60 *Goblins Will Get You* * 12/4/65

Tennessee and Chumley go trick-or-treating. Tennessee eats too much candy and falls asleep and has a nightmare about a wicked witch and her goblins that live in a haunted forest. In the dream, Mr. Whoopee resembles Wizard and helps Tennessee with his problems. The witch and the goblins plan to get Tennessee and Chumley, but, fortunately, Tennessee wakes up.

Tennessee Tuxedo #61 *The Cheap Skates* * 12/11/65

Tennessee suggests that Yak call his cousin Sewonya Button to ice skate in their show. She falls in the ice, but everyone rescues her. Sewonya refuses to skate unless there is a rink, so Tennessee, Chumley, Yak and Baldy all go to Mr. Whoopee to learn about ice and lakes. After learning, they build their own ice-skating rink. Sewonya tries it out, but it doesn't support her, so it's back to Mr. Whoopee. He offers an easier type of rink to make. The show goes on as scheduled. They earn $200 and that's enough to buy skates, but then everyone, including Sewonya, takes their cut, leaving only $50 left, enough for one pair, so Yak, Baldy, Tennessee and Chumley get on each other's shoulders and skate on that one pair.

Tennessee Tuxedo #62 *Going Up* 12/18/65

Synposis unavailable.

Tennessee Tuxedo #63 *Monsters from Another Park* 12/25/65

Synposis unavailable.

Tennessee Tuxedo #64 *Signed and Sealed* 1/1/66

Synposis unavailable.

Tennessee Tuxedo #65 *The Barbers* * 1/8/66

Tennessee and Chumley buy a barbershop, but they don't know the first thing about cutting hair and shaving. Before working on any further customers, they decide to call Mr. Whoopee. Whoopee recommends barber school, but before they can go, Rocky Monanoff comes in demanding a change in his looks. T&C decide to go to Mr. Whoopee about this additional information about makeup, which transforms a bust of a boy into one of Abraham Lincoln. Rocky and Pretzel rush back to the barbershop after his bank robbery to apply the makeup and make Rocky look like Abraham Lincoln! The police arrive and are not fooled and pull off the mask and take Rocky in. Note: This episode is available on DVD on *The Ultimate Underdog Collection Volume 2*.

Tennessee Tuxedo #66 *Catch a Falling Hammock* * 1/15/66

Tennessee and Chumley are battling aggressive termites that are chewing up the trees preventing them from raising a hammock and knocking down Yak and Baldy's tree house. The boys try many things to defeat the termites, but as an exploding bomb backfires, they struggle their way to Mr. Whoopee. They learn about insecticides and battle the insects, but the insects are tough. Finally, they use their ultimate weapon and get rid of all the bugs, but, unfortunately, all of the trees, too.

Tennessee Tuxedo #67 *Peace and Quiet* 1/22/66
   Synopsis unavailable.

Tennessee Tuxedo #68 *Robot Revenge* * 1/29/66
   Yak and Baldy are tired of working for Stanley, so they build robots to do their work for them. Tennessee and Chumley laugh hysterically about this and go to sleep still ridiculing them. Soon, they are awoken by robots that want to toss them into the melting pot for making fun of them. Tennessee reasons that the Regal Robot needs a heart, so they escape to see "The Friendly Robot With All the Answers" to learn about how a heart works. This is a robot version of Mr. Whoopee. Later, they build a heart, which explodes. The robots still want to send them to the melting pot, but they wake up. Just then, two robots enter the room and terrify Tennessee and he passes out. It turns out to be Yak and Baldy who have given up on building robots, and made robot costumes instead. Note: This episode is available on DVD on *The Ultimate Underdog Collection Volume 3*.

Tennessee Tuxedo #69 *There Auto Be a Law* * 2/5/66
   Tennessee wants to build a racecar to win money in the big race. Their first cars fail, so eventually Tennessee, Chumley, Yak and Baldy go to Mr. Whoopee's to learn about cars. They build an assembly line of cars, but still lose the race.

Tennessee Tuxedo #70 *Samantha* * 2/12/66
   Chumley wakes up Tennessee to see Samantha, a new female walrus at the zoo. Chumley wants Samantha to like him, but keeps annoying rather than attracting her. Tennessee and Chumley go see Mr. Whoopee for love advice. Whoopee explains about knights and chivalry and Tennessee thinks that's all there is to it and gets in a footrace to prove his love, but Yak wins. So, back to Mr. Whoopee, who explains the "Rules of Etiquette" and how to be a gentleman. Chumley tries out his new skills on Samantha, but Tennessee helps from behind the scenes to correct Chumley's mess-ups and, as a result, it works for Chumley and Samantha.

RIDDLES
(31 EPISODES)

Type 1: ("You have a riddle, Chumley?")
   #1 * Why does an Indian wear feathers in his hair? Because he wants to keep his wigwam.

#2* Why did the lobster get embarrassed? Because it saw the salad dressing.

#3* Why isn't my nose twelve inches long? Because that would make it a foot.

#4* How can five men stand under one umbrella and still nobody gets wet? Because it isn't raining.

#5* Why is the farmer cruel to his corn? Because when it's grown, he pulls its ears.

Type 2: ("C'mon Chumley, we better get back to the zoo before Stanley misses us.")

#6* If a blue stone falls into the Red Sea, what will it become? Wet.

#7* Why is it bad to leave a clock at the head of the stairs? It might run down.

#8* What letter is never found in the alphabet? The letter that I put in the mailbox.

#9* Ten birds on a wire, scare one away, how many are left? None, they all fly away.

#10* Why does the Statue of Liberty stand in New York Harbor? Because it can't sit down.

Type 3: (Rocket Crash)

#11* What has four legs and one foot? A bed.

#12* What has only one foot and is alive? Your leg.

#13* What has a head, and tail, but no body? A penny.

#14* What has a foot at each end and another foot in the middle? A yardstick.

#15* What has six feet, one tail, and four ears? A man on horseback.

Type 4: ("Tell me, Mr. Whoopee")

#16* What should I take when I'm run down? The license plate of the car that hit you.

#17* What can run, but can't walk? Water.

#18* Why are fish well educated? Because they travel in schools.

#19* What did Paul Revere say at the end of his famous ride? Whoa!

Type 5: (Rocket to Space)

#20* What is it that is even smarter than a talking horse? A spelling bee.

#21* What is it that asks no questions, but gets many answers? A doorbell.

#22* What is it that has 18 legs and catches flies? A baseball team.

#23* What is it that only has one horn, is white and give milk? A milk truck.

Type 6: (Diving Board)

#24* What is the biggest bow in the world? The rain-bow.

#25* What is the smallest room in the world? A mush-room.

#26* What is the most famous bus in the world? Colum-bus.
#27* What is the biggest pencil in the world? Pennsylvania.

Type 7: (Mountain Climbing)
#28* What do they call a monkey who sells potato chips? A chip-monk.
#29* What do they call a duck who's smart in school? A wise-quacker.
#30* What do they call a person who keeps borrowed books? A book-keeper.
#31* What do they call a cat that drinks lemonade? A sour-puss.

OPENING AND CLOSING

Bumpers:
"So long, Mr. Whoopee, we've got to get back; something big is going to happen!"
"There's more fireworks in the rest of our show" leading to Goodness Pack promo.
"Tennessee and Chumley will be right back with more cartoon fun."
"Let's get back for our next show."

FrostyO's Commercial:
Baldy sings "Little Chocolate Donuts" with Tennessee and Chumley in pursuit.
Baldy disguises himself as a little girl to try to get "FrostyO's."
Baldy teaches Chumley magic in order to get "FrostyO's."

Soaky Toys Commercial:
Tennessee Tuxedo with Superman.

Version 1: Tennessee and Chumley on a Boat and bullfight sung by Mexican singers. Emphasis on "see, see, see" sounds more like "si, si, si"
Version 2: Same as Version 1, but sung by Don Adams and Bradley Bolke.
Version 3: A football game featuring the Tennessees playing the Chumleys.
Version 4: Tennessee and Chumley chased by a train. This version features different lyrics about Mr. Whoopee.

Come on and see, see, see
Tennessee Tuxedo,
See, see, see
Tennessee Tuxedo.

He will be
Parachuting for your pleasure,
Sailing seas in search of treasure,
Anything so he can measure
Up to men
That's Tennessee Tuxedo.
A small penguin,
Who tries but can't succeed-o.

Though he may fail
As he vies for fame and glory,
Still he tries in each new story-tale.
That's Tennessee Tuxedo and his Tales.

Closing:
A preview of our next show with Mr. Whoopee.
Tennessee and Chumley unroll a giant scroll.

UNDERDOG
(124 EPISODES)

FIRST SEASON: 10/3/64-3/27/65
NBC (52 EPISODES, 2 PER SHOW)

Underdog #1 *Safe Waif* * (pilot; no on-screen title shown) 10/3/64

This episode introduces the world to Underdog. Underdog is shown as being far more clumsy and accident-prone than in later episodes. Also, this episode is played for laughs more than later stories. A small boy is trapped in a bank safe and it's Underdog to the rescue. Note: This episode is also available on DVD on *Underdog Collectors Edition* and as a bonus feature on the 2007 theatrical *Underdog* movie.

Underdog #2 *March of the Monsters* * 10/3/64

Sweet Polly reports on giant robot monsters in this more serious single-part episode. It is discovered by a robot scientist that the monsters are controlled by a single glass tube, so Underdog uses his high-frequency voice to break the tubes, but he overdoes it and breaks all the city's windows and other glass items. Note: This episode is available on DVD on *Underdog Collectors Edition*.

Underdog #3 *Simon Says* * 10/3/64

Simon Bar Sinister sets out to conquer the world by taking people's picture. When Simon says, "Hold it," it turns the subject he photographs into a photograph. Simon's plan is to take Underdog's picture and tear it up. When Simon takes Underdog's picture, Underdog holds up a mirror and Simon turns into a photograph. Underdog then reverses the lens of the camera and changes all of the photographs back into people. Note: This is the first story to feature Simon Bar Sinister. This episode is available on DVD on *Underdog Collectors Edition*.

Underdog #4 *Go Snow* Part 1 * 10/10/64
Underdog #5 *Go Snow* Part 2 * 10/10/64
Underdog #6 *Go Snow* Part 3 * 10/17/64
Underdog #7 *Go Snow* Part 4 * 10/17/64

Sweet Polly investigates a snowstorm in July and discovers Simon Bar Sinister and his snow gun. Simon threatens to turn everyone into snowmen unless he gets, "Money and power and money and power and money and power!!" from atop a high building. Underdog arrives and shakes the building to cause Simon to fall, but the building owner says that other people will be hurt if he doesn't stop shaking, so Underdog goes after Simon directly. Simon points his gun at

Underdog and says, "Go snow," and turns Underdog into a snowman, and he falls to Earth. The people try to defrost Underdog to no avail. Simon orders everyone to go home, but Underdog escapes from his snowy prison under his own volition. Underdog goes after Simon again, but flies at amazing speeds in order to avoid getting zapped by the snow gun again. The dizzying feats cause Simon and Cad to get dizzy and Underdog captures them and sends them to jail.

Underdog #8 *Zot* Part 1 * 10/24/64
Underdog #9 *Zot* Part 2 * 10/24/64
Underdog #10 *Zot* Part 3 * 10/31/64
Underdog #11 *Zot* Part 4 * 10/31/64

King Klobber's daughter, Princess Glissando, wants a husband, so the King declares a fight to the finish for his daughter's hand. Seymour wins, but Goggol is ordered to find a stronger man and he discovers Underdog. Goggol goes to Earth with a number of flying saucers to bring Underdog back to Zot. Underdog refuses and soon a mighty space battle takes place. Ultimately, he gives in to Klobber and agrees to marry Glissando when Polly is placed in a precarious position. Before the wedding is to take place, a giant two-headed dragon named Ralph and Irving attacks (in one scene one of the heads calls the other "Clyde"). Underdog defeats the dragon and comes back to Earth as Glissando has fallen in love with Goggol. Note: Goggol is featured in Sugar Jets commercials. The four episodes are available on DVD on *The Underdog Chronicles*.

Underdog #12 *The Great Gold Robbery Part 1* * 11/7/64
Underdog #13 *The Great Gold Robbery Part 2* * 11/7/64
Underdog #14 *The Great Gold Robbery Part 3* * 11/14/64
Underdog #15 *The Great Gold Robbery Part 4* * 11/14/64

Riff Raff and his gang are again robbing a bank, with Underdog in pursuit. He does this many times and Underdog always triumphs, causing Riff Raff to drop from Public Enemy #1 down to Public Enemy #5280. Riff hears about a train carrying a huge amount of gold. The robbery of this train will reinstate him back #1. Riff captures Sweet Polly and places her in a hot air balloon and recordings of Polly's voice in dozens of other hot air balloons. Underdog comes to the rescue, but is confused by the many balloons. Riff now is free to sabotage the train and steal the gold. Meanwhile, the real Sweet Polly's balloon had sprung a leak and is dropping quickly, but finally Underdog rescues the real Polly after he battles some interfering alligators. Underdog also is able to stop the trains from crashing into each other and captures Riff and his gang. Note: This is the first story to feature Riff Raff. Part 2 of this story was always aired with the sound out of sync in syndication. These four episodes are available on DVD on *The Ultimate Underdog Collection, Volume 2*.

Underdog #16 *Fearo Part 1* * 11/21/64
Underdog #17 *Fearo Part 2* * 11/21/64
Underdog #18 *Fearo Part 3* * 11/28/64
Underdog #19 *Fearo Part 4* * 11/28/64

 O.J. Skweez, President of TTV, wants to put on a big spectacle on television and wants Polly to go to an island populated by ancient creatures and a gigantic ape. Shoeshine Boy just happens to be shining Skweez's shoes and decides he better tag along on the trip as it sounds dangerous. A prehistoric creature starts attacking the ship, but Polly grabs onto Shoeshine preventing him from changing into Underdog. Finally, she lets go and Underdog does the job. Later, there is a mutiny and Polly, Shoeshine and the Captain are tossed overboard, but Underdog rescues everyone. Polly asks where Shoeshine went and Underdog explains that he took him home. Finally, at the island, they encounter more dinosaurs and finally Fearo. By this time, Underdog is very weak. Polly helps with the energy vitamin pill. Underdog defeats Fearo and they take him back for Skweez's TV show. Polly feeds Fearo on the show, but Fearo eats the spoon and goes nuts grabbing Polly in the process. Shoeshine Boy hears Polly's screams, but Riff Raff stops by and demands a shine. Finally, Shoeshine gets away long enough to change into Underdog and beat up Riff Raff. He tames Fearo with bananas, saves Polly and takes Fearo back home. Note: These four episodes are available on DVD on *The Ultimate Underdog Collection, Volume 1*.

Underdog #20 *The Big Shrink Part 1* * 12/5/64
Underdog #21 *The Big Shrink Part 2* * 12/5/64
Underdog #22 *The Big Shrink Part 3* * 12/12/64
Underdog #23 *The Big Shrink Part 4* * 12/12/64

 Simon says, "Sniff" and douses the sniffer of his flower with his new formula that shrinks people. Soon, Simon is the biggest person in the world. He even shrinks Cad, Sweet Polly and Underdog. After a series of adventures with a large toaster and ball of twine, Underdog uses the twine and sets up a trap to trip Simon and Cad. Meanwhile, Simon goes to get his cloud machine in order to douse more people at one time and falls for Underdog's trap. Underdog and Polly escape Simon's grasp but Underdog is severely weakened. Now, giant rats are after the two. Polly helps Underdog with his energy vitamin pill. Now he defeats the rats easily. Then after encountering a large rattrap, a giant bird takes Polly away. With everyone shrunk, the people use music to put Simon to sleep. While sleeping, they shrink Simon smaller than everyone else and tickle him to submission. Simon reveals how to return everyone back to normal and they are. Note: These four episodes are on DVD on *The Ultimate Underdog Collection, Volume 2*.

Underdog #24 *The Bubbleheads Part 1* * 12/19/64
Underdog #25 *The Bubbleheads Part 2* * 12/19/64
Underdog #26 *The Bubbleheads Part 3* * 12/26/64
Underdog #27 *The Bubbleheads Part 4* * 12/26/64

A land beneath the sea is ruled by a group of people called the Bubbleheads, who are ruled by an Emperor, who in turn is ruled by an Empress. They want to take over the land above. Scientist #1 creates a volcano machine which Underdog stops. Scientist #2 creates a drill machine to split the earth and this fails too. These two scientists are fed to a giant clam. Scientist #3 creates a huge agitator to create a huge tidal wave to wash away the land people above. Meanwhile, Sweet Polly and Professor Moby Ahab wonder what the source is for the giant waves, which annoys the Empress. Underdog comes to help and battles a school of whales. Eventually, Underdog destroys the agitator and brings the Bubbleheads in line.

Underdog #28 *From Hopeless to Helpless Part 1* * .1/2/65
Underdog #29 *From Hopeless to Helpless Part 2* * .1/2/65
Underdog #30 *From Hopeless To Helpless Part 3* * .1/9/65
Underdog #31 *From Hopeless To Helpless Part 4* * .1/9/65

TTV station owner O.J. Skweez is excited about a news story about the Hopeless diamond on display at a big society party. Riff Raff and Mooch see the same story and plan to be at the same event. Shoeshine Boy is shown the story as well and is told to go as people may need their shoes shined. At the party, Sweet Polly is a hors d'eurves girl and is captured by Riff Raff. Meanwhile, as Shoeshine can't get in to the party, he changes himself into Underdog when he hears Polly's screams. He rescues Polly and then goes after Riff Raff. Underdog hires an impersonator to get the diamond and uses Tap Tap the Chiseler. With Underdog's costume, he looks exactly like Underdog except for the cigar and his voice. Tap Tap steals the diamond and intends to cut the diamond, while the real Underdog is sent to jail. Tap Tap cannot cut the diamond; it's too hard. Riff Raff, Mooch and Tap Tap break Underdog out to cut the diamond. Underdog agrees, but when he gets to their hideout, he takes the diamond and captures the criminals. Note: This episode appears on DVD on *Underdog Collectors Edition*.

Underdog #32 *Tricky Trap by Tap Tap* * 1/16/65

Underdog checks on the local prison, the one that holds Tap Tap. While he checks out everything, Tap Tap uses the situation to his advantage and escapes. Tap Tap captures Polly and threatens to blow up the city with a bomb he's obtained from the Adams Bomb Company. He'll let everyone go for a million bucks. Underdog pretended to think it over, but he really is melting the handcuffs.

He then captures Tap Tap easily after the bomb goes off. Note: The news article about Underdog's visit to the prison was written by Treadwell Covington. This episode is the sequel to the four-part story "From Hopeless to Helpless." This episode is available on DVD on *Underdog Collectors Edition*.

Underdog #33 *The Witch of Pickyoon Part 1* * 1/23/65
Underdog #34 *The Witch of Pickyoon Part 2* * 1/23/65
Underdog #35 *The Witch of Pickyoon Part 3* * 1/30/65
Underdog #36 *The Witch of Pickyoon Part 4* * 1/30/65

The wicked witch of Pickyoon has found out that Underdog has no weakness except Sweet Polly Purebred. She captures Polly and makes her drink a sleeping potion. Underdog goes to Pickyoon and questions the villagers who are in fear of the witch and warn Underdog that she will cast a spell on him. Underdog meets up with the witch who wants him to battle various monsters in an arena. Underdog wins and the witch wants Underdog to complete three tasks. These tasks are all illegal, but Underdog figures out a way to do them legally. Eventually, Underdog disposes of the witch and he tells the villagers they are now free. Unfortunately, Sweet Polly is still sleeping for 1000 years. Underdog gives a kiss to the sleeping Polly before leaving, and she wakes up. Note: These four episodes are available on DVD on *Underdog Nemesis*.

Underdog #37 *Weathering the Storm Part 1* * 2/6/65
Underdog #38 *Weathering the Storm Part 2* * 2/6/65
Underdog #39 *Weathering the Storm Part 3* * 2/13/65
Underdog #40 *Weathering the Storm Part 4* * 2/13/65

Simon has invented a machine that controls the weather, but he and Cad claim they need to go to the moon in order to work the controls properly. Sweet Polly is going to the moon with two astronauts, but they aren't astronauts at all, but Simon and Cad. The real astronauts are tied up. A call goes out for Underdog to help with the spaceship, but he was busy helping stop a war (shades of Vietnam). Finally, he shows up just as the spaceship with Simon, Cad and Polly lands on the moon. Cad sets up the weather machine, and Simon plans to wipe out the Earth. He sends rain, lightning, and a tornado. Then, if the Earth doesn't agree to make Simon dictator, he will press all of the buttons at once. Underdog takes a super energy pill to prepare to battle all of these storms. Cad, meanwhile, strikes Simon and they get into a fight. It turns out that Underdog is using super speed to manipulate Cad's arms. Note: These four episodes are available on DVD on *The Ultimate Underdog Collection, Volume 3*.

Underdog #41 *The Gold Bricks Part 1* * 2/20/65
Underdog #42 *The Gold Bricks Part 2* * 2/20/65

Underdog #43 *The Gold Bricks Part 3* *..........................2/27/65
Underdog #44 *The Gold Bricks Part 4* *..........................2/27/65

It is decided that Underdog will drive an armored car containing a billion dollars of gold bricks. Meanwhile, Riff Raff and Mooch are planning to steal the gold. They put up a phony tollbooth in order to switch the armored car. After the switch, Underdog is driving an empty truck. After the delivery of the empty truck, Underdog is arrested and thrown in jail. Polly's boss, O.J. Skweez tells Polly to report Underdog on the news, but she refuses. Instead, she finds and follows Riff Raff and Mooch in a helicopter until she is shot down. Polly then goes to a haunted house to find help. Underdog, by this time, is in court and is found guilty and is sentenced to 30 years in jail. It turns out that the haunted house was faked by Riff Raff and Mooch, who, by this time, have painted the gold bricks to look like real bricks. Underdog breaks out of prison to save the frightened Sweet Polly and discovers the ghost machine. Eventually, Underdog catches Riff Raff and Mooch and clears his name. Note: These four episodes are available on DVD on *The Ultimate Underdog Collection, Volume 1*.

Underdog #45 *The Magnet Men Part 1* *..........................3/6/65
Underdog #46 *The Magnet Men Part 2* *..........................3/6/65
Underdog #47 *The Magnet Men Part 3* *..........................3/13/65
Underdog #48 *The Magnet Men Part 4* *..........................3/13/65

The Olympics are underway, but athletes begin to disappear. Scientists figure out that there is a planet pulling these athletes away to this new planet that magnetizes people and drags them there. The Magnet Men also capture Underdog and Sweet Polly with their giant electro-magnet gravity gun. The Magnet Men want metal and they plan to pull Earth away from the Sun to get all of Earth's metal. Underdog and Polly are sent back to Earth to tell everyone to give up all of their metal. Viewers did not agree with Polly's news report, and also did not believe it, despite Underdog verifying that it was true what the Magnet Men said. Soon, Earth is pulled away from the Sun and people panic. Eventually, Polly and Underdog neutralize the power on their bracelets and rings, and he beats up the Magnet Men and pushes Earth back to its proper place.

Underdog #49 *The Phoney Booths Part 1* *..........................3/20/65
Underdog #50 *The Phoney Booths Part 2* *..........................3/20/65
Underdog #51 *The Phoney Booths Part 3* *..........................3/27/65
Underdog #52 *The Phoney Booths Part 4* *..........................3/27/65

Simon and Cad replace real phone booths with "phoney booths," phone booths that jump and spin and put everyone who enters them under Simon's power. The people affected have a light bulb implanted into their heads. Various people with various professions enter the booths, all ending up with the same fate, under Simon's control. Shoeshine Boy enters a phoney booth to become Underdog and he too, becomes a slave to Simon's power. O.J. Skweez, Polly's boss, tells her that Underdog is under Simon's power and she takes it upon herself to destroy the phoney booths with an ax. Simon commands Underdog to destroy Sweet Polly. This creates havoc with Underdog's brain and he shatters his head light bulb. Simon then sends the Army to destroy Underdog. A piece of shrapnel hits the General's bulb and shatters it, and he is no longer under Simon's power. Soon, Underdog and the Army take over and blow up Simon's lab and in the end Simon and Cad land in a tree, defeated, with all the phoney booths destroyed.

SECOND SEASON: 9/18/65-2/5/66
NBC (44 EPISODES, 2 PER SHOW)

Underdog #53 *Pain Strikes Underdog Part 1* * 9/18/65
Underdog #54 *Pain Strikes Underdog Part 2* * 9/18/65
Underdog #55 *Pain Strikes Underdog Part 3* * 9/25/65
Underdog #56 *Pain Strikes Underdog Part 4* * 9/25/65

It's Underdog birthday, but Underdog's required to carefully guard the Excalibur sword collection en route to San Francisco. Underdog saves the Excalibur sword collection from Riff Raff, but he is now in constant pain. "When I stay straight, I'm as right as rain, but when I bend over there's a stabbing pain," exclaims Underdog. "And tomorrow's his birthday," adds Sweet Polly. While Underdog is in the hospital undergoing a battery of tests, Riff Raff and Mooch plan to get the swords again from the San Francisco Museum, and succeed. Riff Raff then dips the swords in wax and disguises them as candles. Sweet Polly goes to buy candles for Underdog's birthday to cheer him up, but she gets dipped in wax and is headed for the wick cutter on the assembly line. Underdog comes to the rescue and he becomes a candle as well, but he breaks free and beats up Riff Raff and Mooch. Underdog melts all the candles and they have his birthday, despite Underdog still being in pain. Then it is discovered that they are missing one of the swords, and Underdog realizes that one of the swords has been stabbing him the entire time.

Underdog #57 *The Molemen Part 1* * 10/2/65
Underdog #58 *The Molemen Part 2* * 10/2/65
Underdog #59 *The Molemen Part 3* * 10/9/65
Underdog #60 *The Molemen Part 4* * 10/9/65

Large amounts of crops have gone missing, and Sweet Polly is reporting the bad news. She calls for Underdog, but he is in the middle of a battle with some giant squid. In the meantime, Polly decides to do some investigating of her own and falls in a deep hole. Mange, the king of the Molemen, reveals himself and says he is taking all of the crops. Polly says that Underdog will stop them, but Mange says that the mole-hole gun will defeat him. The mole-hole gun does not bore a hole in Underdog, but it does slow him down. Since the gun doesn't work, the Molemen let loose a giant ant, and a big fight ensues, and Underdog begins to weaken. The Molemen take Polly and Underdog to a cage and have them sealed in silk by a giant caterpillar. While trapped, Polly helps Underdog take his energy vitamin pill and, with his new strength, he defeats the caterpillar and the giant ant. While this is happening, a giant spider grabs Polly and soon Underdog and the spider are fighting. Afterwards, Underdog flies to the surface for help, but everyone is too weak from hunger. After rescuing Polly, he puts his energy vitamin pill in every reservoir and Polly tells everyone to drink water, so that they can all defeat the Molemen and the ants. Everyone is as strong as Underdog, all the people escape and the Army defeats Mange and his mole-hole gun.

Underdog #61 *The Flying Sorcerers Part 1* * 10/16/65
Underdog #62 *The Flying Sorcerers Part 2* * 10/16/65
Underdog #63 *The Flying Sorcerers Part 3* * 10/23/65
Underdog #64 *The Flying Sorcerers Part 4* * 10/23/65

King Kup is searching for a baker to bake a good cake. He sends his sons, Bric and Brac, to other planets, including Zot and the Magnet Men's planet, but their cakes are no good, either. Finally, Bric and Brac see Sweet Polly baking a chocolate cake on TV, and kidnap her, bringing her back to their home planet. Underdog hears Polly's cries, and follows them to their planet. Polly is their prisoner and makes King Kup a cake, then 50, then 500! Underdog has been changed into a rubber ball and keeps reverting back every time he gets out. Polly is overwhelmed by making so many cakes and falls into the giant mixer. Underdog takes one of his super energy pills to give him extra strength and defeats the Flying Sorcerers and rescues Polly. Polly gives King Kup her recipe, so that he can make cakes himself.

Underdog #65 *The Forget-Me-Net Part 1* * 10/30/65
Underdog #66 *The Forget-Me-Net Part 2* * 10/30/65
Underdog #67 *The Forget-Me-Net Part 3* * 11/6/65
Underdog #68 *The Forget-Me-Net Part 4* *. 11/6/65

Simon is robbing banks, but Underdog stops him again. Cad suggests that the only way they can defeat Underdog is to make him forget he's Underdog. Simon creates the Forget-Me-Net to drop on him so that he will forget. Then he commits a series of robberies in order for the people to call Underdog, but Underdog doesn't show up. Simon and Cad kidnap Sweet Polly and finally Underdog shows up and they throw the net on him. Underdog forgets who he is until someone says his name, so Simon disguises Underdog as a little old lady selling apples. But Apple Mary still has the same powers and people almost say, "That was exactly like Underdog." Now, Simon has created a huge net to throw over Washington and make them all forget. Meanwhile, Apple Mary and Sweet Polly meet up with each other and Mary eventually remembers her name and successfully helps Sweet Polly. Polly realizes Apple Mary is really Underdog but doesn't know to say his name, but eventually his name is said and Underdog catches Simon and Cad in their own net, prompting them to forget each other's name.

Underdog #69 *Whistler's Father Part 1* *....................... 11/13/65
Underdog #70 *Whistler's Father Part 2* *....................... 11/13/65
Underdog #71 *Whistler's Father Part 3* *....................... 11/20/65
Underdog #72 *Whistler's Father Part 4* *....................... 11/20/65

Riff Raff hires the best crooks to steal the painting of "Whistler's Father" at the Midtown Art Museum. Together they want to use guerilla warfare tactics, including camouflage and sabotage, in order to steal it. Underdog is personally guarding the painting, but at one point has to leave to check out an explosion, with Polly in charge. Underdog uses one of his super energy pills for extra strength to repair the door and then he gets another call to fix some leaky pipes and a heating system in the museum. Meanwhile, two villains disguised as columns finally steal the painting, but Underdog gets it back again. This time Underdog carries the painting with him wherever he goes and unbeknownst to him leaves a trail of birdseed as planted by Riff Raff who calls it a sneak attack. Riff Raff discovers that Underdog is Shoeshine Boy because of following him and will tell everyone, but Underdog quickly changes back and forth from himself to Shoeshine and back to give the illusion that they are two separate people and he finally defeats the crooks. Note: These four episodes are available on DVD on *The Underdog Chronicles*.

Underdog #73 *Simon Says…No Thanksgiving Part 1* *............. 11/25/65
Underdog #74 *Simon Says…No Thanksgiving Part 2* *............. 11/25/65
Underdog #75 *Simon Says…No Thanksgiving Part 3* *............. 11/27/65
Underdog #76 *Simon Says…No Thanksgiving Part 4* *............. 11/27/65

Simon has a new plan with three airplanes, three tanks and 12 soldiers taking over the city. Sweet Polly overhears this plans and runs to the police, who laugh at her. Polly wants to tell Underdog, but he's in the midst of stopping a major earthquake. Simon then tells Cad about two special buttons attached to a light pole. Simon explains that the top button will sound an air raid siren and the bottom button will lock every door in the city after the entire population scurries inside the buildings. Simon says he will be master of the city. When he tries to do what he wants to do, a Thanksgiving Parade is underway and Simon cannot get to the buttons. Cad says the only way they can get rid of the Thanksgiving Parade is to get rid of Thanksgiving. Simon uses his time bomb to go back in time to 1621 to end Thanksgiving by making the Indians fight the Pilgrims. After Simon and Cad leave, Underdog and Polly follow by also going back in time. Underdog helps the Pilgrims out to prove that they are friends. Simon, meanwhile, is stirring up the Indians with Cad's help and they attack. Then, Simon and Cad come back to the present just in time to see the parade disappear. Of course, Underdog solves the problems with the Pilgrims and the Indians and Thanksgiving Day and the Parade goes on without a hitch, as Simon still isn't able to press his buttons. The ending has Underdog making a reference to his own balloon. Note: The first two episodes originally aired on Thanksgiving Day. The soundtrack for these episodes was issued on a 45RPM record in 1965.

Underdog #77 *The Silver Thieves Part 1* * 12/4/65
Underdog #78 *The Silver Thieves Part 2* * 12/4/65
Underdog #79 *The Silver Thieves Part 3* * 12/11/65
Underdog #80 *The Silver Thieves Part 4* * 12/11/65

Ghost creatures are stealing silver from everyone. A call goes out for Underdog, but he is resting after battling giant sharks. Then, the silver thieves come to steal Underdog's silver ring. Underdog refuses and the silver thieves' lightning jolts him and they steal the ring. It is done easily due to Underdog's weakened condition. The people come to Underdog's rescue. Underdog discovers that the silver thieves are not ghosts but really cloud men and they need silver for their silver linings. Underdog must go to planet Cumulus to get back his ring and the other silver. Sweet Polly goes with him to help and a battle on Cumulus ensues, resulting in a weakened Underdog and Polly running on a conveyor belt into a giant silver melting vat. Underdog finds his ring on the conveyor belt with him and takes one of his energy vitamin pills and defeats the cloud people. They come up with a resolution that the cloud people will trade gold for silver. Note: These four episodes are available on DVD on *Underdog Nemesis*.

Underdog #81 *Riffraffville Part 1* * 12/18/65
Underdog #82 *Riffraffville Part 2* * 12/18/65
Underdog #83 *Riffraffville Part 3* * 12/25/65
Underdog #84 *Riffraffville Part 4* * 12/25/65

Riff Raff once again tries to rob a bank in person and by helicopter, and Underdog once again stops him. Riff Raff has a new plan to paint cars as they go through a tunnel, but Underdog stops this, too. Then, Riff Raff tries to steal an armored car and Underdog stops him for the ninth time that month. Finally, Riff Raff gives up and leaves town to go West and to live in a small Western town. He soon takes over and renames it "Riffraffville." Back in the city, Sweet

Polly reports that there is no more crime, and Underdog is reduced to rescuing cats out of trees. Riff Raff and Mooch decide to mess with Sweet Polly and offer her a free vacation to Riffraffville shortly after she has turned Underdog's ring in for repair. Underdog finds out Polly is tied up, and soon he heads West without his ring, and as a result, is getting weaker by the moment. Riff Raff challenges Underdog to a gun duel. It turns out Polly didn't take Underdog's ring after all, and Underdog takes the super energy pill just in time. Note: There is a folk music version of the *Underdog* theme that plays in the background of episode four. These four episodes are available on DVD on *The Ultimate Underdog Collection, Volume 3*.

Underdog #85 *The Tickle Feather Machine Part 1* * 1/1/66
Underdog #86 *The Tickle Feather Machine Part 2* * 1/1/66
Underdog #87 *The Tickle Feather Machine Part 3* * 1/8/66
Underdog #88 *The Tickle Feather Machine Part 4* * 1/8/66

Simon is legally elected dictator because everyone is laughing due to Simon's tickle feather machine. Sweet Polly is assigned to put on an entertainment special. She sings the *King Leonardo* theme song. Underdog discovers that Simon wasn't legally elected as he is not registered to vote and everything goes back to normal. Underdog uses his atomic breath to blow all of the tickle feathers into outer space. Note: These four episodes are available on DVD on *The Underdog Chronicles*.

Underdog #89 *Underdog vs. Overcat Part 1* * 1/15/66
Underdog #90 *Underdog vs. Overcat Part 2* * 1/15/66
Underdog #91 *Underdog vs. Overcat Part 3* * 1/22/66
Underdog #92 *Underdog vs. Overcat Part 4* * 1/22/66

People are pouring into Metropolitan Stadium to see the battle of Underdog vs. Overcat. Overcat is the overbearing ruler of a cat planet called Felina. Overcat came to Earth when he found out that Felina no longer has any milk. So, Overcat launches a fleet of rocket trains to capture all the cows on Earth, which they do by vacuuming up all the cows. Now, Earth is milk-free, making it a worldwide disaster. Underdog comes to the rescue looking for the missing cows. Meanwhile, on Felina the cats are trying to figure out how to get milk out of the cows. Overcat sends a couple of his henchman back to Earth to get someone who knows how to milk a cow, and they capture Sweet Polly who mentions in her news report that she knows how to milk a cow. When Underdog comes to Felina to rescue Polly from her predicament, they capture him inside a gigantic rubber ball, which weakens him significantly and soon he is released from the ball and thrown in with Polly to milk cows. Polly helps Underdog regain his strength by giving him his energy vitamin pill. With newfound strength, Underdog clobbers all the cats. He then takes all the cows and Polly back home. So, Overcat challenges Underdog to a fight to the finish for the cows. Underdog wins, and helps Felina with their milk problems by planting coconut trees. In the end, Overcat is banished from Felina, but will he be back? Note: This episode is available on DVD on *Underdog Collectors Edition*.

Underdog #93 *The Big Dipper Part 1* *..........................1/29/66
Underdog #94 *The Big Dipper Part 2* *..........................1/29/66
Underdog #95 *The Big Dipper Part 3* *...........................2/5/66
Underdog #96 *The Big Dipper Part 4* *...........................2/5/66

    Simon Bar Sinister creates a small vacuum-type machine he calls "The Big Digger." Cad pours water on the floor and Simon says, "Dry up." After some failed attempts, Simon succeeds and starts sucking up all the water in the world and saving it in little glass jars. Sweet Polly overhears Simon's plans, but the police don't have enough information to arrest him, and also Underdog is busy battling a pack of killer whales. When Underdog does become available, he builds high fences around the remaining bodies of waters, but it does no good, as Simon still gets all the water in the world, except the Atlantic Ocean, and then he gets that, too. Simon makes the world his slave unless they get no water. Sweet Polly calls again for Underdog, but now he's stuck in the mud of what used to be the bottom of the Atlantic Ocean. Meanwhile, Simon is selling water at $1,000 a glass or for slave work. In the end, Underdog takes an energy vitamin pill and goes to battle Simon. Simon threatens to break all the jars and throws them at Underdog. Ultimately, Underdog has all the bottles and Simon has none. Underdog takes over the machine and washes Simon and Cad away, and returns all the water to where it belongs. Note: These four episodes are available on DVD on *The Ultimate Underdog Collection, Volume 1*.

THIRD SEASON: 9/10/66-12/10/66
CBS (28 EPISODES, 2 PER SHOW)

Underdog #97 *The Just in Case Part 1* * 9/10/66
Underdog #98 *The Just in Case Part 2* * 9/10/66
Underdog #99 *The Just in Case Part 3* * 9/17/66
Underdog #100 *The Just in Case Part 4* * 9/17/66

    The police department is nervous about Riff Raff's latest plan to get a new gang together while in prison, and they call Sweet Polly to call Underdog. The new mob is a laughing stock: a tailor, a blacksmith, a carpenter and a globular character referred to as "just in case." Shoeshine hears Polly's cries, but the closest phone booth is occupied. Riff Raff and the gang break out of jail and use their respective talents to build a boat. Finally, Underdog is available and looks for Riff Raff. Riff Raff and his gang now have a ghost ship and rob boats, ships and yachts of all types. The other members of the gang are getting resentful that "just in case" isn't doing anything. Riff Raff assures everyone that he's there "just in case." Sweet Polly has stowed away on the ghost ship, but is eventually discovered and a cry goes out for Underdog after she's tied up. As Underdog is arriving, "just in case" is revealed to be a Witch Doctor who uses a voodoo doll on Underdog. Whatever the doll does, Underdog does. The Witch Doctor gives the doll to a seagull to fly away with while Riff Raff and the gang rob the *Queen May*. Then a monkey gets hold of the Underdog doll and plans to drop it into a volcano. Underdog knows that the only way to break the spell it to eat an Underdog super energy pill. He breaks the spell, paints the invisible ship visible and clobbers Riff and the gang.

Underdog #101 *The Marble-Heads Part 1* * 9/24/66
Underdog #102 *The Marble-Heads Part 2* * 9/24/66
Underdog #103 *The Marble Heads Part 3* * 10/1/66
Underdog #104 *The Marble Heads Part 4* * 10/1/66

    A brilliant white light flashes across the sky and the stars of *My Fair Lady* are among the witnesses. Eventually, the strange object crash-lands. Scientists begin examining the strange sphere. Polly does the news report and calls for Underdog. Underdog realizes that everything is under control, so he leaves as does everyone else. Afterwards, two marble men leave their round spaceship and began eating rocks and other stone structures. They also shoot a gun that turns people into stone, including Sweet Polly and Shoeshine Boy. Captain Marble Head is pleased as he wants slaves for his planet – Planet Granite. The Army tries to stop the marble men, but to no avail as they just turn all of them into stone. Soon, the Marble Heads take their cargo back to Planet Granite. Captain Marble Head wants the slaves to mine the rocks for them to eat. Sweet Polly calls for Underdog, but Shoeshine can't change into Underdog for fear of revealing his true identity, so he suggests mutiny in order to change amidst the chaos. Underdog takes over and even though he is turned to stone with the granite gun, he easily breaks free and the Marble Heads give up, and the former slaves return home. Note: The title of the episode is hyphenated for parts 1 and 2, but not parts 3 and 4. These four episodes are available on DVD on *The Ultimate Underdog Collection, Volume 2*.

Underdog #105 *Simon Says Be My Valentine Part 1* * 10/8/66
Underdog #106 *Simon Says Be My Valentine Part 2* * 10/8/66
Underdog #107 *Simon Says Be My Valentine Part 3* * 10/15/66
Underdog #108 *Simon Says Be My Valentine Part 4* * 10/15/66

    Simon invents a machine called the Valentine Vault that turns people into Valentines. Cad then goes out and captures Sweet Polly. Shoeshine Boy witnesses the kidnapping and allows himself to get beaten up in order not to reveal his secret identity. Later, he waits in line for the phone booth, while Polly is bound and gagged. Shoeshine finally changes into Underdog, but is turned into a Valentine by Simon's machine. Then, Simon tells Cad to take the machine to City Hall to turn the Mayor into a Valentine. The bound Polly is forced to look at her Underdog Valentine. Polly finally breaks free and frees Underdog by feeding him a paper vitamin energy pill. Underdog then flies to City Hall and rescues the Mayor while Polly makes Valentines out of Simon and Cad.

Underdog #109 *Round and Round Part 1* * 10/22/66
Underdog #110 *Round and Round Part 2* * 10/22/66
Underdog #111 *Round and Round Part 3* * 10/29/66
Underdog #112 *Round and Round Part 4* * 10/29/66

    Two outer space men (one named Zorb and one named Crum) want to take over the Earth and need to destroy Underdog. To attract Underdog to outer space, they meddle with a spaceship in flight. They greet Underdog and give a necklace to him as a gift that makes him dizzy. "Things are fine when I sit down, but when I get up, things spin around," Underdog claims. Meanwhile, scientists are doing tests on Crum and cage him up. As he doesn't like this, he increases up to giant size and keeps growing. Doctors are also doing tests on Underdog to figure out why he's getting dizzy. Underdog is aware of the giant, and tries to help, but is too dizzy to do much. The Army, Navy and Air Force try to help, but the giant easily defeats them. Underdog still insists on helping and a struggle ensues with Polly, who tries to keep him in his hospital bed, and accidentally rips the necklace off. Underdog, no longer dizzy, easily defeats the giant, and socks him back to his home planet. Note: These four episodes are available on DVD on *The Ultimate Underdog Collection, Volume 3*.

Underdog #113 *A New Villain Part 1* * 11/5/66
Underdog #114 *A New Villain Part 2* * 11/5/66
Underdog #115 *A New Villain Part 3* * 11/12/66
Underdog #116 *A New Villain Part 4* * 11/12/66

    A powerful thunderstorm ravages the city and inscribes a message on the side of a building with "To Underdog, a rhyme in time saves nine." Polly takes the message to Officer Flim Flanagan (from *The Hunter*) and he says it's the work of a new villain called The Slippery Eel and his partner, Fish. They were in prison and sent to a jail with an electric fence by Underdog. Eel plans to make his escape by scaling the fence. The guards turn on the electricity, but instead of electrocuting him, it electrifies him. Officer Flanagan suggests giving the mysterious clue to Shoeshine Boy to decipher, and he does. He concludes that the riddle means that Underdog should go to Big Ben in London as the Eel and his gang plan to rob some diamonds from a jeweler there. Eel is planning for Underdog's arrival and creates an electric cage to trap him. Virtually defeated, Underdog says to not throw him into the lake, which is exactly what the Eel does. Thinking he is free from Underdog, the Eel launches a major crime wave. The Eel and his gang head to Washington, D.C., to take over the country, but Underdog comes back. The water actually helped Underdog recover his powers. He then creates a giant glass jar and traps the Eel inside, where he can no longer harm anyone with his electric powers.

Underdog #117 *Batty Man Part 1* *............................11/19/66
Underdog #118 *Batty Man Part 2* *............................11/19/66
Underdog #119 *Batty Man Part 3* *............................11/26/66
Underdog #120 *Batty Man Part 4* *............................11/26/66

Yet another new villain is terrorizing the country and it's up to Underdog to figure out who is causing the latest crime wave. He discovers that it is the work of Batty Man, a Dracula-like vampire character. Polly and Underdog investigate the goings-on at Batty Man's castle. Batty Man's bats attack the duo and they are soon overcome and are chained up. While captured, Batty Man and his bats raid Fort Knox. They press the stolen gold into gold bowling balls, which they paint black. They plan to pass as bowling ball salesmen. They also place Underdog and Polly on the conveyor belt to turn them into bowling balls as well. The steam from the machine loosens Polly's chains and she feeds Underdog his super energy pill. Underdog battles the bad guys and throws them in jail and returns all the gold to Fort Knox. Note: The incredible popularity of *Batman* in 1966 inspired this story.

Underdog #121 *The Vacuum Gun Part 1* *.........................12/3/66
Underdog #122 *The Vacuum Gun Part 2* *.........................12/3/66
Underdog #123 *The Vacuum Gun Part 3* *........................12/10/66
Underdog #124 *The Vacuum Gun Part 4* *........................12/10/66

Simon comes up with another devastating new weapon, a vacuum gun. With it, he sucks up everything in sight, including Cad, by saying "Simon says, 'Come here.'" Ultimately, he uses it to clean up crime and sucks up Riff Raff, Batty Man, the Electric Eel and all of their related henchmen. Meanwhile, Underdog is called off to rescue a sinking ocean liner, the *Lusitanic*. It turns out that Simon cleaned up crime to build an army of bad guys. Meanwhile, Sweet Polly is spying and is captured by Simon. Underdog is finally available and comes to the rescue. Note: These four episodes are available on DVD on *Underdog Collectors Edition*.

"Thanks, Shoeshine Boy. You're humble and loveable."

OPENING AND CLOSING

When criminals in this world appear
And break the laws that they should fear
And frighten all who see and hear
The cry goes up both far and near for Underdog!
Underdog!

Speed of lightning
Roar of thunder
Fighting all who rob or plunder
Underdog!
Underdog!

When in this world the headlines read
Of those whose hearts are filled with greed
Who rob and steal from those who need
To right this wrong with blinding speed goes
Underdog!
Underdog!

Speed of lightning
Roar of thunder
Fighting all who rob or plunder
Underdog!
Underdog!

Show Opening #1: Billboard with Go Go Gophers.
Show Opening #2: Poster with The Hunter.

Syndicated Show Opening:
"Don't touch that dial" with Underdog fanfare and origin.
Underdog flies by and a giant *Underdog* logo appears.
Underdog crashes into a stone *Underdog* logo, knocking him dizzy.
Underdog gets tangled in a banner.
Underdog makes his name out of smoke.

Segment Opening 1: Simon Bar Sinister with Claw Machine
Segment Opening 2: Riff Raff shakes money from news dealer.
Segment Opening 3: Generic giant monster tears up the city.

Closing:
On our next show
Don't miss our next show
Post No Bills

Cheerios Commercial:
Simon turns Cheerios into tiddlywinks.

GO GO GOPHERS
(48 EPISODES)

FIRST SEASON: 10/3/64-3/27/65
NBC (AS PART OF *THE UNDERDOG SHOW*)
(26 EPISODES)

Go Go Gophers #1 *Moon Zoom* * 10/3/64
   Colonel Kit Coyote asks Sergeant Okey Loma how many Indians are left and the Sergeant reveals that there are only two left, so the Colonel says that they should be easy to defeat. The gophers create a teepee disguised like a rocket to retaliate. The gophers put a lot of "Keep Out" signs around the teepee, which attracts the Colonel and the Sergeant, and they are soon propelled to the moon. Note: This episode is available on DVD on *The Best of Go Go Gophers* and *The Underdog Chronicles*.

Go Go Gophers #2 *Trojan Totem* 10/10/64
   Synopsis unavailable.

Go Go Gophers #3 *Introducing General Nuisance* * 10/17/64
   General Nuisance arrives on the scene to find out why the Colonel and Sergeant have not captured the gophers Indians. He doesn't understand why it's so difficult to capture two Indians. The Colonel is about to be fired, so the Indians help out by scaring the General and acting scared of the Colonel. The General is happy and leaves the scene. Note: This episode is available on DVD on *Underdog Nemesis*.

Go Go Gophers #4 *Gatling Gophers* * 10/24/64
   The Colonel has received a huge Gatling gun in order to get rid of the gopher Indians for good. He demonstrates the gun and destroys his office in the fort. The Indians hear about this gun and make up a plan to retaliate. They make a cutout of themselves in a canoe and are shot at by the Colonel and the Sergeant who fall off a waterfall trying to shoot them. Next, the gophers saw down a tree that the Colonel and Sergeant are in. Finally, the gophers roll a huge boulder on top of them and succeed in taking out the gun as well. Note: This episode is available on DVD on *The Best of Go Go Gophers*.

Go Go Gophers #5 *The "Cleveland Indians"* * 10/31/64
   The Colonel has finally figured out how to get rid of the Indians; send them to Cleveland! When they get there, they set up camp in the middle of Main

Street. They get out of that fix and the Colonel tries to sign up the gophers to the Cleveland Indians baseball team. They don't want to join as the baseball players do not wear feathers. The Colonel then tries to get them to a hotel, which causes more chaos. Finally, the Mayor of Cleveland boots them out, but to take advantage of the situation, the gophers ask what the Colonel will do for them to get them to go back to Gopher Gulch. Note: This episode is available on DVD on *The Best of Go Go Gophers*.

Go Go Gophers #6 *Medicine Men* * 11/7/64

The supply wagon arrives with a large amount of bologna, the Colonel's favorite. Meanwhile, the two gopher Indians wave a white flag of surrender. They want to trade a blanket for some bologna. Colonel says no and kicks them out and also hides the bologna in a cannon. Soon, the Indians attack and the Colonel fires the cannon, forgetting that it was full of bologna and shoots it all to them. Note: This episode is available on DVD on *The Best of Go Go Gophers*.

Go Go Gophers #7 *Mesa Mess* * 11/14/64

The Colonel is making more plans to get rid of the gopher Indians. They receive a note mentioning where their secret hideout is, sent by the Indians themselves. The Indians lead the Colonel and the Sergeant, with explicit directions, to a trap door and box them up. Note: This episode, not "Up in the Air," is available on DVD on *The Best of Go Go Gophers*.

Go Go Gophers #8 *Termite Terror* * 11/21/64

The Colonel's secret weapon is a book featuring many tips on how to take care of the gopher Indians. The gopher Indians retaliate with an Indian termite that eats up everything in sight. Ultimately, the Colonel and Sergeant end up with a pile of sawdust. Note: This episode is available on DVD on *The Best of Go Go Gophers*.

Go Go Gophers #9 *Who's a Dummy?* * 11/28/64

The Colonel is determined to capture the gopher Indians without using guns. The gophers retaliate by creating wood dummies of themselves. The Colonel and the Sergeant are fooled time and time again. Finally, the Colonel gives up and the final time, they didn't use dummies at all.

Go Go Gophers #10 *Tapping the Telegraph* * 12/5/64

General Nuisance gives orders via telegraph to the Colonel and the Sergeant to get those gopher Indians. The new strategy doesn't work any better than the others and in the end they are thrown into the guardhouse.

Go Go Gophers #11 *Bold as Gold* * 12/12/64

    Settlers are pouring into California after a gold strike, so the Colonel wants to repeat the same thing in Gopher Gulch. The Colonel tries at an abandoned mine, but does not find anything but trouble. The Indians suggest panning for gold and so the Colonel and the Sergeant go at it. Meanwhile, the gophers un-dam the river and wash them out. Then, they discover a trail of gold, but it turns out to be rocks painted by the two Indians. Finally, the Indians pour a pile of the "gold" rocks on top of them. Note: Bullwinkle makes a cameo as a moose head on the wall! This episode is available on DVD on *The Best of Go Go Gophers*.

Go Go Gophers #12 *Up in the Air* * 12/19/64

    The Colonel and Sergeant obtain an airplane to drop bombs on the gopher Indians. Note: This episode is not on *The Best of Go Go Gophers* DVD. It is really "Mesa Mess."

Go Go Gophers #13 *The Big Banger* * 12/26/64

    The Colonel is trying to get the gopher Indians with a booby trap, but it backfires on General Nuisance. Nuisance says that he needs to use the cannon called the Big Banger to get the Indians. The gophers set up their share of booby traps and every attempt to use the Big Banger fails.

Go Go Gophers #14 *He's For The Berries* * 1/2/65

    The Colonel and the Sergeant go berry picking. The gopher Indians hear that he's going to eat gopher berries and the Indians try to stop him. The Colonel eats the berries and he suddenly grows into a giant. As a giant, the Colonel feels he can really defeat the gophers. He still can't do it as when he does corner them, he shrinks down to a midget. It all turns out to be a dream. Note: This episode is available on DVD on *The Best of Go Go Gophers*.

Go Go Gophers #15 *Swamped* * 1/9/65

    The Colonel has a new plan to get rid of the gopher Indians; he's going to go through the swamp. The Indians retaliate by building an alligator submarine. The sub leads to a wild chase and an explosion that leaves the Colonel and Sergeant up a tree. From the tree, they see the Indians tee-pee. The Colonel and the Sergeant attack, but are still being chased by the alligator submarine. Note: This episode is available on DVD on *The Best of Go Go Gophers*.

Go Go Gophers #16 *Tanks to the Gophers* * 1/16/65

    The Colonel gets another box; this one filled with a tank. The Colonel's plan is to roll over the gopher Indian tee-pee. The gophers set a gasoline fire to get the Colonel and Sergeant to retreat and they waterlog the tank. Next, the gophers dig a hole and trick them into falling in. The tank is now in really bad shape, but the Colonel isn't giving up and tries again. He drives right off a cliff thinking they are driving over the Indian's tee-pee. Note: This episode is available on DVD on *The Best of Go Go Gophers*.

Go Go Gophers #17 *Indian Treasure* * 1/23/65

The gopher Indians drop a rock with a map on the Colonel and he and Sergeant consult the Indians to decipher the code on the map. This takes the Colonel and the Sergeant on a dangerous route to the treasure. Eventually, they do get to the treasure chest. They open it and it explodes in their faces. Note: This episode is available on DVD on *Underdog Nemesis*.

Go Go Gophers #18 *The Carriage Trade* * 1/30/65

The gophers are sold a horseless carriage, which they can barely drive and they careen through Gopher Gulch. They want their old horse and wagon, but they have no money. The Indians want to trade their car for a horse and wagon with the Colonel. The Colonel decides to make a bet that his horse and wagon is faster than their car. If they win, the Colonel will make the trade. If he wins, the gophers agree to leave Gopher Gulch. Of course, the gophers win. Note: This episode is available on DVD on *The Best of Go Go Gophers*.

Go Go Gophers #19 *Honey Fun* * 2/6/65

The Colonel and the Sergeant are checking the supplies and some honey is missing. The gopher Indians have been stealing supplies. The Colonel and the Sergeant are on the trail, but end up rolling off a cliff in a log. Back to checking supplies, the Colonel and Sergeant discover even more honey is missing. On the trail again, they jump into a cactus disguised as Running Board. Finally, the last jar of honey is stolen and the Indians lead the Colonel and Sergeant into a bear's cave. Note: This episode is available on DVD on *The Best of Go Go Gophers*.

Go Go Gophers #20 *The Colonel Cleans Up* *. .2/13/65

Another box is sent to the Colonel to clean up Gopher Gulch containing a super vacuum cleaner. The Colonel plans to disguise the nozzle as a tee-pee and suck up the Indians. The Indians want the Colonel to go inside first to show them the tee-pee and he gets sucked up. The Colonel tries again, but the Indians have placed a mountain lion inside their tee-pee and that gets sucked up. The Colonel tries again but they suck up a couple sticks of lit dynamite. Note: This episode is available on DVD on *The Best of Go Go Gophers*.

Go Go Gophers #21 *The Raw Recruits* * 2/20/65

Part 1: The Colonel tells the Sergeant that if he can't capture the gopher

Indians, he will draft them into the Army. The Colonel tells the gophers about drills and the obstacle course, but the mischievous gophers have the upper hand, as usual.

Go Go Gophers #22 *Tenshun!* * 2/27/65
Part 2: The Colonel is still determined to make soldiers out of Ruffled Feather and Running Board. He takes them to the rifle range, which turns out to be a disaster, as they destroy the range, and then shows them how to march. Finally, the Colonel shows the Indians how to shoot the cannons and ends up being shot himself.

Go Go Gophers #23 *Cuckoo Combat* * 3/6/65
Part 3: The Colonel is still trying to make soldiers out of the gopher Indians. He shows the duo some basic self-defense skills, but is not very successful. Note: This episode is available on DVD on *The Ultimate Underdog Collection, Volume 3*.

Go Go Gophers #24 *Kitchen Capers* * 3/13/65
Part 4: The gophers throw a live grenade in through the Colonel's window. He's still trying to make soldiers out of the Indians and he puts them in the kitchen. The gophers make a special spicy soup for the Colonel and Sergeant. After drinking a lot of water, the Colonel teaches the Indians how to make biscuits, but the crafty duo use gunpowder instead of baking powder. The Colonel has had enough and discharges the gophers. Note: This episode is available on DVD on *The Best of Go Go Gophers*.

Go Go Gophers #25 *The Great White Stallion* * 3/20/65
Colonel Coyote wants to catch the Great White Stallion, but there's no such animal, according to the gopher Indians, so they decide to disguise themselves as one. Many chases occur, but the Colonel and Sergeant don't quite catch him. Instead, the gopher Indians capture the Colonel and Sergeant and roll them down a steep hill while trapped in a wooden cage. Note: This episode is available on DVD on *The Best of Go Go Gophers* and on *The Ultimate Underdog Collection, Volume 2*.

Go Go Gophers #26 *Blankety-Blank Blanket* * 3/27/65
Ruffled Feathers and Running Board are freezing and stop a passing stagecoach and take their blanket. Colonel Coyote and the Sergeant are after them, leading to a snowball fight and the Colonel falling into the icy water. In the end, the Colonel knits a brand-new blanket to replace the one the Gopher Indians stole. Note: This episode is available on DVD on *The Best of Go Go Gophers* and on *The Ultimate Underdog Collection, Volume 1*.

SECOND SEASON: 9/18/65-2/5/66
NBC (AS PART OF *THE UNDERDOG SHOW*)
(22 EPISODES)

Go Go Gophers #27 *The Ironclad* 9/18/65
Colonel Kit Coyote has a secret weapon, the Unsinkable Ironclad, a battleship with a cannon to defeat the gopher Indians. The gophers decide to build their own ship to retaliate. At first, the gophers don't have a chance, as they sink with the first shot. The gophers battle back and sink the Unsinkable Ironclad. Note: This episode is available on DVD on *The Best of Go Go Gophers* and on *The Ultimate Underdog Collection, Volume 2*.

Go Go Gophers #28 *Crash Diet* 9/25/65
Colonel Coyote is going to bite into a piece of pie, but before he can eat, the gopher Indians grab and eat the pie. The gopher Indians feel that Coyote is getting fat and play a trick on him, by sending a phony note to him from General Nuisance. Then, the gopher Indians pretend to help Coyote and put him on a diet and take all of the food that he used to eat. The real General Nuisance stops by and claims that he sent no message, causing Coyote to angrily chase the Indians. Note: This episode is available on DVD on *The Best of Go Go Gophers* and on *The Ultimate Underdog Collection, Volume 1*.

Go Go Gophers #29 *Wild Wild Flowers* 10/2/65
Part 1: A new shipment of pickles has arrived at the fort and the Indians are excited. Meanwhile, Aunt Flora has come for a visit, planting flowers everywhere and annoying the Colonel. The Indians use this opportunity to steal the pickles. The Colonel calls for the Sergeant, but apparently he's under the weather, so Corporal Crimp arrives to help. The camp can't attack due to the numerous flowers. The Colonel tries to fire a cannon, but it also backfires due to the flowers. Note: This episode is available on DVD on *The Best of Go Go Gophers*.

Go Go Gophers #30 *Look Out! Here Comes Aunt Flora* 10/9/65
Part 2: Aunt Flora is coming to visit again, but the Colonel is not happy. Corporal Crimp asks why. He feels that she will cause too much trouble and put flowers everywhere, so much so that he can't concentrate on the gopher Indians. The gophers hear about this and decide to have a little fun. The Colonel is trying to prevent her arrival. The Indians are trying to help her to come, and, of course, she does. Note: This episode is available on DVD on *The Best of Go Go Gophers* and on *The Ultimate Underdog Collection, Volume 3*.

Go Go Gophers #31 *Root Beer Float* *............................10/16/65
Corporal Crimp makes a deal with the Indians, trading water for root beer. The Indians have put hiccup drops into the root beer and everyone in the fort drinks it, causing severe hiccups. The Colonel, Corporal and Sergeant all have hiccups as well. The Colonel finds out what the Indians have done and chases the Corporal off for making such a bad trade. Note: This episode is available on DVD on *The Best of Go Go Gophers*.

Go Go Gophers #32 *Amusement Park* *.........................10/23/65
The Colonel is tired of battling the gopher Indians, so he and the Sergeant take the Indians to the amusement park to have a little fun. At the park, the gophers insist that the park has been built on Indian land and take free rides.

Go Go Gophers #33 *Tricky Teepee Trap* 10/30/65
Synposis unavailable.

Go Go Gophers #34 *3-Ring Circus*.............................11/6/65
Synposis unavailable.

Go Go Gophers #35 *Don't Fence Me In*.........................11/13/65
Synposis unavailable.

Go Go Gophers #36 *Locked Out* 11/20/65
Synposis unavailable.

Go Go Gophers #37 *Hotel Headaches* 11/25/65
Synposis unavailable. Note: this episode originally aired on Thanksgiving Day.

Go Go Gophers #38 *Choo Choo Chase*...........................11/27/65
Synposis unavailable.

Go Go Gophers #39 *Rocket Ruckus*..............................12/4/65
Synposis unavailable.

Go Go Gophers #40 *Go Go Gamblers* 12/11/65
Synposis unavailable.

Go Go Gophers #41 *Radio Raid*................................12/18/65
Synposis unavailable.

Go Go Gophers #42 *Steam Roller* 12/25/65
   Synposis unavailable.

Go Go Gophers #43 *Mutiny a Go-Go* 1/1/66
   Synposis unavailable.

Go Go Gophers #44 *Marooned on Cannibal Island* 1/8/66
   Synposis unavailable.

Go Go Gophers #45 *The Indian Giver* 1/15/66
   Synposis unavailable.

Go Go Gophers #46 *The Big Pow-Wow* 1/22/66
   Synposis unavailable.

Go Go Gophers #47 *Back to the Indians* 1/29/66
   Synposis unavailable.

Go Go Gophers #48 *California Here We Come* 2/5/66
   Synposis unavailable.

OPENING AND CLOSING

Opening 1:
A narrated opening telling of how the Go Go Gophers are the last two gopher Indians. This rarely seen opening shows the Go Go Gophers as much more savage than later on.

Opening 2:
Two little Indians,
All others gone,
Two little Indians,
Left all alone.

No buffalo to run,
No tribe to lead,
What can they do for fun?
(gibberish)

Go Go Gophers,
Watch them go go go,
Go Go Gophers,
Watch them go go go.

Here comes the Colonel with his Sergeant,
Both are a roarin' and a chargin'.

Go Go Gophers,
Watch them go go go,
Go Go Gophers,
Watch them go go go.

Go Go Gophers, watch them go go go!

COMMANDER McBRAGG
(48 EPISODES)

FIRST SEASON: 10/3/64-3/27/65
NBC (AS PART OF *THE UNDERDOG SHOW*)
(26 EPISODES)

Commander McBragg #1 *Over the Falls* * 10/3/64
McBragg tells of how he went over the Ranchopokee Falls to escape a tribe of a thousand savages.

Commander McBragg #2 *Fish Story* * 10/10/64
McBragg tells of a time he caught a giant fish by tying two masts together to form a prop to hold the fish's jaws open. When the man who "really must be going" expresses interest in seeing the fish, McBragg claims that rowing the giant fish made him so tired and hungry that he ate it.

Commander McBragg #3 *The Himalayas* * 10/17/64
McBragg climbs up the Himalayas, and an avalanche and blizzard overtakes his crew. He is then chased by abominable snowmen, but he eventually melts them with a small blowtorch and uses one of their shields to slide down the mountain to safety.

Commander McBragg #4 *The North Pole* * 10/24/64
McBragg leads a party through the snow and ice to the North Pole, and is soon separated from his party. He meets a band of polar bears, fires a shot, but the cold freezes the bullet. So, McBragg runs and climbs up what turns out to be the North Pole. Using his "mighty weight," he breaks off the pole, and pole-vaults over the bears, back to the safety of the nearby ship.

Commander McBragg #5 *Khyber Pass* * 10/31/64
McBragg tells of how he escaped 10,000 screaming tribesmen. McBragg is ambushed and soon he is out of ammunition. He begins firing a disabled cannon and the recoil propels him to safety. Note: This episode is available on DVD on *The Underdog Chronicles*.

Commander McBragg #6 *Ace Of Aces* * 11/7/64
McBragg takes down five enemy planes in France. At first, the five destroy McBragg's plane while he's flying it. He looks like a goner, but quickly grabs the falling wings and flaps his arms and flies with them. The shocked enemy planes all crash into each other staring at the sight.

Commander McBragg #7 *Niagara Falls* * 11/14/64

McBragg is thrown over the falls in a barrel of his own design. Unfortunately, the falls freeze and his barrel starts falling apart. Thinking quickly, McBragg fashions a pair of skis out of two-barrel staves and skis to safety.

Commander McBragg #8 *Dodge City Dodge* * 11/21/64

McBragg cleans up Dodge City, not Wyatt Earp as often claimed. Soon, McBragg is up against 20 of the roughest bad guys with only five bullets. Thinking quickly, he shoots at a nearby water tower, flooding out the villains. Note: This episode is available on DVD on *Underdog Nemesis* and *The Ultimate Underdog Collection Volume 3*.

Commander McBragg #9 *Football By Hex* * 11/28/64

McBragg wins the football championship single-handedly after all of his teammates are felled by injuries by tossing a high forward pass and sneaking quickly through the line to catch a touchdown. He wins the game 6-3. Note: Even though McBragg is apparently English, he seems to have attended an American college, as he plays American football. The man who "really must be going" is reading *Punch*. This episode is available on DVD on *The Ultimate Underdog Collection Volume 1*.

Commander McBragg #10 *Rabelasia* * 12/5/64

A send-up of James Bond-like gadgetry with McBragg driving an auto that dispenses banana peels causing the other spies to slide off the road. McBragg takes a recording of Rabelaisian secrets and at one point loses his front wheel. He replaced the wheel with the long-playing record and drives to safety. Note: the man who "really must be going" gets a chance to say "quite." Rabelasia is not a real place, unlike most places McBragg talks about.

Commander McBragg #11 *Okeefenokee Swamp* * 12/12/64

McBragg is captured by a gigantic black snake. Realizing that this was an American snake, McBragg starts whistling the "Star Spangled Banner" and the snake stands at attention. McBragg gets free and captures the still-erect snake.

Commander McBragg #12 *The Flying Machine* * 12/19/64

McBragg claims he flew a long time before Wilbur and Orville. After a few failed attempts, McBragg succeeds in flying, though not for long. His airplane eventually crashes and creates a deep hole. By the time McBragg climbs out of the hole, the Wright Brothers have received credit for inventing the airplane. Note: This episode is available on DVD on *Underdog Nemesis*.

Commander McBragg #13 *The Giant Elephant* *................12/26/64

McBragg encounters a giant angry elephant while on safari in Africa. The natives run off in fear, leaving McBragg to his own devices. The elephant is about to stomp on McBragg when McBragg notices a thorn in the elephant's front foot. The thorn is removed and the grateful elephant chases McBragg to Paris, London, and even to his home at the time this story is being told!

Commander McBragg #14 *The Great Bird* *......................1/2/65

McBragg accompanies the man who "really must be going" outside as he tells of his adventures with a giant bird. Alice, Jeffrey and Seymour are the names of the bird's children who are dropped out of the nest to fly and be on their own. McBragg can't fly so the mother bird took McBragg under her wing, apparently for good, as McBragg is swooped away at the end of the episode.

Commander McBragg #15 *Chicago Mobster* *....................1/9/65

McBragg cleans out the racketeers in Chicago and brings in the leader Al Baloney. He disguises himself as a vacuum cleaner salesman with a number of weapons. The mobsters take away McBragg's weapons and so he defeats Baloney by vacuuming him up.

Commander McBragg #16 *The Monster Bear* *..................1/16/65

At the Arrora Borealis Islands [sic], McBragg gets shipwrecked on an island with a giant polar bear. He defeats the polar bear by crying tears that freeze instantly and fires them at the polar bear with a slingshot, knocking the bear out.

Commander McBragg #17 *The Kangaroo* *......................1/23/65

McBragg is hired to locate the escaped giant kangaroo in Australia. He finds the kangaroo, which proceeds to box with him. Eventually, McBragg holds up a log, the kangaroo punches it and it splinters into hundreds of pieces, caging him in perfectly.

Commander McBragg #18 *The Giant Mosquito* *.................1/30/65

McBragg tells of battling a giant mosquito from the north swamps. Nothing kills the giant insect, so he ran away and hid in a nearby shack. The mosquito stings the house and McBragg hammers the stinger so that the mosquito is trapped. The mosquito starts flying with the house, and McBragg saws off the stinger so that the mosquito falls to his doom. McBragg fashions a makeshift parachute and lands the house and himself to safety.

Commander McBragg #19 *The Black Knight* *...................2/6/65

McBragg encounters the Black Knight in England, and battles and defeats him. When all looks lost, McBragg escapes out the back hatch of his suit of armor and sneaks around to clobber the Black Knight with a smoking pipe.

Commander McBragg #20 *The Flying Pond* * .2/13/65
McBragg discovers a way to release a bunch of ducks that have been frozen in a pond causing the ducks to fly with the frozen ice pond still attached.

Commander McBragg #21 *The Old Ninety-Two* *. 2/20/65
Abilene is the site where McBragg is a train engineer on the Old '92. The James Boys are attacking from the rear, but McBragg points the smokestack and steams them away. Then, the James Boys blows up the bridge. McBragg can't stop in time and travels on the bottom of the river, steaming up the water to a boil. He gets to Abilene on time with a trainload of cooked fish.

Commander McBragg #22 *Our Man in Manhattan* * 2/27/65
McBragg has to deliver a brief case, but is stopped repeatedly by a number of spies. He defeats them with a number of far-fetched inventions, including using his belt, which turns into a rattlesnake, and gluing his shoes together, which creates a machine gun. Eventually, McBragg turns in the briefcase to headquarters.

Commander McBragg #23 *Oyster Island* * 3/6/65
McBragg saves a native and is given many gifts from the other natives on the island, including a string of pearls. McBragg then goes pearl diving and spots a gigantic pearl. He soon is trapped by the giant oyster, but tickles the oyster to gain his freedom and also to gain the pearl.

Commander McBragg #24 *The Steam Car* * 3/13/65
McBragg tries hard but fails to invent the horseless carriage.

Commander McBragg #25 *Swimming the Atlantic* * 3/20/65
McBragg swims in the Atlantic Ocean for kicks, when a school of man-eating sharks starts chasing him. McBragg breaks away as such speed that he starts cutting a trench that leads him to the Pacific Ocean. He soon realizes that he has just cut the Panama Canal!

Commander McBragg #26 *Fort Apache* * 3/27/65
McBragg becomes the sole survivor at Fort Apache. He tricks a band of savage Indians by playing a recording of the cavalry, convincing them the Indians to retreat.

SECOND SEASON: 9/18/65-2/5/66
NBC (AS PART OF *THE UNDERDOG SHOW*)
(22 EPISODES)

Commander McBragg #27 *The Flying Trapeze* *.................9/18/65

McBragg is selling balloons at a traveling circus when an opening for a trapeze artist opens up. McBragg is competing against Nasty McNasty for the job. Nasty causes trouble by damaging the trapeze, causing McBragg to fall, but McBragg uses one of his balloons to bounce back up, fix the trapeze, and get the job.

Commander McBragg #28 *Around the World* *...................9/25/65

McBragg desires to travel around the world by balloon in 79 days. Along the way, he encounters many different sights, including a band of natives who attack him and pop his balloon. McBragg blows up a bubble gum balloon and floats to safety.

Commander McBragg #29 *Indianapolis Speedway* *...............10/2/65

McBragg wins the Indianapolis 500, but not before his tire goes flat. He fixes his own tire (no pit crew) with a small bicycle pump. He does this twice before his engine explodes. In the end, McBragg uses the pump-to-pump air to propel him across the finish line. Note: This episode is available on DVD on *The Ultimate Underdog Collection Volume 1*.

Commander McBragg #30 *The Rhino Charge* *...................10/9/65

A cricket is caught in a huge spider web, and McBragg saves him. Soon, a charging rhino chases McBragg to the side of a cliff; the rhino goes off the side but traps McBragg in a precarious position after he crashes at the bottom. McBragg uses the grateful cricket to leap and tie a rope across the gap and McBragg uses the taut rope to pull himself to safety.

Commander McBragg #31 *Mystifying McBragg* *................10/16/65

McBragg is locked in a mailbox and tossed in the Hudson River. He escapes flawlessly every time until a giant octopus traps him on one occasion. McBragg scribbles a note and "mails" it to the surface. A postman on the surface receives the letter and they torpedo the octopus, and McBragg swims to safety.

Commander McBragg #32 *Mamouth Cavern* *...................10/23/65

McBragg tells of how his discovered the great Mamouth Caverns, by firing his new rifle. The kick of the gun drives him into the cave inside the cliff. Trapped at the bottom of a hole, McBragg fires both barrels of the rifle toward the ground and is propelled out of the cavern.

Commander McBragg #33 *The Astronaut* * 10/30/65
McBragg becomes the first man in space. Scientists prepare special food for his flight but McBragg refuses, instead only wanting to ingest "McBragg's Marvelous Mixture." Suddenly, the fuel light goes on and McBragg is forced to pour the rest of "McBragg's Marvelous Mixture" into the fuel tank to safely return to Earth.

Commander McBragg #34 *Dam Break* * 11/6/65
River City has been exposed to rain for 40 days and 40 nights, so much rain that the dams bust. McBragg thinks quickly and purchases a store's entire supply of sponges, which soak up all of the excess water, and saves the city.

Commander McBragg #35 *The Eclipse* * 11/13/65
McBragg is captured by hostile natives and claims that if he isn't let go, he will make the sun disappear. They do not, and just then, an eclipse of the sun begins to start. In the darkness, McBragg escapes and makes his way to safety.

Commander McBragg #36 *Ship of the Desert* * 11/20/65
McBragg is attacked by Arabs while riding on a camel. McBragg fires back, but soon runs out of bullets. He then digs a deep hole, strikes water and floods the desert, using his camel as a "ship" and sails to safety while the bobbing Arabs look on. Note: McBragg turns the gun on himself to check to see if there are any bullets! This episode is also available on DVD on *The Ultimate Underdog Collection Volume 3*.

Commander McBragg #37 *Egypt* * 11/25/65
Egypt is the destination where McBragg is chased by an army of tanks. Crashing his jeep into a pile of stone blocks, McBragg takes out the inner tube of his tire, fashions a giant slingshot and shoots brick after brick at the tanks, enclosing them and creating the great pyramids! Note: This episode originally aired on Thanksgiving Day.

Commander McBragg #38 *The Singing Cowboy* * 11/27/65
McBragg sings "Where the Buffalo Roam" while Indians attack. He shoots arrows with his guitar but is eventually trapped. McBragg sings at the top of his lungs and causes an avalanche and captures the entire Indian party with one lasso.

Commander McBragg #39 *The Lumberjack* * 12/4/65
The North Woods Lumber Company hires McBragg to chop trees. He's so good that there is soon a logjam in the river. McBragg decides to blow up the

jam with TNT, but quickly builds a log cabin to keep him safe after the explosion. Afterwards, his log cabin floats to safety. Note: This episode is available on DVD on *The Ultimate Underdog Collection Volume 2*.

Commander McBragg #40 *The Bronco Buster* * 12/11/65

Arizona is the spot where McBragg becomes a rodeo champion and tames a giant bucking bronco. At one point, McBragg has the beast roped but, as he is being dragged along, his spurs rip into the dirt, eventually creating the Grand Canyon!

Commander McBragg #41 *Echo Canyon* * 12/18/65

McBragg discovers an echo canyon while riding on his horse and carrying a load of gold. Soon, he is chased by a band of robbers intent on stealing the gold. McBragg is chased into a corner, but shouts out, "You're surrounded! Drop your weapons!" The echoing voice sounds like many and McBragg easily rounds up the gang and leads them to jail.

Commander McBragg #42 *Tightrope* * 12/25/65

In Victoria Falls, McBragg walks across on a tightrope and performs a number of daring feats but loses his footing on one. While falling, he spins his balancing pole and creates a helicopter effect and flies himself to safety.

Commander McBragg #43 *Lake Tortuga* * 1/1/66

All of the fish in a small village are being eaten by a giant snapping turtle, causing the inhabitants to starve. McBragg tries to lasso the turtle, but fails. He then fires a cannon ball, which bounces off the turtle's shell. Finally, he fires numerous cannonballs, which boil the water and create a giant lake of fish and turtle soup.

Commander McBragg #44 *Coney Island* * 1/8/66

McBragg wins $2,000 at Coney Island by diving from a high tower into a barrel of water. After he takes a test dive at 100 feet, McBragg climbs up to the very top to do the final dive. While diving, McBragg realizes that there is no more water in the barrel as his clothes have soaked it all up. Quickly, he wrings out the soaked water and lands in the refilled barrel just in time.

Commander McBragg #45 *Rainbow Island* * .1/15/66

Penniless, McBragg is asked to come to the US for work, provided he starts the next day. He misses his plane and charters a private plane. While flying, McBragg stands up to take a photo of a rainbow and falls out of the cockpit. The plane crashes, McBragg slides down the rainbow to safety and is able to pay for everything with the pot of gold at the end of the rainbow.

Commander McBragg #46 *The Insect Collector* * 1/22/66

McBragg tells of how he bagged a lion without firing a shot. He is looking at an insect with a giant magnifying glass when a lion starts chasing him. At a cliff, with nowhere else to go, McBragg looks through the glass and gives a roar that scares the life out of the lion.

Commander McBragg #47 *Lost Valley* * 1/29/66

McBragg works out with the man who "really must be going" and tells of his story of how he obtained his hula-hoop. He helps a giant in Lost Valley by pulling a thorn out of his foot. As a reward, McBragg gets the ring from his finger. Note: The jazzy McBragg theme music used in this episode is quite cool.

Commander McBragg #48 *The Orient Express* * 2/5/66

McBragg outwits the enemy Secret Service on the Orient Express while he is in his pajamas.

OPENING AND CLOSING

Openings: (George S. Irving, Sandy Becker and Kenny Delmar sing)

Natives and rhinos:
This is the World of Commander McBragg.
Your hair will curl in the World of McBragg.
He fights monsters galore
And then asks for still more
Or so says the brag of McBragg.

Arabs:
This is the World of Commander McBragg.
Your head will whirl in the World of McBragg.
He can do anything!
In his world he's a king!
Or so says the brag of McBragg.

Marines:
When on the hill the Marines plant the flag,
They may be led by Commander McBragg.
With a cannon in hand
He can beat any *band!*
Or so says the brag of McBragg.

Endings:
Snake charmer breaks his flute.
McBragg comes out of a pipe.
Barrel with fuse does not explode.

"Did I ever tell you abouy you about the time that I..."

KLONDIKE KAT
(26 EPISODES)

FIRST SEASON: 9/10/66-12/10/66
CBS (AS PART OF THE UNDERDOG SHOW)
(14 EPISODES)

Klondike Kat #1 *Honor at Steak* * 9/10/66
Savoir Fare is stealing steaks under the eyes of Klondike Kat and Major Minor. He then escapes with the help of Malamutt. Klondike tries to catch Savoir Fare, but can't control his skis. Soon, Klondike asks an old prospector for help in finding Savoir Fare, but it is Savoir Fare. Ultimately, Klondike gets his mouse. Note: This episode is available on DVD on *The Underdog Chronicles* and *The Ultimate Underdog Collection Volume 3*.

Klondike Kat #2 *Secret Weapon* * 9/17/66
Klondike is putting up Wanted posters to get Savoir Fare and Savoir Fare keeps taking them down. Klondike retaliates by getting a giant cannon to blow up Savoir Fare's secret hideout. The gun backfires, sending Klondike on a wild ride backwards. Klondike tries again, but fails, until finally he inadvertently captures him.

Klondike Kat #3 *The Big Fromage* * 9/24/66
Major Minor tells Klondike to guard a giant round of cheese. Malamutt and Savoir Fare smell the cheese and decide to steal it. Klondike sets up a booby trap with electrical wires that backfire. Savoir Fare then steals the cheese. Klondike chases him with a gun and when he is about to shoot, he drops the gun, which causes Savoir Fare to drop the cheese, which shatters in a thousand pieces, but Klondike Kat always gets his mouse. Note: Malamutt, normally mute, says, "Cheese."

Klondike Kat #4 *Hard To Guard* 10/1/66
Synopsis unavailable.

Klondike Kat #5 *The Candy Mine* * 10/8/66
Savoir Fare has been stealing the candy coming out of the candy mine and Klondike is assigned to monitor the candy shipments. Klondike is keeping track, but Savoir Fare takes a mine car into the mine anyway. Inside the mine, Savoir Fare starts packing a mine car with candy. Klondike comes to stop him, but is soon chased by Savoir Fare's car. Eventually, both Savoir Fare and Klondike ride off the rails in one of the cars, and Klondike finally captures him. Note: This episode is available on DVD on *The Ultimate Underdog Collection Volume 2*.

Klondike Kat #6 *Rotten to the Core* 10/15/66
   Synposis unavailable.

Klondike Kat #7 *Trap Baiting* 10/22/66
   Synposis unavailable.

Klondike Kat #8 *Gravy Train* * 10/29/66
   Klondike is assigned to transport a package of roast beef on a train and stores it in a safe, but Savoir Fare steals it after distracting Klondike. Klondike is thrown off the train, but before Savoir Fare can eat the beef, Klondike catches up and arrests him. Note: This episode is available on DVD on *The Ultimate Underdog Collection Volume 1*.

Klondike Kat #9 *Cream Puff Buff* * 11/5/66
   Major Minor asks Klondike to buy a dozen cream puffs for the Governor's visit from the local bakery, but to watch out for Savoir Fare. Unfortunately, Savoir Fare gets the puffs and runs off with Malamutt. Klondike chases him and gets trapped, but Savoir Fare "rescues" him. Finally, Klondike chases him again and captures him while disrupting Major Minor and the Governor's dinner.

Klondike Kat #10 *Plane Food* * 11/12/66
   Major Minor tells Klondike to take a plane to get more food for the camp and to keep Savoir Fare away. Savoir and Malamutt follow Klondike and don disguises in order to steal the food on Klondike's plane. Savoir takes over the plane. Klondike tries to take it back and they tailspin back down to the camp, and food rains on the hungry Mounties plates. Note: This episode is available on DVD on *Underdog Nemesis* and on *The Ultimate Underdog Collection Volume 2*.

Klondike Kat #11 *Banana Skinned* * 11/19/66
   Major Minor assigns Klondike to guard some bananas. Of course, Savoir Fare gets into them. Savoir gets away by shooting bananas at Klondike, causing him to slip all over the place. Klondike plans to replace the bananas with dynamite. Major Minor comes back just in time to catch Savoir with the lit dynamite bunch. A scuffle ensues where Klondike is trying to give the dynamite back to Savoir and Minor keeps snatching the bunch back. Klondike reveals that it is dynamite about the time that the bunch explodes. Note: This episode is available on DVD on *Underdog Nemesis*.

Klondike Kat #12 *Up a Tree* * 11/26/66
   Klondike tries to catch Savoir Fare and Malamutt, who are feasting up in a tree, but fails time and time again.

Klondike Kat #13 *Pie Fly* * 12/3/66
Klondike sets a number of booby traps involving pies in order to catch Savoir Fare.

Klondike Kat #14 *Jail Break* * 12/10/66
Klondike captures Savoir Fare and puts him in jail. However, with Savoir Fare caught, Klondike has nothing to do, so he forced to set Savoir Fare free.

SECOND SEASON: 9/10/66-11/26/67
CBS (AS PART OF *THE BEAGLES*)
(12 EPISODES)

Klondike Kat #15 *Fort Frazzle Frolics* 9/10/66
Synposis unavailable.

Klondike Kat #16 *Sticky Stuff* 9/17/66
Synposis unavailable.

Klondike Kat #17 *Who's a Pill* * 9/24/66
With Savoir Fare stealing all the food, Klondike goes to the doctor to get a pill that will force Savoir Fare to do anything Klondike wants. However, the pill backfires and Klondike ends up doing Savoir Fare's bidding.

Klondike Kat #18 *Getting the Air* * 10/1/66
Klondike arrives from New York with some special cheese and in order to keep Savoir Fare from taking it, Klondike is told to go back to camp in a hot air balloon. Savoir Fare is wise to this, and makes a jump from the Empire State Building to the balloon. After a struggle, Klondike wins the battle and captures Savoir Fare.

Klondike Kat #19 *If I'd-a Known you was Comin'* * 10/8/66
Major Minor is making a cheesecake. Klondike comes running in to stop Minor so he can use it as an opportunity to stop Savoir Fare. While trying to stop Savoir Fare, Klondike gets trapped on a spinning record and also gets electrocuted and an ironing board falls on him and he gets trapped in a Murphy bed. Savoir Fare finishes making the cheesecake, but Klondike catches him just in time at the end.

Klondike Kat #20 *The Big Race* * 10/15/66
It's the 73rd Annual Sled Race, which Savoir Fare always wins. This time Klondike has a motor so Savoir Fare needs to depend on sneaky tactics to win. After many failed attempts, Klondike does indeed win the race using rocket

power until Major Minor points out that rockets are not acceptable and Savoir Fare is declared the winner yet again.

Klondike Kat #21 *Date on the Desert* *..........................10/22/66
Klondike is in the Klondobi Desert and Major Minor makes a call to check up on him. Klondike has a whole case of dates that he's protecting from Savoir Fare, and is bringing back to Fort Frazzle. Klondike is in disguise so he isn't bothered, but it doesn't work. Savoir Fare tries to get the dates by trading a glass of water for the dates. Klondike is very thirsty, but he refuses. When Klondike opens the case of dates for the Major, Savoir Fare has eaten the dates and a chase ensues through fadeout.

Klondike Kat #22 *Klondike Goes to Town* *.....................10/29/66
Klondike goes to the Branchwater Café to check out Savoir Fare, who is apparently hiding there. Klondike doesn't realize that the bartender is just Savoir Fare on stilts. Klondike picks a fight with Two-Gun Pete thinking that he's Savoir Fare. He finally catches the bartender when he falls off his stilts.

Klondike Kat #23 *Motorcycle Mountie* *........................11/5/66
Savoir Fare has the fastest sled in the territory, and Klondike reveals his new motorcycle to capture Savoir Fare. Major Minor wonders if he can drive it. He can…barely. Savoir and Malamutt enjoy the dinner they have stolen but they realize that Klondike is in pursuit on his motorcycle. They seem to get rid of Klondike and resume their meal. Klondike captures Savoir Fare, but his motorcycle has run off. Klondike whistles for the bike back and it returns! Klondike takes Savoir Fare to jail.

Klondike Kat #24 *Island in the Sky* 11/12/66
Synposis unavailable.

Klondike Kat #25 *The Island Hideout*..........................11/19/66
Synposis unavailable.

Klondike Kat #26 *The Kat Napper*.............................11/26/66
Synposis unavailable.

OPENING AND CLOSING

Opening 1:
Klondike Kat,
He's after Savoir Fare,

What a rat,
He's stealing everywhere,
Klondike Kat,
Will track him to his lair,
He always gets his mouse.
Klondike Kat,
He's always on the trail,
Klondike Kat,
Through rain or snow or hail,
Klondike Kat,
That cat will never fail,
He always gets his mouse.

Opening 2:
"Savior Fare has stolen my cheeses"

Savior Fare is *everywhere!*

GENE HATTREE
(1 EPISODE)

Gene Hattree #1 *The Trap* *
produced 9/64; first aired in syndication on *The Underdog Show* in 1973

Rabbit Foot runs in and wants to capture Tortilla Fats and his gang, who have just robbed the Parchesi Junction First National Bank, but Gene Hattree informs him that catching crooks is for sheriffs, sweeping is for deputies, but, first, time for a little song. Rabbit Foot wants to set a trap for the bandits where the bandits go on a ramp and get clobbered with a rock. Unfortunately, Gene Hattree gets clobbered and Rabbit Foot is sent back to sweeping. Rabbit Foot doesn't give up and tries a net trap, which catches Hattree again. Running gags include Hattree's continual bad singing and his need to replace his shot-up hat. Eventually, Rabbit Foot does capture Fats' gang, but Hattree gets all the glory, prompting Rabbit Foot to say that he's the unluckiest Rabbit Foot in the world.

CAULIFLOWER CABBY
(2 EPISODES)

Cauliflower Cabby #1 and #2 *Introducing The Champion!* *
produced circa 1964; first aired in syndication on *The Underdog Show* in 1973

The pilot for *Cauliflower Cabby* appears in syndication with the final episodes of *The Underdog Show*. It is not known whether this aired originally during the '60s, but what is known is that the pilot was produced and that General Mills owned it and was free to do anything they wanted with it. Boston Bully and Shifty rob a bank and escape in their invisible getaway car. At one robbery, Cauliflower Cabby is run down by the gang making another escape. Pinky Knees wonders why Cauliflower doesn't do anything about it and stop being a wimp. Little does she know, he's really The Champion! The Champion chases the crooks but loses them due to their invisible paint. The Champion discovers that Pinky has been captured which makes him livid. Champion sprays ink on Boston's car, making it visible again. Catching up with the crooks, the Champion tricks Boston by claiming that there are invisible policemen surrounding him.

THE BEAGLES
(36 EPISODES)

FIRST SEASON: 9/10/66-1/7/67
CBS (36 EPISODES, 2 PER SHOW)

Note: episodes 1-18, 23-26 and 31-34 are unavailable for viewing.

The Beagles #1 *Ghosts, Ghouls and Fools Part 1* 9/10/66
The Beagles #2 *Ghosts, Ghouls and Fools Part 2* 9/10/66
  Song: *Looking for the Beagles*

The Beagles #3 *Dizzy Dishwashers Part 1* 9/17/66
The Beagles #4 *Dizzy Dishwashers Part 2* 9/17/66
The Beagles #5 *Dizzy Dishwashers Part 3* 9/24/66
The Beagles #6 *Dizzy Dishwashers Part 4* 9/24/66
  Song: *Sharing Wishes*

The Beagles #7 *Drip, Drip, Drips Part 1* 10/1/66
The Beagles #8 *Drip, Drip, Drips Part 2* 10/1/66
The Beagles #9 *Drip, Drip, Drips Part 3* 10/8/66
The Beagles #10 *Drip, Drip, Drips Part 4* 10/8/66
  Song: *What More Can I Do?*

The Beagles #11 *Tubby Troubles Part 1* 10/15/66
The Beagles #12 *Tubby Troubles Part 2* 10/15/66
The Beagles #13 *Tubby Troubles Part 3* 10/22/66
The Beagles #14 *Tubby Troubles Part 4* 10/22/66
  Song: *You Satisfy*

The Beagles #15 *I'm Gonna Capture You Part 1* 10/29/66
The Beagles #16 *I'm Gonna Capture You Part 2* 10/29/66
The Beagles #17 *I'm Gonna Capture You Part 3* 11/5/66
The Beagles #18 *I'm Gonna Capture You Part 4* 11/5/66
  Song: *I Wanna Capture You*

The Beagles #19 *Foreign Legion Flops Part 1* * 11/12/66
The Beagles #20 *Foreign Legion Flops Part 2* * 11/12/66
The Beagles #21 *Foreign Legion Flops Part 3* * 11/19/66
The Beagles #22 *Foreign Legion Flops Part 4* * 11/19/66

Scotty wants The Beagles to play their new song, *I'd Join the Foreign Legion*, to get ideas on how to promote the song. He decides to have Stringer and Tubby join the Foreign Legion, but only as honorary members, but the Foreign Legion has other ideas, and actually signs them up. Stringer and Tubby sing their song again to see if they'll let them go. Later, Stringer and Tubby are taken prisoner, but everything works out in the end.

The Beagles #23 *The Braves Part 1* 11/26/66
The Beagles #24 *The Braves Part 2* 11/26/66
The Beagles #25 *The Braves Part 3* 12/3/66
The Beagles #26 *The Braves Part 4* 12/3/66
   Song: *Indian Love-Dance*

The Beagles #27 *The Man in the Moon Part 1* * 12/10/66
The Beagles #28 *The Man in the Moon Part 2* * 12/10/66
The Beagles #29 *The Man in the Moon Part 3* * 12/17/66
The Beagles #30 *The Man in the Moon Part 4* * 12/17/66

Scotty wants to hear The Beagles latest song, so they sing, *Thanks to the Man on the Moon*. Scotty says it's a good song but they need to do a publicity stunt to get their new song noticed. They want to blast Stringer and Tubby to the moon, but are thrown out. Eventually they meet up with Professor X, who has a private rocket to the moon. Scotty only wants to take publicity photos, but soon Stringer and Tubby launch into space and are trapped. While in space, they play their new song again. Then they are in real trouble as their rocket crash lands on another planet and encounter a space monster. Eventually, they do get home.

The Beagles #31 *Captain of the Ship Part 1* 12/24/66
The Beagles #32 *Captain of the Ship Part 2* 12/24/66
The Beagles #33 *Captain of the Ship Part 3* 12/31/66
The Beagles #34 *Captain of the Ship Part 4* 12/31/66
   Song: Be the Captain

The Beagles #35 *I Feel Like Humpty Dumpty Part 1* * 1/7/67
The Beagles #36 *I Feel Like Humpty Dumpty Part 2* * 1/7/67

Scotty comes in and demands yet another new song for a movie being made for Epic Pictures. The result is the song Humpty Dumpty. To attract movie director C.B. Schlemiel, Stringer dresses up like an egg to be thrown off a wall to convince Schlemiel to use the song. They try a few attempts before Schlemiel sees them, and when he finally does, he says the Scotty that he could use their song in his picture.

OPENING AND CLOSING

Opening:
Laughing Man in rubber ring in pool introducing The Beagles saying "Don't touch that dial."
Laughing Man skydiving and introducing The Beagles.
Laughing Man surfing and introducing The Beagles.
Looking for the Beagles song with The Beagles running.
Laughing man on tightrope saying, "Next episode in today's show."
Laughing man mountain climbing with a preview of next show.
Laughing man pumping up inflatable bed saying see you next time.

Credits:
Created and Produced by Total Television Productions (Watts Biggers, Chet Stover, Joe Harris, Tread Covington)
Animated by Gamma Studios (Harvey Siegel, Jaime Torres V., Sam Kai, Joseph Montell)
Voices: Allen Swift, Kenny Delmar, Mort Marshall
Storyboards: Gary Mooney, Marty Murphy
Animation Direction: Sal Faillace, Lucifer Guarnier, Pete Dakis
Music Direction: Charles Fox
Songs by Total Television Productions (Watts Biggers, Chet Stover, Joe Harris, Tread Covington)

THE SING-A-LONG FAMILY
(3 EPISODES)

CBS (FIRST AIRED IN 1966 AS PART OF *THE BEAGLES*.)

The Sing-a-Long Family #1 *Picnic* *
Song: *Nothing Like a Picnic*

The Sing-a-Long Family #2 *Skating* *
Song: *Skating's Such Fun to Do*

The Sing-a-Long Family #3 *Fair* *
Song: *There's a Great Affair, That You Can Share, When the Fair Comes to Your Town*

Note: *The Sing-a-Long Family* cartoon titles listed above are unofficial and do not appear on screen.

TWINKLES
(52 EPISODES)

Twinkles #0 (*Cereal Introduction*) *
This is an ad that is part live-action, part-animated that introduces the "Twinkles" cereal and all of the major characters, including Twinkles the Elephant, Wilbur the Monkey, Sanford the Parrot and Fulton the Camel, and the storybook package on the back. Not really part of the series, but included here for completeness' sake.

Twinkles #1 *Twinkles and the Sailboat*
Sanford, the parrot, takes Twinkles for a boat ride and uses an umbrella for a sail.

Twinkles #2 *Twinkles and the Trip to China*
Wilbur, the monkey, and Sanford, the parrot, run into trouble digging to China.

Twinkles #3 *Twinkles and the Bull Fight*
On Twinkles' picnic, the bull in the pasture meets El Sanfordo, the great Matadoro.

Twinkles #4 *Twinkles and the Airplane*
Sanford boasts to Twinkles and Wilbur that he can fly a plane, and Wilbur puts him to the test.

Twinkles #5 *Twinkles and the Honey Bees*
Fulton, the camel, shows Twinkles his new invention for taking honey from the bees.

Twinkles #6 *Twinkles and the Big Fan*
Fulton's new invention for beating the heat causes unexpected trouble, with Twinkles to the rescue.

Twinkles #7 *Twinkles and the Fishing Trip*
Wilbur gets a head start on Twinkles so that he can catch all the fish, but he runs into thin ice.

Twinkles #8 *Twinkles and the Roller Skates*
Fulton thinks his jet skates are just what he needs to win the race against Harley, the horse.

Twinkles #9 *Twinkles and the Carnival*
Sanford, "the lone parrot," gets thrown by the electric bucking horse, and the Ferris wheel makes matters worse.

Twinkles #10 *Twinkles and the Bananas*
Wilbur and Twinkles visit Terrible Mike, the gorilla, who is captain of the banana tugboat.

Twinkles #11 *Twinkles and the Mountain Climb*
Twinkles, Sanford and Wilbur get into trouble when Wilbur's trick starts an avalanche.

Twinkles #12 *Twinkles and the Pirate*
Fulton's invention for seeing parades over other people's head has surprising results.

Twinkles #13 *Twinkles and the Haunted House* *
Wilbur says that a ghost lived in the haunted house. Sanford says it's nonsense until they go to the house. After being scared, they discover that it's Herman Hyena scaring them.

Twinkles #14 *Twinkles and the Horse Show* *
Jimmy the Zebra disguises himself as a horse to compete in a horse show, but ends up winning as "Best Zebra in a Horse Show."

Twinkles #15 *Twinkles and the Snow Shovel*
Wilber volunteers to clear Twinkles' walk of snow with Fulton's new invention.

Twinkles #16 *Twinkles and the Rubber Raft*
Sanford and Wilbur have a race with rubber rafts and who should turn up but Mr. Whale. Note: There is a handwritten note on the schedule stating "Show 29," so was this originally aired in show #29 of *King Leonardo and his Short Subjects*, from October 14, 1961?

Twinkles #17 *Twinkles and the Desert Rescue*
Twinkles tells how Fulton started making inventions, even though they never work.

Twinkles #18 *Twinkles and the House Boat* *
Wilbur and Sanford decide to build a raft instead of a houseboat that Twinkles was building, but the houseboat proves to be more seaworthy.

Twinkles #19 *Twinkles and the Leaping Robber*
Twinkles and Fulton go to see Twinkles' Uncle Jumbo and meet a train robber on the way.

Twinkles #20 *Twinkles and the Flying Saucer*
"Sharp-eye" Sanford is sure he's seen a flying saucer and rushes out to tell all his friends. Note: There is a handwritten note on the schedule stating "Mar. 4," so was this originally aired in show #21 of *King Leonardo and his Short Subjects*, from March 4, 1961 or maybe show #20 of *King Leonardo and his Short Subjects*, actually aired March 4, 1961?

Twinkles #21 *Twinkles and the Little Boy*
Twinkles and Sanford, out for a walk, help Little Boy Blue who has lost his horn.

Twinkles #22 *Twinkles and the Big Fish*
Sanford, "the world's greatest fisherman," catches a big one, and he swims right over the dam.

Twinkles #23 *Twinkles and the Swimming Pool**
Wilbur digs a swimming pool, but eventually the steam shovel breaks down. Twinkles helps build the swimming pool and all is well.

Twinkles #24 *Twinkles and the Balloon*
Fulton takes Twinkles for a ride in his strange new invention, but doesn't know how to come down again.

Twinkles #25 *Twinkles and the Musical Band*
Twinkles and Sanford form a band, and Thomas, the octopus, proves to be quite a musician.

Twinkles #26 *Twinkles and the Amateur Show*
Twinkles shows Fulton, Wilbur and Sanford how teamwork can win.

Twinkles #27 *Twinkles and the Rodeo*
"Never-Fall Sanford, the Bronco King" is in for a surprise when Wilbur plays a monkey trick.

Twinkles #28 *Twinkles and the Show Boat*
Twinkles hates to miss the show but when the big paddle wheels break, the show must go on.

Twinkles #29 *Twinkles and the Boat Ride*
   Wilbur, Sanford and Twinkles try out Wilbur's boat, but Wilbur makes it go too fast.

Twinkles #30 *Twinkles and the Climbing Shoes*
   Wilbur thinks Fulton's unfinished invention is just what he needs to get to the best coconuts.

Twinkles #31 *Twinkles and the Falling Leaves*
   The fast Sanford rakes leaves, the faster they fall, until Twinkles discovers Wilbur is up to monkey tricks.

Twinkles #32 *Twinkles and the Big Storm*
   A rainstorm almost ruins the picnic until Twinkles puts his magic trunk to work to prove that every cloud has a silver lining.

Twinkles #33 *Twinkles and the Trailer*
   Fulton, the camel, invents a motor made of soap for his boat. The motor works just fine until it gets suds in Fulton's eyes.

Twinkles #34 *Twinkles and the Bird Cage*
   Sanford decides that the life of a pet parrot is best, but he soon discovers he's only a bird in a little wire cage.

Twinkles #35 *Twinkles and the Soap Boat*
   Sanford thinks he's the greatest driver in the world and takes Twinkles and Wilbur for a wild ride in a trailer.

Twinkles #36 *Twinkles and the Game*
   Twinkles and his friends play "hide and seek." Twinkles finds everyone but Jimmy, the zebra, who hides himself in a funny way.

Twinkles #37 *Twinkles and the Parachute* *
   Fulton invents a parachute and wants to test it by jumping off of a cliff with it. Twinkles suggests he just jumps off the roof. The parachute fails and Fulton is grateful.

Twinkles #38 *Twinkles and the Lawnmower*
   Sanford's lawnmower breaks down, and he's out of a job until Twinkles comes along and thinks of a strange way to make the lawnmower work.

Twinkles #39 *Twinkles and the Baby Sitter*
Twinkles and his friends start a babysitting business, and just when everything is going wrong, Twinkles gets an idea to make the children behave.

Twinkles #40 *Twinkles and the Lemonade Stand*
Sanford and Wilbur have a lemonade stand but no customers until they decide to take the lemonade to the customers.

Twinkles #41 *Twinkles and the Tractor*
Wilbur and Sanford become farmers and all goes well until Sanford wrecks the tractor.

Twinkles #42 *Twinkles and the Kite*
Fulton invents a "camel-carrying kite" and when he tries it out, he runs into trouble because Wilbur has played a monkey trick.

Twinkles #43 *Twinkles and the Little Girl*
Twinkles and Sanford, out for a walk, meet Miss Muffet, who tells them about a huge spider that has just frightened her.

Twinkles #44 *Twinkles and the Gold Mine*
Sanford and Wilbur explore an old lost gold mine in search of treasure, but part of the ceiling falls down and they can't get out.

Twinkles #45 *Twinkles and the Mechanical Man*
Fulton, the camel, invents a mechanical man that works but won't do anything right, and Twinkles discovers that the mechanical man has a tail that looks like a monkey's.

Twinkles #46 *Twinkles and the Volunteer Fireman*
Mrs. Horse's house is on fire and Wilbur and Sanford, the volunteer firemen, go to her rescue. Luckily, they take Twinkles with them.

Twinkles #47 *Twinkles and the Sports Car*
Sanford takes Twinkles for a fast ride in his sports car, but the car runs out of gas in the middle of heavy traffic.

Twinkles #48 *Twinkles and the Missing Fish*
Twinkles and Fulton go fishing and have wonderful luck, but then they discover that their fish are gone…and they also discover why.

Twinkles #49 *Twinkles and the Birthday Party*
Twinkles is sad because he thinks he's being left out of a birthday party for someone special — then he gets a big surprise.

Twinkles #50 *Twinkles and the Toboggan*
Sanford, Wilbur and Twinkles go to the top of Slippery Hill to slide does on their toboggan. On their way down, they run into trouble.

Twinkles #51 *Twinkles and the Sheep*
Coming home from a picnic, Twinkles and Sanford meet Little Bo Peep who has lost her sheep. Twinkles thinks of a way to help her.

Twinkles #52 *Twinkles and the Carousel*
Wilbur, Sanford and Twinkles go to the Carousel in the park. Sanford boasts that he can catch the brass ring but he reaches out too far.

Twinkles cereal box stories:

Series 1:
Sleepy the Baby Kangaroo
The Frozen Pool
Wilbur the Monkey
The Buried Treasure
The Lion who Loved Himself

Series 2:
Wilbur's Birthday
The Wild West
The Unknown Creature
The Lost Kitten
The Amazing Little Elephant
The Tin Soldiers

Series 3:
The Beanstalk
The Double Bubbles
The Day of Rest
The Moon Man
The Sanford Tree

Series 4:
The School Below the Sea
The Teddy Bear
The Magic Lamp
The Butterfly Hunt
The Island Vacation
The Trouble Maker

Series 5:
The Little Kangaroo
Firehouse No. 99
Casey Jones
The Telescope
Bradley Bighorn the Mountain Sheep
The Penguin Family

Series 6: Regular
The Balloon Machine
The Lost Geese
The Iceberg
The Monkey Trick

Series 6: Sugar Sparkled
The Live Scarecrow
The Elephant Carnival
The Duck Call
The Sad Circus Owner
The Wicked Pirates
The Money Trees

Series 7: Sugar Sparkled
The Hound Dog

Series Unknown:
The Animal Circus
The Balloon Breaker
The Platypus

APPENDIX

PUBLISHING

COMIC BOOKS

King Leonardo and his Short Subjects:
Four Color #1242 (11-1/62)
Four Color #1278 (2-4/62)
Dell #01290-207 (7/62)
#1 (10/62) - #4 (9/63)

The Colossal Show #1 (10/69) (Gold Key)

Underdog:
#1 (7/70) - #10 (1/72) (Charlton)
1974 Kite Fun Book
#1 (3/75) -#23 (2/79) (Gold Key)
March of Comics #426 (1977), #438 (1978), #467 (1980), #479 (1981)
3-D #1 (#43) (6/88) (Blackthorne)
#1 (1987) - #2 (1987) (Spotlight)
Summer Special #1 (10/93) (Harvey)
#1 (11/93) - #5 (7/94) (Harvey)

BOOKS

King Leonardo and the Royal Contest (1962)
Twinkles and Sanford's Boat (1962)
Tennessee Tuxedo and the Sailboat Race (1965)
Tennessee Tuxedo and Old 97 (1965)
Underdog (1965) Note: In this book Riff Raff is referred to as "Cad Lackey" repeatedly.
Underdog and the Disappearing Ice Cream (1975)

COLORING BOOKS

King Leonardo – 1
Tennessee Tuxedo – 5
Twinkles – 1
Underdog – 8

APPENDIX

A WHO'S WHO OF TOTAL TELEVISION PRODUCTIONS

Don Adams (1923-2005) *voice: Tennessee Tuxedo, Pretzel, Mayor of Megapolis*
Maggi Alcumbrac (1917-1975) *animation: TV Spots*
Frank Andrina (1933-   ) *animation: TV Spots*
Roman Arambula (1935-   ) *animation: Gamma*
Jackson Beck (1912-2004) *voice: King Leonardo, Biggy Rat, Professor Messer, vo on General Mills commercials, narrator on* Gene Hattree, *Tortilla Fats, announcer on* The Dudley Do-Right Show
Sandy Becker (1922-1996) *voice: Mr. Wizard the Lizard, Lois Loon, Horrors Hunter, announcer on* Tennessee Tuxedo and his Tales, *Tiger Tornado, the man who "really must be going," Savoir Fare, Sergeant Okey Homa, Ruffled Feathers, Gene Hattree, Rabbit Foot, announcer on* The Beagles
W. Watts "Buck" Biggers (1927-   ) *creator, writer, songwriter*
Ellie Bogardus *animation: TV Spots*
Bradley Bolke (1925-   ) *voice: Chumley, Jerboa Jump, Slippery Hood*
Shull Bonsall (1917-2002) *animation: TV Spots*
Martha Buckley *animation: TV Spots*
Bill Butler (?-1998) *animation: TV Spots*
Angel Canton *animation: Gamma*
Cesar Canton *animation: Gamma*
Jerry Capp *writer and artist on* Twinkles *and brother of* Li'l Abner's *Al Capp*
Roger Carlin *representative for Leonardo and P.A.T.*
Dale Case (1938-   ) *animation: TV Spots*
Treadwell D. Covington (1926-   ) *creator, producer, business, voice talent*
Wally Cox (1924-1973) *voice: Shoeshine Boy/Underdog, various cloud people, various voices on* Underdog
Pete Dakis *animation direction*
Chris Decker *animation: TV Spots*

Kenny Delmar (1910-1984) *voice:* The Hunter, *narrator for The Hunter, Mr. Mad, narrator for* Tennessee Tuxedo, *Flunky, Yak, Sergeant Badge, Mr. Hothead, Commander McBragg, Colonel Kit Coyote, Corporal Crimp, narrator for* The Beagles, *C.B. Shlemiel*
Phil Duncan *animation: TV Spots*
Izzy Ellis (1910-1994) *animation: TV Spots*
Sal Faillace (1930-?) *animation direction: Gamma*
Eli Feldman *co-producer on the aborted* Parrot Playhouse
Charles Flekal *animation: TV Spots*
Charles Fox *music direction*
Bob Gannon (1909-1972) *associate producer: TV Spots*
Joyce Gard *animation: TV Spots*
John Garling *animation: TV Spots*
Herschel Burke Gilbert (1918-2003) *music composer*
Bob Gore *animation: TV Spots*
Norm Gottfredson (1925-   ) *animation: TV Spots*
Edwin A. "Bud" Gourley *animation: Gamma*
Lu Guarnier (1914-2007) *animation direction*
Joe Harris (1928-   ) *creator, artist, character designer*
Charles Hatton
Tex Hansen *animation: Gamma*
Dave Hoffman *animation: TV Spots*
Charlie Hotchkiss *P.A.T.*
Charlotte Huffine *animation: TV Spots*
George S. Irving (1922-   ) *voice: various on King Leonardo, Death Valley O'Days, General Custard, The Black Baron, Mr. Mad, narrator for* Twinkles, *narrator for* Underdog, *various cloud people, Tap Tap, Just in Case the Witch Doctor, narrator for* Klondike Kat, *Major Minor, Running Board, General Nuisance*
Gordon Johnson (1929-1988) *DFS account executive representing General Mills*
George Jordan *animation: TV Spots*
Samuel S. Kai (1917-2006) *animation: TV Spots, animation: Gamma and Animation Supervisor*
Phil Kaye *animation: TV Spots*
Leonard Key (1920-   ) *co-founded Leonardo and P.A.T. with Peter Piech; brother of Ted Key*
Charles Kimball *post-production: Gamma*
Bill Kohn *animation: TV Spots*
Roy Laufenburger *animation: TV Spots*
Norma MacMillan (1921-2001) *voice: Sweet Polly Purebred*
Fred Madison *animation: TV Spots*

Carlos Manriquez (1908-1981) *animation: Gamma*
Mort Marshall (1918-1979) *voice: various on* The Hunter, *Stanley Livingstone, Baldy Eagle, Big Bill Bear, Mr. Stonecutter, plumber, Klondike Kat, Tubby, Professor X*
Jack Mathis *DFS account executive representing "Twinkles" cereal*
Jesus "Chuy" Martinez *animation: Gamma*
Chuck McCann (film editor) *animation: TV Spots*
Chuck McCann (1934-   ) *voice: Tennessee Tuxedo on "FrostyO's" commercials*
Tom McDonald *animation: TV Spots*
Frank Milano (1918-1962) *voice: various on* King Leonardo
Lee Mishkin (1927-2001) *animation: TV Spots*
Joseph Montell *animation: Gamma and Layout Supervisor*
Gary Mooney (1930-2008) *storyboard artist*
Marty Murphy *storyboard artist*
Sam Nicholson *animation: TV Spots*
Casey Onaitis (1918-1999) *animation: TV Spots*
Barbara Orme *animation: TV Spots*
James Partch *animation: TV Spots*
Peter M. Piech (1918-1999) *executive producer of Leonardo and P.A.T.*
Sy Plattes *General Mills and inspiration for Platypus in Tennessee Tuxedo*
Jack Pleis (1917-1990) *music conductor, orchestrator*
Bernard "Barney" Posner *animation: TV Spots*
John Pratt *animation: TV Spots*
Thelma Raider *animation: TV Spots*
Anna Lois Ray *animation: TV Spots*
Gerald Ray (1924-1983) *associate producer: TV Spots*
Julian E. Raymond *animation: TV Spots*
Dunbar "Dun" Roman (1914-1980) *animation: Gamma*
Philip Roman (1930-   ) *animation: TV Spots; later founded his own animation studio*
Norman Rose (1917-2004) *voice: various on* King Leonardo
Beverly Rowe *animation: TV Spots*
Bob Schleh *animation direction: Gamma*
Glen Scott *animation: TV Spots*
Alberto Severns *animation: TV Spots*
Winston Sharples (1909-1978) *stock music used in earlier TTV shows, composed music for Paramount's Famous Studios cartoons*
Harvey Siegel (1945-2004) *animation: TV Spots (misspelled "Spiegle" on* King Leonardo *credits), co-owner: Gamma and Production Director*
George Singer (1923-2002) *animation: Gamma*

Delo States *voice: King Leonardo's mama, Carlotta Colognie, Lynetta Lion, Sewonya Button, the duchess, Samantha, Princess Glissando, Bubblehead Empress, Pinky Knees, the lady who says, "It's a frog!," the wicked witch of Pickyoon, Aunt Flora, all female voices on all TTV shows except Sweet Polly Purebred*
Ben Stern (1923-   ) *sound engineer, father of radio DJ Howard Stern*
Ben Stone *voice: The Fox, Officer Flim Flanagan, Rocky Monanoff, Cad Lackey, Cauliflower Cabby/The Champion*
Larry Storch (1923-   ) *voice: Phineas J. Whoopee, the platypus*
Chet A. Stover (1925-   ) *creator, writer*
Allen Swift (1924-   ) *voice: narrator for* King and Odie, *Odie Colognie, Itchy Brother, Duke, Earl, Tooter Turtle, Simon Bar Sinister, Riff Raff, Mooch, King Klobber, Goggol, Irving and Ralph, the two-headed dragon, O.J. Skweez, King Cumulus, Mange the Mole King, Bubblehead Emperor, Overcat, Captain Marble Head, Boston Bully, Shifty, Scotty*
Ernest Terrazas (1909-1995) *animation: Gamma*
Stuart Upson *DFS*
Gustavo Valdez *studio owner, Gamma*
Jaime Torres Vasquez (1943-   ) *co-owner, Gamma and Associate Director*
Norm Vizentz *animation: TV Spots*
Fred Von Bernewitz (1938-   ) *film editor, negative cutter*
Ben Washam (1915-1984) *animation director: TV Spots*
Dave Weidman *animation: TV Spots*
Ray Young *animation: TV Spots*
Gordon Zahler (1926-1975) *musical director, supervisor*

Unknown voices: Gopher brothers, beaver brothers

BIBLIOGRAPHY

A&E Biography: Don Adams VHS. A&E Home Video, 2004.

Adams, Don. *Would You Believe?* Los Angeles: Price Stern Sloane. 1966.

Arnold, Mark. "Whatever Happened to Total TeleVision productions?" *Hogan's Alley* #15, 2007.

Basile, Nancy. "Underdog Cartoon Becomes Live Action Movie" (Interview with Creator and Illustrator Joe Harris). About.com, 2007.

Biggers, Buck, and Stover, Chet. *How Underdog Was Born*. Boalsburg, PA: BearManor Media, 2005.

Brodsky, Leigh Anne. "Flying High With Underdog" *Animato!* #38 Summer-Fall 1997.

Christensen, Paulington James, III. "Exclusive Interview: *Underdog* Creator Joe Harris Speaks!" Movieweb.com, 2007.

Cox, Wally. *My Life as a Small Boy*. New York: Simon and Schuster, 1961.

Fischer, Stuart. *Kids' TV: The First 25 Years*. New York: Facts on File. 1983.

Green, Joey. *The Get Smart Handbook*. New York: Collier Books, 1993.

Grossman, Gary H. *Saturday Morning TV*. NewYork: Dell Publishing Co. 1981.

Hall, Jim. *Mighty Minutes*. New York: Harmony Books. 1984.

Harris, Joseph. "Life With Underdog" *Animato!* #38 Summer-Fall 1997.

Krell, David. "Underdog the Canine Crusader" *Animato!* #38 Summer-Fall 1997.

Lawson, Tim, and Persons, Alisa. *The Magic Behind the Voices*. Jackson: University Press of Mississippi. 2004.

Lenburg, Jeff. *The Encyclopedia of Animated Cartoons*. New York: Facts on File. 1991.

McNeil, Alex. *Total Television, 4th Edition*. New York: Penguin Books, 1996.

Scott, Keith. The Moose That Roared. New York: St. Martin's Press. 2000.

Ulrich, Charles. "Who Was Who" *The Frostbite Falls Far-Flung Flier* V.4 #3, March 1990.

Underdog Chronicles, The DVD. New York: Sony Wonder, 2001.

Underdog Collectors Edition DVD. New York: Sony Wonder, 2000.

Various, "International Movie Database", IMDB.com.

Various, "Social Security Death Index", SSDI, com.

Various, "Wikipedia", Wikipedia.com.

CREATED AND PRODUCED BY TOTAL TELEVISION PRODUCTIONS

INDEX

1st Books Library 10
3DBB 138-139, 148

A&E Biography 140
Aarondale, Frank 11
ABC 13-14, 137, 218
Academia de San Carlos School of Fine Arts 120
Action for Children's Television (ACT) 219
Adams, Don 19, 23, 137-138, 140-143, 145, 158, 163
Adventures of Superman, The 162
Aesop and Son 14, 121
Airport 1975, 142
Al Brodax Productions 202
Allen, Dayton 36, 142, 146-147
Allen, Fred 35, 73
Allen, Woody 164
Allen's Alley 73, 141
Amos 'n' Andy 39
Andrina, Frank 38-40
Animato!, 9, 22, 30, 38
Arambula, Roman 120-123, 166, 219
Archies, The 201
Arnaz, Desi 262
Arngrim, Alison 165
Arngrim, Thor 164
Around the World in 80 Days 246
Arthur Godfrey's Talent Scouts 140
ASCAP 245
Aura Recording Studios 145-146
Australia 215, 246
Autrey, Gene 211
Avondale Estates, GA 10

Baldwin, Alan, 223
Baldwin, Alec, 144
Baldy the Eagle, 138, 141, 147, 150, 154, 221
Ball, Lucille, 162

Ballantine Books 10
Bamberger Books 10
Banana Splits, The 207
Baron Munchausen 189
Barron, Jack 36
Barrymore, Lionel 165
Bart, Ernie 126
Basile, Nancy 189
Baum, Marty 35
BBD&O 146, 222
Beagles, The 122, 141, 197-198, 201-208, 212, 215, 222, 250
Beatles, The 201-202
Beany and Cecil 39
Beck, Jackson 34, 36-37, 140
Beck, Max 36
Becker, Sandy 97, 179
Beetle Bailey 39
Belly Book, The 241
Benny, Jack 216
Beverly Hills, CA 141
Big Cartoon Database 251
Biggers, Earl Derr 10
Biggers, W. Watts "Buck" 9-25, 27-29, 33-35, 37-38, 73-74, 97, 119, 125, 137-138, 140, 163, 165-166, 190, 201-203, 211, 215-223, 245-246, 248, 251
Biggy Rat 33, 43, 46-71
Bill Dana Show, The 140
Bluto 37
Bogart, Humphrey 165
Bolke, Bradley, 74, 138, 140-144, 146-147, 157, 165
Bongo Congo 33
Bonsall, Shull 39
Boomerang 223
Boris Badenov 238-239
Boston, MA 19, 222
Boston Bully 212

Bounty towels 11
Brando, Marlon 164
Britt, Ponsonby 18
Broadway Video 203, 223
Brodax, Al 202
Bronx, The, NY 142
Browne, Dik 217
Bruszewski, John 153, 182, 199, 205, 224
Brutus 37
Bullwinkle and Rocky Fan Club, The 14
Bullwinkle (character) 129, 162, 211, 237-239
Bullwinkle Show, The 13-14, 33, 119, 129, 162, 189
Bullwinkle's Corner 14, 163
Bullwinkle's Restaurant 138, 221, 237-239
Burgos, Daniel 121
Buzzy the Crow 37

Cad Lackey 74, 165, 172, 174, 226-227, 247
California 145
Calvin and the Colonel 39
Canton, Angel 121
Canton, Cesar 121
Cantor, Charlie 143
Cape Cod, MA 12, 97
Cap'n Crunch cereal 14
Captain America 222
Captain Kangaroo 147
Carlin, Roger 26
Carter, Boake 144
Cartoon Cut-Ups 218
Casper, the Friendly Ghost 165, 246
Cauliflower Cabby (character) 74, 212
Cauliflower Cabby (segment) 211-212
CBS 137-138, 161, 202, 224
Champion, The 74, 212
Chapel Hill, NC 18
Charlie Brown 222
Charlie Chan novels, 10
Charlotte, NC 18, 20
Charlton Comics 221, 225
Check it Out 141
Cheerios cereal 21, 166-167, 175, 181
Cheerios Kid 11, 15
Chicago, IL 145
Chief Running Board 168, 179-183, 186-187, 240
Chihuahua, Mexico 121
Children's Television: The First 35 Years 139

Christensen III, Paulington James 162
Chuck E. Cheese's Pizza Time Theatre 221
Chumley the Walrus 138-140, 142-143, 146-151, 153-155, 179, 221, 238-240
Clarabelle the clown 147
Classic Media 138, 223, 247-248
Clifton Finnegan 143
Clint Clobber 35
Clock, The 218
Cocoa Puffs cereal 11
Cocoa Puffs Kids 11
Coke / Coca-Cola 162, 222
Colman, Ronald 34
Colonel Kit Coyote 168, 179-180, 182, 240
Colonius, Lars 11-12, 21
Colossal Show, The 139, 215-218, 224
Columbia Pictures 25, 36, 252
Columbia Records 207
Columbia University 10
Commander McBragg (character) 9, 121, 189-193, 195
Conried, Hans 13
Conversations With Woody Allen 142, 164
Cool Cat 142
Coral Gables, FL 18
"Counterfeit Wants" 76-94
Covington, Treadwell "Tread" 2, 9, 12, 18-20, 22, 24-25, 34-35, 38, 48, 53, 73-74, 76, 97-99, 114, 125, 130, 138, 140-143, 145-148, 164-165, 190, 198, 201-203, 216, 219-222, 245-246, 248, 250-251
Cox, Wally 19, 23, 34, 141, 163-164, 166, 176, 190, 222-223
Crowther, Duane 11-12, 21
Crusader Rabbit 39
Czechoslovakia 40

Da Vinci, Leonardo 34
Dakis, Pete 23-24
Dallas, TX 122
Dana, Bill 140
Dancer-Fitzgerald-Sample (DFS) 9-12, 14-18, 20, 22, 25, 38, 97, 119-120, 122, 125, 166, 202-203, 212, 217-218, 246, 251
Davey and Goliath 165
Davey Hanson 165
De La Torre, Sergio 121
Deitch, Gene 35
Dell Comics 45, 97

Delmar, Kenny 73-74, 141, 201, 216
Deluxe Toys 202
DePatie-Freleng 219
Deputy Dawg 146-147
Detroit, MI 163
Dickie-Raymond 19
Dickinson College 10
Disney (Walt Disney Productions) 11-12, 21-22, 120, 122, 164, 247
Don Adams Screen Test, The 141
Dora the Explorer cereal 126
Dudley Do-Right (character) 237-239
Dudley Do-Right of the Mounties (segment) 13-14, 121, 197
Dudley Do-Right Show, The 37, 218, 252
Duffy's Tavern 143
Dumplings, The 74, 141

"Eclipse, The" 194
Ed Sullivan Show, The 140
Einstein, Albert 97
Ellis, Tom 222
Emory University Law School 10
England 36
Entertainment Rights 223
Evanston, IL 164

F Troop 142
Faillace, Sal 122, 197-198
Family Guy 222
Famous Studios 37, 211, 246
Fantasia 11
Fat Albert 201
Feiffer, Jules 217
Feldman, Eli 19, 137
Feldon, Barbara 158
Fibber McGee and Molly 148
Filmation 215, 219
Filmtel International Corporation 25
First Family, The 165
Fleischer Studios 37, 211
Flunky 141
Fort Frazzle 197
Four Feathers, The 189
Fox, The 46-47, 73-95, 97, 168
Fractured Fairy Tales 14, 38, 121, 163
Fractured Flickers 13
Fred Allen Show, The 73, 141
Frees, Paul 221

Friends 162
Frosted Flakes cereal 10
FrostyO's cereal 139, 142, 150
Frosty the Snowman 147
Fulton the Camel 128-134

Gamma Productions 9, 13-14, 25-26, 38, 40, 119-121, 123, 138, 166, 197, 215, 218-219
Ganon, Bob 39
Gartenberg, John 203
Gary Moore Show, The 140
Gaynor & Ducas 19
Gene Hattree (character) 211-212
Gene Hattree (segment) 211
General Mills 9-15, 19-23, 25-26, 33-34, 37-38, 119-120, 123, 125-126, 137, 142, 150, 161, 163, 166, 197, 201-203, 212, 215, 218-221, 246, 251
George of the Jungle 12, 14
Get Smart 140-142, 158
Ghost Busters, The 142
G.I. Joe 37
Gifford & Kim 11
Gifford, Lou 11
Gilligan's Island 139-140
Glen Glenn Sound 122
Go Go Gophers (characters) 9, 168, 179-184, 186-187, 240
Go Go Gophers (segment) 9, 121, 123, 141, 143, 162, 171, 179-187, 240, 250
Go Go Gophers Show, The 179, 220
Gold Key Comics 45, 97, 221, 224, 226-227
Gold Medal flour 20-21
Golden Books 203, 217, 223
Gonzara, Rodolfo 122
Gourley, Bud 122
Gracie Films 120
Grade, Lew 36
Grant, Bud 215
Great Race, The 142
Greenwich Village, NY 164
Griffin, Bob 247-248
Groovy Guru 142
Guadalajara, Mexico 120
Guarnier Lu 24
Guerrero, Julio 122
Gunsmoke 137, 218

Hagar the Horrible 217

Hallmark 220
Hanna-Barbera Productions 16-17, 25, 39, 122, 212, 218-219, 252
Hansen, Tex 122
Harley the Horse 130-134
Harmony Records 207
Harris, Joe 9-10, 14-17, 19-24, 30, 34, 38, 40, 119, 126, 137, 162, 165, 176, 187, 189-190, 197-198, 201, 203-204, 211, 216, 218-224, 229, 241, 246-248
Harvey, Paul 9
Harvey Comics 221, 228
Hatfields and the McCoys, The 220
Hayde, Michael 208
"Helicopter Hi-Jinx" 139
Here Come the Beagles 122, 202, 207
Hiram Holiday 163
Hold Back the Tide 9
Hollywood, CA 12
Hollywood Squares 164, 176
Hoppity Hooper (character) 238-239
Hoppity Hooper (series) 14, 121, 138, 162, 189, 198
Horrors Hunter 75, 168
Hotchkiss, Charlie 25-26
How Underdog Saved the Thanksgiving Day Parade! 172
How Underdog Was Born 9, 12, 125
Howdy Doody (character) 36
Howdy Doody Show, The 35-36, 147
Huckleberry Hound 17
Huckleberry Hound Show, The, 16
Hunter, The (character), 46-47, 73, 75-95, 97, 168
Hunter, The (segment), 14-17, 73-74, 76-95, 137, 162-163, 179, 218, 250
Hurtz, Bill, 122
Hyperion Productions, 122

I Love Lucy 162
"I Wanna Capture You" 208
Impala, Vinnie 222
Inspector Gadget 141
Irene 74
Irving, George S. 74, 126, 141, 179
Ishi, Chris 12, 20-23
Itchy Brother 33, 35, 43, 46-71

Japan 26, 123, 219

Jay Ward Productions 9, 12-15, 25-26, 37-39, 119-120, 138, 162-163, 189, 197-198, 212, 218, 221, 237
Jerboa Jump 143
"Jerkey Jockey or ("Kenducky Derby")" 99, 109-113
Jimmy the Zebra 128, 131, 133
Johnson, Gordon 12-15, 20, 22, 24-26, 33-34, 38, 120, 122, 125, 162, 246
Joker, The 142

Kansas City 217
Keeshan, Bobby (Robert) 147
Kennedy, Edgar 141
Kennedy, John F. 165
Key, Len 25-26, 120
Kim, Paul 11
King and Odie (segment) 14, 33, 38, 43, 48-71, 121, 125, 137, 202, 246, 250
King and Odie, The (series) 38, 125, 218, 246
King Leonardo (character) 33-34, 37, 43-71, 125, 127, 129
King Leonardo and his Short Subjects 9, 13, 19-20, 22, 33, 38-39, 43, 45-47, 73-75, 97-98, 119, 121, 123, 125, 137, 139, 161, 201-202, 215, 219-220, 246, 250, 252
King Leonardo and the Royal Contest 44, 97
King Vitaman cereal 14
Kirwood Derby 14
Kix cereal 11, 21
Klondike Kat (character) 197-199
Klondike Kat (segment) 123, 162, 171, 197-199, 203, 250
Knotts, Don 163
Koko the Clown 142
Korea 40
Kraft Music Hall, 142
Krell, David 9
Kurer, Ron 33

LaMarche, Maurice 189
"Lamplighters, The" 143
Lancelot Productions 203
Laurel & Hardy 138-139
Lee, Spike 144
Leonardo Productions 24-25, 38, 203, 221, 223
Life magazine 17
Linus the Lionhearted 39

INDEX

Litchfield, CT 97
Little Caesar Pizza 37
"Looking for The Beagles" 207
Los Angeles, CA 38, 121-122, 219
Los Angeles Comic Book and Science Fiction Convention 29
"Lossie – Doggone Dope" 99-108
Love, Andy 20
Lucky Strike cigarettes 146

Mackey, Pat 39
MacMillan, Norma 164-166
Macy's Thanksgiving Parade 17, 125, 161-162, 173, 222
Magnet Man 225
Major "Blast-Off" Connel 74
Major Minor 197
Malamutt 197-198
"Man From the Moon, The" 48-53, 65-71
Man Inside, The 10
Manhattan, NY 15, 73
Manley's Marauders 218
Manriquez, Carlos 121, 123
Marbleheads, The 165
March, Fredric 37
Marshall, Mort 11, 74, 141, 201, 216
Martin, Dean 201
Martinez, Jesus 121-122
Marvel Productions 122
Marvel superheroes 222
McCann, Chuck 142
Messing, Debra 144
Maxwell Smart 158
Mexico 13, 24-26, 33, 38, 40, 119-123, 138, 197-198, 215, 245-246
Mexico City, Mexico 40, 120-122, 198
MGM 120
Miami, FL 18, 20
Mickey Mouse 122
Michaels, Lorne 223
Mike the Gorilla 130
Milano, Frank 97
Milton-Bradley 246
Minneapolis, MN 20
Minow, Newton R., 139
Monkees, The 201
Montgomery Burns 189
Mooney, Gary 24
Moore, Artie 35

Moose That Roared, The 9, 14, 25-26, 120, 123
Morgan, Frank 141-142
Mortimer Snerd 97
Mouse Factory, The 164
Mr. Know-it-All 14, 189, 211
Mr. Magoo 189
Mr. Peepers 163
Mr. Wizard the Lizard 46, 97-117
My Life as a Small Boy 163

Nander, Jack 21
Natasha Fatale 238-239
National Association of Broadcasters (NAB) 139
NBC 19, 22, 33, 38, 137, 161, 216
Nellie Olson 165
New Casper Cartoon Show, The 165
New Jersey 221
New York City, NY 10, 12, 18-21, 23, 35, 38, 74, 123, 140-142, 144-145, 164, 198, 202, 216, 224
New York University 144
New Yorker, The 161
Noah's Lark 218
North Georgia Military College 10
"Nug of Nog, The" 222

Odie Colognie 33-35, 43-71
Officer Flim Flanagan 73-95, 168
Olivares, Eduardo 121
One Brick Films 10
"One Where Underdog Gets Away, The" 162
Otter Side, The 218, 224
Otters, The 218, 224

Paisley, Al 39
Palace, The, 36
Palladium, The, 36
Pallette, Eugene, 34-35
Pangborn, Franklin, 141
Paramount Pictures 211, 246
Parrot Playhouse 137, 140, 218
Partners, The 141
Payne, John 37
Peabody's Improbably History (Peabody and Sherman) 14, 121
Pelican Films 19, 137
Pennell, William 37
Pepsi 221

Perry Mason 39
Peterson, Bob 20-21
Phineas J. Whoopee 138-139, 141-142, 146-148, 150-151, 154-155
Phineas T. Bluster 147
"Phunnie Munnie" 153
Piech, Peter 24-26, 123, 218, 221-223
Pillsbury Doughboy 11
Pinky Knees 212
Pintoff, Ernie 21, 40
Pip the Piper 129
Plattes, Sy 23
Platypus (character) 23
Pluto 16
Ponsonby Britt 18
Popeye 37, 41-42, 246
Popeye show 35, 41-42
Powell, William 140
Producer's Associates of Television (P.A.T.) 24-26, 37, 203, 218, 221, 223
Program Exchange 212
Providence, RI 247

Quake cereal 14
Quaker Oats 14
Quisp cereal 14

Rabbit Foot 211
Raft, George 165
Rankin-Bass 35, 74, 146-147
Ray, Gerry 39
Reddy 17
Reeves, George 162
Rhino Home Video 203
Richfield, CT 10
Riddles 147
Riff Raff 35, 165, 167-168, 174, 228, 236, 240
Robinson, Edward G. 34
Rocky and Bullwinkle (segment) 14, 119, 121, 138, 162
Rocky and his Friends 13-15, 17, 26, 123, 129
Rocky (character) 237-239
Rocky Monanoff 74
Roosevelt, Franklin D. 144
Roosevelt, Theodore (Teddy) 179
Rose, Norman 35
"Royal Amnesia" 53-65
Rudolph, the Red-Nosed Reindeer 147
Ruff and Reddy 17, 252

Ruffled Feather 168, 179-184, 186-187, 240

Saatchi and Saatchi 11, 251
"Safe Waif" 163
Sally Hanson 165
Sandoval 122
Sandy Becker Show, The 97
Sanford the Parrot 126-128, 130-134
Saturday Night Live 223
Savoir Fare 197-198
Schleh, Bob 24, 121-123
Scorcese, Martin 144
Scott, Bill 12-13, 119
Scott, Keith 9, 25
Scotty 201, 206
Scranton PA, 10
Screen Gems 25, 252
"Seemingly Never Ending Story, The" 189
Senator Claghorn 73, 141
Sergeant Badge 141
Sergeant Bilko 216
Sergeant Okey Homa 168, 179-180, 182, 240
Sharples, Winston 246
Shelasky, George Irving 74
Shifty 212
Shoeshine Boy 163, 236
Shout Factory 203
Siegel, Harvey 121-123, 197-198, 201
Silverman, Fred 202, 215, 218-220
Silvers, Phil 216
Simon Bar Sinister 35, 165-168, 172-175, 222, 225-228, 236, 247
"Simon Says...No Thanksgiving" 161, 172
Simpsons, The 120, 189
Sing-a-Long Family, The 162, 211
Sisters Grimm, The 204
Smith, "Buffalo" Bob 36
Smith, C. Aubrey 189
Smothers Brothers, The 201
Smurfs, The 218
Snidely Whiplash 13, 239
Sobol, Jack 215-216
Southampton, NY 216
Space Kidettes 212
Sparks, Ned 141
Spider-Man 222
Spotlight Comics 221, 228
"Spoofs 'n' Saddles" 137, 218
Springfield, MA 74

Stadlin, Ira 35-36
Stanley Livingstone 74, 139, 141
States, Delo 74
"Steam Roller, The" 185
Stern, Ben 143, 145-146, 157
Stern, Howard 145-146, 157
Steve Allen Show, The 140
Stewart, James G. 122
Stewie 222
Stone, Ben 74, 165
Storch, Larry 141-143, 145
Stover, Chester A. "Chet" 9-10, 12-17, 19-23, 25, 27-28, 33-34, 38, 97, 125, 137-138, 140, 162-163, 165-166, 190, 201, 203, 218-220, 222-223, 246, 248
Stringer 201, 205-208
Sugar Frosted Twinkles cereal 126
Super Bowl 222
Superchicken 14
Superman 163
Sweet Polly Purebred 74, 164-169, 173-175, 221, 226-228, 234-235, 238-239, 247-248
Swift, Allen 35-36, 41-42, 97, 140, 147, 165-166, 190, 201, 216
Swift, Jonathan 35

"Telephone Terrors or Dial 'M' for Mayhem" 139
Tennessee Tuxedo (character) 9, 29, 74-75, 138, 142, 146-155, 163, 199, 221, 238-240, 245
Tennessee Tuxedo (segment) 15, 121, 138, 140-141, 143, 148-149, 153-156, 165, 179, 240, 246, 250
Tennessee Tuxedo and his Tales 9, 23, 38, 73-75, 121, 137-140, 142-143, 147-149, 153, 161, 165, 179, 189, 218, 220-221, 240, 246, 250
Tennessee Tuxedo and Ol' 97 149
Tennessee Tuxedo and the Sailboat Race 149
Terrazas, Ernesto 121-122
Terry-Toons 35, 120, 146, 216-217, 220, 224
Thin Man, The 140
Thomas the Octopus 132
Thor 222
Three Caballeros, The 121
Thurber, James 220
Tisch School of Arts 144
Tom Corbett: Space Cadet 74
Tom Slick 14

Tom Terrific 217
Tom the Water Baby 218
Tony the Tiger 10
Toonerville Trolley 97
Toonerville Turtle 97, 99-117
Toontracker 33, 203
Tooter Turtle (character) 35, 46-47, 97-117, 138, 221, 239
Tooter Turtle (segment) 14, 39, 97-117, 138, 250
Tortilla Fats 212
Total TeleVision productions (TTV) 2, 9, 12-15, 17-20, 22-23, 25-26, 33-35, 37-38, 74, 97, 119-120, 122-123, 125-126, 137-139, 141-143, 146-147, 161-163, 165, 189, 198, 201-203, 208, 212, 215, 218-221, 223, 235, 237, 240, 245-247, 250-251
Tracey Ullman Show, The 120
Trix cereal 10-11, 21, 121
Trix Rabbit 10-11, 74
TTV-Leonardo 25, 137, 218
Tubby 201, 205-208
TV Guide 251
TV Spots 9, 38-40, 119, 125
Twinkles and Sanford's Boat 126-127
Twinkles cereal 125, 128, 189
Twinkles (segment) 125-134, 189, 250
Twinkles the Elephant 11, 125-134

Uncle Waldo 14, 218
Underdog balloon 17, 161-162, 173, 222
Underdog (book) 174
Underdog (character) 9, 17, 22-23, 25, 29-30, 38, 75, 138, 162-169, 172-176, 212, 221-223, 225-242, 245, 247-249
Underdog Collectors Edition 119
Underdog (feature film) 247-249
Underdog float 173
Underdog (segment) 74, 121, 139, 162, 165, 170-171, 190, 212, 222-223, 240, 250
Underdog Show, The 9, 17, 73, 121, 139, 141, 161-163, 165, 167, 170-171, 175, 179, 189, 197-198, 201-202, 211, 219-222, 225, 240, 250-251
Underdog Theme Song, The 172, 245
"Underdog vs. Overcat" 252
Union Seminary 10
University of Minnesota 10
University of North Carolina 18, 20

"Up a Tree" 199
UPA 23

Valdez, Gustavo 26
Val-Mar Productions 120, 122-123
Vancouver, BC 164
Vasquez, Jaime Torres 122-123
Victory Over Violence 10
Visa Check Card 222, 242
Volkswagen 11

Walt Disney Productions (see Disney)
Walter Lantz Productions 120
Ward, Jay 9, 12-14, 18, 119, 189, 197-198, 221, 223
Warner Bros. 122
Washington, DC 139
Wayne, John 179
Westchester County, NY 217
White, Larry 215
White Deer, The 220

Whitman Comics 221, 226-227
Who Framed Roger Rabbit? 247
Wikipedia 9, 38, 189, 215, 223
Wilbur the Monkey 127-134
Will and Grace 144
Wizard of Oz, The 141
Wonderama 97
Woolery, George W. 139
World Hunger Year 222
World of Commander McBragg, The 9, 138, 189-195, 211, 218, 250
Wynn, Ed 144

Yak 141, 147
Yarmy, Donald James 140
Year Without a Santa Claus, The 74, 147
Yellow Submarine 12, 202

Zamora, Rudy 122
Zot, 166, 228 240

COMING IN 2010 FROM FUN IDEAS AND BEARMANOR

IF YOU'RE CRACKED YOU'RE HAPPY!

WRITTEN BY MARK ARNOLD

Bear Manor Media

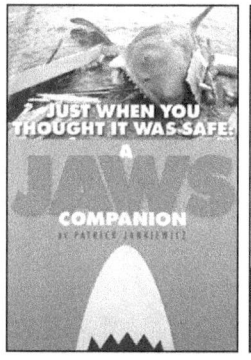

Classic Cinema.
Timeless TV.
Retro Radio.

WWW.BEARMANORMEDIA.COM

www.ingramcontent.com/pod-product-compliance
Lightning Source LLC
Chambersburg PA
CBHW071951220426
43662CB00009B/1080